HEALING MOVEMENTS

Healing Movements

*Chicanx-Indigenous Activism and
Criminal Justice in California*

Megan S. Raschig

NEW YORK UNIVERSITY PRESS
New York

NEW YORK UNIVERSITY PRESS
New York
www.nyupress.org

© 2024 by New York University
All rights reserved

A previous version of chapter 3 was published as Megan Raschig, "*Cargas* Coming Down: Chronic Stress, Chicana-Indigenous Spiritual Healing, and Feminist Fugitive Potentiality," *Feminist Anthropology* 4 (1): 36–58.

Please contact the Library of Congress for Cataloging-in-Publication data.
ISBN: 9781479827060 (hardback)
ISBN: 9781479827077 (paperback)
ISBN: 9781479827107 (library ebook)
ISBN: 9781479827091 (consumer ebook)

This book is printed on acid-free paper, and its binding materials are chosen for strength and durability. We strive to use environmentally responsible suppliers and materials to the greatest extent possible in publishing our books.

Manufactured in the United States of America

10 9 8 7 6 5 4 3 2 1

Also available as an ebook

CONTENTS

A Guide to Identity Terms — vii

Introduction: It's the Ollin — 1

1. Occupying the Narrative: From Criminalization to Cultural Healing — 29
2. Making the Movement of Healing: Navigating Paths to La Cultura — 45
3. *Cargas* Coming Down: Chronic Stress and New Possibilities in the Women's Healing Circle — 73
4. Homegirl *Noble*: Relational Ethics across Affiliated Generations — 92
5. This Is Where We Walk Together: "Raw" Women's *Movidas* amid Police Homicides — 117
6. The Work and Play of Healing: Making Fugitive Spaces for Joy — 143

Conclusion: Closing the Circle — 165

Acknowledgments — 175
Notes — 177
Bibliography — 183
Index — 193
About the Author — 200

A GUIDE TO IDENTITY TERMS

There are numerous fine-grained distinctions and contestations among the variety of identity terms used in this book, which have changed significantly in recent years. This guide provides a brief introduction to these terms as well as my reasons for employing them.

- MEXICAN AMERICAN refers to people born in the United States and of Mexican ancestry.
- CHICANO/A/X/E refers to a political identity claimed by some Mexican Americans, reclaiming a former racist and classist slur. Chicano refers to a male-identified person; Chicana to a female-identified person; Chicanx and Chicane are gender-neutral terms. I use Chicanx throughout this text unless referring to particularly gendered people.
- XICANA describes a Chicana feminism rooted in Indigeneity and reclaims the Nahuatl phonetic sound "shee" as represented by the *X*. I use this primarily in reference to Xicana feminist thinkers and activists who claimed this specific spelling of the term.
- CHICANX-INDIGENOUS refers to an identity claimed by some Chicanx peoples to articulate and emphasize Indigenous ancestry, typically linked to various Mesoamerican, Uto-Aztecan Indigenous groups in what is now Mexico and the US Southwest. Some interlocutors in this text prefer the term "Indigenous," claim a particular tribal identity, or separate the terms (Chicano, Chicana, or Chicanx and Indigenous) rather than hyphenate them. Still, I use this term to specify those who embrace both their politicized Chicanx identity and their Indigenous ancestry without necessarily knowing the specifics of the latter. I discuss this further in chapter 2.
- *MEXICANO/A* is the Spanish-language term for Mexican, typically used to refer to someone more recently arrived from Mexico or strongly associated with that nation. Speakers in Salinas often code-switch to the Spanish term even when otherwise speaking in English, and I follow their use of this term in the text, with the masculine *Mexicano* serving as a collective

noun for a mixed-gender group. In italicizing this name, I indicate it is a Spanish-language term and thus pronounced meh-hee-CA-no.
- *MEXICA* is another name for the Aztec or Nahuatl peoples of Mesoamerica. It follows Nahuatl phonetics in being pronounced meh-SHEE-ca.
- LATINO/A/X/E refers to people of broadly Latin American ancestry. Throughout this text it replaces "Hispanic," which is considered to be an imposed colonial category by most people featured in this book. Still, I use it sparingly, as it does not reflect how most of my interlocutors identify themselves, and I have been strongly urged by some interlocutors to use more specific terms instead.

Introduction

It's the Ollin

Circling Up

We could hear the chants—*we want peace, we want peace*—muffled by the walls and competing with the sound of speeding cars and honking. It was gray and overcast outside on this early evening in May. Still, we kept the lights off in the little office of the BreadBox community center in East Salinas where we gathered, every Monday and Thursday, for the healing circle of La Colectiva de Mujeres, the Women's Healing Collective.

Most of us Mujeres had just been out there on the sidewalk, which was packed with people in protest. We hung back to watch as young people held up signs that read No More Violence or *Amor y Paz* (Love and Peace). Women, comfy in colorful sweatsuits after long days spent working in the fields that surrounded Salinas, joined their children at the curb, holding up signs with slogans scribbled onto construction paper or cardboard. Men with brown weather-beaten skin and ranchero hats clapped along to the rhythms of the chanting. Daniel, a member of another Salinas healing collective named MILPA, had crouched down to light a piece of charcoal, placing it in a wide abalone shell.[1] Out of a small plastic bag, he pulled apart pieces of copal, a resinous medicine sourced in Mexico, so fresh it stretched like warm taffy. He laid a thick strand of copal on top of the glowing charcoal, and it started to smolder. Holding the abalone shell, Daniel walked between the street and the line of protesters, letting the sweet white smoke wash over each of them.

This moment of ceremonial blessing was a prelude to the community healing circle that would be held inside the BreadBox after the protest. It enacted the idea, at that time increasingly prominent in Salinas, that *la cultura cura*: culture (specifically the practices and relationships considered to be ancestral and indigenous to Mexican Americans) heals (has a transformative and positive impact).

There was much to heal from in this working-class community. Two days earlier, an officer from the Salinas Police Department had shot a man named Carlos Mejía outside a neighborhood bakery. Nine days ago, a different officer had shot another man, Osmar Hernández, outside of Mi Pueblo supermarket. Mejía was a gardener, Hernández a *lechuguero* (lettuce cutter), both from El Salvador. Angel Ruiz, who was Mexican American, had already been shot by the police a couple months earlier in the parking lot of a chicken wing chain. It would be another month or so when Frank Alvarado Jr., also Mexican American, would meet the same end before sunrise in front of his mother's home. These police homicides, happening in rapid succession in this small agricultural city of 165,000, ignited residents who typically kept to themselves and their work, abiding the ongoing affronts of living in an overpoliced and underresourced place. As footage of Mejía's murder circulated through the community, residents with long-simmering stress, anger, and grief spilled out onto the streets.

As local news crews showed up to report from the protest, Shi, the Colectiva's facilitator, motioned for us to come inside. Buzzing with the energy of all that had happened in the past few days, we found seats as Shi began to light the sage and officially start the circle. She kept her sunglasses on; I could tell she'd been crying. Her voice was sharp, and her body was on edge. Growing up proudly chola and Chicana on the heavily policed East Side of Salinas, and gang-affiliated throughout her youth, Shi had visceral experience at the edges of police brutality.[2] She had mourned more than her share of loved ones. Mejía's and Hernández's murders brought some of those feelings back, while her role in the healing collectives refracted them in new ways. In recent days, she had been intensely committed to being with the victims' families along with some of the other Mujeres.

Our healing circle would be a little different today, Shi explained to us, gesturing to the violence outside and the surging resident response. "But," she added, "we have to come to circle if we're going to do anything about it—if we even want to survive it."

She stood to relight the bundle of sage resting on the altar surrounded by our plastic stacking chairs, blowing on its embers to make more of the cleansing smoke and wafting it toward herself four times before passing the bundle to the left. Like Daniel's copal but with a slightly different purpose, this medicine was meant to sacralize the space, help us shake off the energy we came in with, and prepare us for healing. Its scent hung in the air as Shi left the time open for anyone to talk, passing a gourd rattle as a talking piece. One by one, each of us—Josefina, Lisa, Pamela and her adult daughter Rachel, Yarri and her toddler, Juana, Rosa, Shi, myself, and a new face, Tara—checked in with the group.[3]

Tara went first. She grappled with her anger at her friend Osmar's violent and unjust death and asked us all to support her because she felt her old "street self" coming back these days. She teetered on the edge of her recovery from past alcohol abuse, and on the cusp of concluding her probation, she couldn't handle another violation. This was only her second time in circle with the Colectiva, having just reunited with her old homegirl Shi at a demonstration against Hernández's killing.

Tara passed the gourd rattle to Shi. For her, it was not only about these specific deaths but the repetitiveness of death around her, in East Salinas, her whole life. So many of those losses had been unsolved and never fully mourned, just happening and then happening again. Tears streamed down her face from behind her sunglasses. "Ometeotl," Shi uttered, closing her check-in with the Nahuatl name for a binary deity of creation.

When it was my turn, I wasn't sure what to say. I had been swept up in days of action among friends in anguish, people who had lived their entire lives in a context of state violence that was still new to me as a white woman and anthropology student. I felt riven with their sadness and anger even as I couldn't understand or experience it in the same way.

Throughout these check-ins, the muffled sounds of protest outside pressed on. Pamela took the gourd rattle from me, shook it once, and said, "Palabra." *Palabra* is literally Spanish for "word," but among the healing collectives, it also indexes one's honor and integrity.

"These people," Pamela started, referencing the protesters outside, "have been silenced so long, but no more. This is them screaming out, in sound, but also in actions, because we are never allowed to just yell and let it out!"

Pamela squinted and snarled. Her hands balled into fists. She screamed a deep, piercing, scraping scream. It reverberated for a moment, absorbed by the circle of us, then faded into the streetside din.

There was a moment of pause, and then she screamed again: "Like *that*!"

As if on cue, the heavy, warm drumbeat of a *teponaztli* began outside. Still reeling from Pamela's screams, I felt physically barraged by the noise and, wincing, turned to Rosa, who was turning to me at the same instant and smiling.

Revolution in the 93905

Alongside the protest outdoors and the healing circle inside, the sage smoke in the air, Pamela's screams, my wince and Rosa's grin, something *otherwise* was happening in Salinas. We felt it—a quickening, palpable pulse of change. "That's the Ollin," Shi, or Daniel, or Rosa's approving smile would announce, referencing the sacred earthquake of their ancestral Nahuatl cosmology. The Ollin was palpable in moments when their ancestral *cultura* was affirmed and leveraged in powerful ways, often against racialized policing, criminalization, and carcerality. These poignant moments surfaced *the movement*, a resurgence of the Chicano Civil Rights Movement but, with revised terms and goals, now oriented by cultural healing.

This book attends to this emerging movement of cultural healing as developed by members of the Salinas healing collectives, MILPA and La Colectiva de Mujeres, spanning a decade of ethnographic engagement from 2013 through 2023. It situates cultural healing as a Chicanx-Indigenous liberatory praxis rich with abolitionist possibility: for endurance, for care, for critical interventions against racialized state violence, for new relations of affirmation and love.

Driven by intersectional feminist commitment, I lift up and move with this praxis as it was borne out by both healing collectives, and especially among the women of La Colectiva de Mujeres. As we will see, these women prepared the ground for critical change in Salinas, creating new forms of presence and practices of nourishment through which self-described "raw" women could be affirmed and equipped to fight back against the carceral state in the spaces of their everyday lives. Their work was essential to that sense of Ollin, of sacred revolution and profound change, in this community. However, the efficacy of the Mujeres' grassroots abolitionist approach and their contributions to this movement have largely been minimized, misrecognized, or erased since the group's dissolution in 2016. In refusal of this disavowal, this book provides perspectives and analyses that demonstrate the complex forms of otherwise transformation engaged in through the Mujeres' work of cultural healing, during but also extending beyond their time as a formal, funded community group. This healing was scented with sage, pierced by their *gritos* (screams), and conditioned by their profound commitment to dismantling the many gendered and racialized facets of carcerality they encountered in their lives.

When I refer to "carcerality," I aim to index not simply institutions like jails, prisons, or policing but their foundational logics of division, isolation, punishment, captivity, and dispossession. These logics are rooted in the capitalist foundations of settler colonial America and continue to structure the core inequalities of American social life in places like Salinas and well beyond (Shanahan and Kurti 2022). Carcerality shapes and sharply limits our imaginations of justice and possibility; cultural healing refracts new avenues to think and build otherwise. Ethnographic attention to the work of both Salinas healing collectives offers important understandings of this deeply potentiated—and precarious—grassroots abolitionist project, launched by those with the most at stake in social change.

* * *

Shi was the lead facilitator of La Colectiva de Mujeres and on the forefront of this emerging movement of healing. Months before the police killings, community healing circles, and protests, we were sitting at her kitchen table with a cool breeze blowing in through the window, trying to plan the themes of the Colectiva's next few circles. As we talked, a Pandora playlist of cumbias interspersed with ads played tinny and loud through her phone's speaker. Her fridge was covered with taped-on photos: of family kicking back and happy; throwbacks of her and her friends in full homegirl splendor; and loving portraits taken with her husband, who was then locked up. This session, and others like it, would stretch on for hours as we discussed Shi's life and experiences, the changes underway in Salinas, and what the Colectiva could and should do to support and organize local women. Most of the Mujeres would describe themselves as homegirls or cholas, Chicanas, *Mexicanas*, or some combination of these; sometimes they would note an Indigenous lineage, like Yaqui, or nod to the province of their family rancho in Mexico, like Michoacán. I was relatively new to town still, and felt conspicuous as one of the only two white women in the Colectiva. Nevertheless, I had formed a quick and close bond with Shi that would last for many years and through many life transitions. She had invited me into the intimacy of imagining and enacting the group's potentiality.

Shi was a lifelong resident of what she proudly called "the 93905," referencing the zip code for the East Side of Salinas. Back in the 1990s, she had been one of the first young women in the area to become a Sureña, a member of a "Southsider" Mexican American gang.[4] She described earning this membership the "honorable way," through fighting, and told stories about the strong relationships and solidarities she had developed with others through this affiliation. She distanced herself somewhat from gang activity as she became a mother of three and sought different work. Eventually becoming employed at a few of the many local nonprofits aiming to address the conditions of structural poverty and racial inequity in Salinas, Shi possessed a level of street savvy that often positioned her on the front lines of violence interruption and first response. In these roles, she centered care for women and youth afflicted by violence while maintaining ambivalence regarding the message she was supposed to be sending about gang deterrence—she knew gangs to be important community formations beyond criminogenic tropes. To criticize them would be to disavow herself and other loved ones whose strength, creativity, and wisdom were rooted on the block and in the barrio (neighborhood).

The healing collectives, Shi explained to me, had a very different vibe from those other nonprofits she had worked for. The collectives were funded by the Building Healthy Communities (BHC) project, an initiative of The California Endowment (TCE), and, as we will see, were beholden to some top-down imperatives, but they weren't trying to impose a way of life on Salinas residents. Instead, the collectives affirmed, even *revered*, the beauty of who these residents were and where they came from, deeper than but inclusive of whichever colors or neighborhood they repped. They code-switched from Spanglish to Caló to Nahuatl, saw water as medicine, and talked about honoring grandparents and dismantling the prison-industrial complex in the same breath.[5]

The movement of cultural healing was being built in a city that Shi had described to me as a place where "nothing ever happens, nothing like activism." "This has never been done before" in Salinas or even Monterey County, she had told me with astonishment, referring to the healing collectives' emergence as fierce and compelling activist organizations on the local scene. Only a handful of months before the police homicides in 2014, the healing collectives MILPA and La Colectiva de Mujeres had come together to contest the county's plans to expand the local juvenile hall. They were united in deep pride in their roots and care for community welfare. With the police homicides, these collectives stepped into greater public prominence. They took up a presence on the streets and in spheres of state power, while consistently holding space in circles for aggrieved community members to reflect, be heard, connect, organize—to heal.

It wasn't exactly true that there was no history of activism in Monterey County, an agricultural powerhouse in a picturesque coastal area. The labor movement has had a strong presence in the region since the 1920s. Nearby Soledad State Prison was an important site in the rise of the Black Panthers. Residents of the Monterey Peninsula have been outspoken in the antiwar movement for decades. Chicano Brown Berets made their mark in neighboring Watsonville, alongside *Mexicana* and Filipina women who led the cannery strikes there in the 1980s and 1990s. But in Shi's lived experience of Salinas, her forty-odd years on the East Side—of people grinding hard with few gains, with many lost to federal antiterrorism sweeps and local gun violence—a revolution was underway, with something otherwise emerging. Rene, an early member of MILPA, described a similar feeling, noting to me how mobilizing community residents through cultural healing "really resuscitated not only previous movements, but also those who were waiting for something new and a generation who was ready to take it to the next level . . . this work reenergized the people, the community, and the hope to bring forth change." Unlike the other movements, this one felt profoundly for people like Shi, Rene, and those they loved: those whose lives had been heavily impacted by carceral systems and logics, whether jails, prisons, and probation, or schools reliant on punitive and individualizing methods of control, or deep-seated associations between criminality and Black and Brown skin that were claimed to justify police surveillance and carceral capture.

I have come to know Salinas as a small city with stark inequalities. Its peaceful, lettuce-lined landscape and temperate climate obscure deep violence: racialized criminalization and overpolicing; exploited labor and profligate use of pesticides; generations of pain from dispossession, migration, and structural poverty. Alongside the swath of rural towns and cities that constitute what Ruth Wilson Gilmore and Craig Gilmore (2004) called "the other California," Salinas and its surrounding area is a fulcrum of California carcerality: a geography shaped by industrialized agriculture and mass incarceration, both in need of a steady population of bodies kept captive to these low-status trajectories. But the Salinas I know best is foremost a place of fierce *palabra*, passion, and persistence. Good, gorgeous things grow here. Profound attempts to dismantle carceral institutions and their racist logics have been underway in this area through a distinctive approach to carceral abolition driven by Chicanx-Indigenous life, love, and *cultura*.

As Shi put it as we sat at her kitchen table, her voice ringing out over the cumbia music, "There's never been anything that *cultural* here, nothing with *that cultural piece*, and I think this is history right now. Everyone is coming together and making it their own, and nobody owns it, and it's just like . . ." She paused, looking for the right words. "It's like something's transforming. It's so beautiful, because it's just like it's starting. Like what we call the Ollin, right? The movement. And that's what it is!"

That Cultural Piece

What Shi called "that cultural piece" is the intentional and affirmative uplift of practices, understandings, and forms of relation, often of Mesoamerican Indigenous origin or association though adapted through life in the US Southwest. I use the broad term "Indigenous" not to collapse or erase the myriad distinctions between different groups throughout time, but, like many of those in the collectives, as an inclusive category that is filled in by individuals as they learn the specifics of their heritage. As we will see, this Indigenous ancestry holds prior and ongoing ways of knowing and relating to others and oneself, and while not 'new' as such it can be leveraged in novel ways.

Patrisia Gonzales, in her text *Red Medicine* (2012), argues that many Indigenous and ancestral cultural practices, knowledges, and relations are already present in majority Mexican American and *Mexicano* populations, who have inherited "body memory of ancestral knowledge" that forms part of the "general cultural competency of many Mexicans" (2012, xxv, 8). However, through intergenerational processes of displacement and "detribalization"—colonialism, migration that is essentially forced, and racialized criminalization—this embodied knowledge was obscured, stigmatized, neglected, or denigrated. Spanish colonizers had sought to demonize and annihilate knowledges that challenged the primacy of their own, though, as Gonzales further notes, many of these ways of knowing were intentionally and implicitly veiled and encoded in practices and rituals that persist in the lifeways of those descending from Mesoamerica today. A *promotora-investigadora* (health promotor–researcher) of Mexican traditional medicine, Gonzales argues that the "re-membering, re-generating, reclaiming, and reframing" of these ancestral knowledges, in settings like the Salinas healing collectives, are generative and liberatory (10); they take on new qualities and ends, offering new possibilities for understanding and acting in contemporary conditions.

In Salinas, such decolonizing practices were strongly inflected by anticarcerality. A key understanding forwarded by the healing collectives, and thus a foundational argument of this book, is that American carcerality has grown alongside and out of the punitive, violent, and reductive practices and logics of colonial oppression. Though the plantation and chattel slavery are well-known antecedents to contemporary mass incarceration, Kelly Lytle Hernández details how settler colonial expansion in the US Southwest was heavily reliant on captivity and incarceration, both among the Tongva in what is now Los Angeles and more broadly across the Southwest after the Mexican-American War and the Treaty of Guadalupe (Hernández 2017; see also Saldaña-Portillo 2016). "Mass incarceration is mass elimination," she writes to open her text *City of Inmates*, revealing through archival research the much deeper colonial roots of American carcerality than is commonly recognized (Hernández 2017, 1). Over the years in this settler colonial nation-state, incarceration became a hegemonic system of racialized class domination and social control (Alexander 2012; Shanahan and Kurti 2022), and carcerality became the dominant form of power (Sojoyner 2021).

Colonial and carceral logics, mutually imbricated but distinct, should be understood in relation to each other. While historically many Black and Indigenous radical projects have focused, respectively, on abolition and anticarcerality, and the restoration of land and sovereignty, recent solidarity work and thought have sought to realize the bridges between these struggles (Lethabo-King, Navarro, and Smith 2020; Maynard and Betasamosake Simpson 2022). These activists and scholars think and act from their productive interstices toward mutual liberation. This Chicanx-Indigenous project of cultural healing draws on these radical practices and dialogues, engaging them from a position of ancestral displacement, dispossession of ways of being and knowing, and criminalization amid erasure in carceral systems. Latinx peoples, particularly those with Mexican heritage, have faced clearly documented "hypercriminalization" in the United States and experienced social exclusion and scapegoating for social ills since the mid-nineteenth century (Rios 2006; Escobar 1999; Salinas 2015). Today, the rates of incarceration of Mexican-origin and Latinx people in the United States are believed to be disproportionately high, yet distressingly undercounted by official carceral demographic data instruments that often leave out "Hispanic" identity or relegate it as secondary to race (Hernandez 2019).[6]

Colonial and carceral processes of displacement and dispossession had resulted in generations of families "who don't know how to take care of each other," as a Mujer named Dolores noted in an interview. She had come to circle as a young woman who had been through sexual abuse, foster care, and juvenile detention, which imparted a deep mistrust of other women. Contemporary families had been severed from ancestral strategies for care, though it was not entirely lost to them, she explained to me. Being in circle together, building a collective sense of possibility with plant medicines at the center, was new to her and many others but felt appealingly familiar—and good. Dolores didn't need to fully understand it to know that healing was "not religious stuff. It's not therapeutic stuff. It's not medication stuff. This feels, *feels* good." She explained that it helped her to "end up understanding I'm Indigenous, you know? Like, this is what my ancestors used to do prior to Christianity, prior to colonization. No wonder it feels right."

From this view, "that cultural piece" could be mobilized to defy and dismantle both the colonial and the carceral, deeply dehumanizing, systems organizing life and death in Salinas and the United States. It felt like it held that incredible potential. When Daniel let copal smoke wash over the protesters, he was reminding them that their lives and futures were valuable, cherished, sacred. He was directly countering the alternative message, acutely weighing on their lives in those days especially, with police homicides of exclusively Chicano and Salvadoreño men revealing a vicious pattern of lethal disregard and disposability. When that *teponaztli* two-tone rhythm rushed over us from the protest outside, Rosa, resplendent, felt power and solace in the sound that she and her ancestors had heard in ceremony. And for Josefina, a member of the Colectiva, something about the "Indian stuff" just felt right to her. Josefina spoke sparingly about the abuse and violence that had shaped her youth. Aware of her Yaqui lineage, she preferred instead to think about and imagine what happened before she was adopted, and what knowing more about being Yaqui could make possible for her. She combed the Colectiva's cultural teachings for ideas and methods for how she could "keep moving forward."

Following Patrisia Gonzales (2012), I use the terms "re-membering" and "reframing" to attend to the intentional, intuitive, and embodied thought and action—the praxis—involved in turning to and uplifting ancestral beliefs, teachings, and practices. I see this as an epistemic and ethical reframing that was experimented with and achieved through its embodied practice, an open-ended explorative process that Ashon Crawley (2016) might call the "living into" of an otherwise. The term "Otherwise," Crawley writes, "announces the fact of infinite alternatives to what *is*." We get the feeling of alternative possibility through our embodied sensory movement through the world, yet "the way we think the world . . . has to be altered to get at what's there" (2016, 2).

The re-membering and reframing of ancestral practices are oriented to such possibility, remaking the carceral conditions shaping lifeways in Salinas, and aligned with broader shifts in liberatory decolonizing and abolitionist social movements in the contemporary United States. In its affirmative and transformational impacts on Daniel, Rosa, Josefina, and others, it is referred to throughout this text as "cultural healing" and more often, simply, "healing." Though concerned with the ancestral, this was not a nostalgic reclamation of the past. It was a praxis of possibility that reframed the past and present to open new possibilities to live into, mobilized in multifaceted efforts to dismantle local institutions of mass incarceration, and to build new institutions of presence and affirmation, in a mode of ceremony and uplift. As the title of this book suggests, this social movement was born through embodied practices of healing, broadly conceived, with *healing movements* unfolding at intimate and more macro scales. The healing collectives' goals were nothing less than to liberate each other, and even all of us, from internalized and embodied colonial subjugation and the carceral institutions that continued to perpetuate this oppression; to build the world otherwise, starting in circle and spiraling out.

Otherwise

"Otherwise" is a theoretical concept deeply bound up with insurgent scholarship (Lethabo-King, Navarro, and Smith 2020; Crawley 2016) and has a parallel lineage in phenomenological anthropology (Zigon 2018; Povinelli 2011, 2012). Laura McTighe and I have conceptualized "otherwise" as naming and framing emergent and radically transformative political potentialities, located in the forms of life that persist and grow despite abounding conditions of carcerality, surveillance, or other forms of attempted lethal oppression (McTighe and Raschig 2019). "Otherwise" gathers and articulates emergent shifts in relation, action, perception, and possibility that do not necessarily conform to mainstream notions of activism or social change but nevertheless build an incrementally transformed world. I use the term "otherwise" throughout this book to articulate the transformations underway through cultural healing in Salinas, often paired with verbs like "building" to emphasize the active work involved.

Sometimes subtle, not always widely recognized as transformative, attending to the intimacies of building otherwise requires a conceptual vocabulary beyond liberalism, the prevailing political philosophy in Western democracies. Scholars across disciplines have reckoned with the failed promises of liberalism (W. Brown 2015; Critchley 2013; Thomas 2011; Zigon 2018; Coulthard 2014): the mythology of linear progress; the attachment to rights that require and entrench the state as arbiter of justice and the individual as its object; and the futile, righteous moralism that often emerges as people reckon with these limitations. These scholars diagnose liberalism's deep flaws while seeking to conceive new understandings and lexicons of political action without leaning on liberal "banisters" (Strong 2013). Indigenous scholars like Glen Coulthard (2014) have debunked liberal rights and recognition frameworks as pathways to Native sovereignty, and others turn to politics of refusal (Simpson 2014) and resurgence (Betasamosake Simpson 2016). Resurgence emphasizes the daily work of building "flight paths or fugitive escapes from the violences of settler colonialism," grounded in Indigenous ways of knowing, being, and relating that defy or ignore state rubrics of sovereignty and Western notions of justice (Betasamosake Simpson 2016, 23). This emphasis on building and emergence is also fundamental to abolitionist work, whose advocates have argued that carceral abolition entails not simply removing prisons from society but experimenting with and creating new institutions of presence and accountability that rework the wide reach of carcerality (Kaba 2021).

A move away from liberal reliance on rights, toward more emergent, affirmative, and embodied concepts and methods, is borne out in the shifting toolkits of contemporary American social justice activism. This is most emblematic in the rise of the "new" civil rights movement of Black Lives Matter (BLM) from 2014 onward (Day 2015). As Americans moved through the second half of the Obama era, reckoning with the realities surfacing out of earlier optimism invested in that presidency, police killings of Black men—not a new phenomenon (Burton 2015)—took on fervent new urgency. The refrain of Black Lives Matter, gaining national prominence in response to the murder of Michael Brown in Ferguson, Missouri, heralded a collective struggle not only against policing but also against the vast racialized systems of control that police embodied and enacted in their perceptions of supposed threat. While this "first crescendo" of BLM resulted largely in liberal capture and "reformist reforms," tinkering with policing rather than attacking its root logics (Maynard and Betasamosake Simpson 2022, 113), George Floyd's murder by police in 2020, early in the COVID-19 pandemic, reignited and deepened this struggle in light of the raced and classed inequities laid bare by the virus (Shanahan and Kurti 2022). "Lives mattering" further resonates with a growing attention to how bodies are shaped by enduring and ongoing oppression, as articulated in the work of adrienne maree brown and the generative somatics movement, and the renewed thinking of radical icons like Angela Davis (a. m. brown 2017, 2019; Van Gelder 2016). They take critical inspiration from Black feminist writers who dared to imagine and write another world into being, with creativity, speculation, and pleasure upheld as powerful knowledge practices.

It should be noted that the initial rise of Black Lives Matter occurred the same summer, 2014, that Salinas was experiencing its second, third, and fourth police homicides in mere months. The historical intervention and specificity of the phrase "Black lives matter" preclude any simple revision to whose lives are at stake (Yancy and Butler 2015). In other words, a "Brown lives matter" movement as such has not emerged, and should not. Instead, we can look to the work of cultural healing in Salinas as aligned with this attention to and affirmation of bodies targeted by the carceral state. Those involved in cultural healing take cues from the "old" Chicano Civil Rights Movement, while renewing it through intentional engagement with Chicana "spiritual activism" in which the spiritual and political are deeply entwined in everyday and embodied acts of resistance and refusal of oppression (Anzaldúa 2015; Facio and Lara 2014). There is no straightforward or transactional justice to be achieved, only worlds to be (re)built where all can flourish.

Though my interlocutors didn't call it "otherwise," throughout my fieldwork I heard the "Ollin." I learned that to invoke Ollin in moments of perceived shift was to articulate the emergence of otherwise: to point out that something was happening, conditions were shifting, even if it wasn't clear quite how that was occurring or what might ensue. As Shi mentioned earlier, the Ollin was transformation in progress. Ollin is a Nahuatl metaphysical modality of movement, specifically earth-quaking, relation-rumbling movement (Maffie 2015), though in its invocation in Salinas it further was understood as driving a *social* movement. For my interlocutors, Ollin refers to the deep transformations of life for peoples of Mesoamerican origin in the long struggle against colonialism. It encompasses but extends well beyond the Chicano Civil Rights Movement and continues today in novel forms. The Ollin is thus not simply a historical comparison or a metaphor; it is an enduring modality of movement and transformation.

In this book I propose Ollin as a grassroots concept of otherwise and think with it to perceive and imagine how social transformations can proceed in ways not limited by liberal tropes or notions of linear progress. In an earthquake, the landscape shifts, imperceptibly or dramatically; infrastructure and people are shuffled; but what was there to begin with is retained and rearranged. Reframing the earthquake from destructive to generative underscores the creative and possibility-laden work of building otherwise through re-membering and reframing what is already available, like one's ancestry and *cultura*. Feeling, knowing, and moving with the earth-quaking, ground-shifting dynamics of Ollin reveals the groundwork of change at an intimate and embodied level.

An Otherwise Anthropology

Paying attention to the moments when Ollin was felt and mentioned taps into the joyous and potentiated affect that permeated much of my early fieldwork especially, teaching me how it could be that the healing collectives could seem so beautiful and so historical to Shi and others. It was a feeling I took up and lived into as well, overlaid for me with marvel at the unexpected and transformative connections of fieldwork. I had moved to Salinas in 2013 to do ethnographic research on a slightly different topic—community health promotion—but connected with the nascent healing collectives just as they were finding their footing to fight local carceral systems and logics.[7] I was invited into the healing circles without planning or intent, and granted *permiso* (permission) to carry out my research in some of the myriad domestic, civic, sacralized, and activist sites of the collectives' movement work. I had a hunch that Salinas would be a good place to study ideas about health as an incitement for social transformation, and had met just enough locals to feel like it would work out before moving there. I can't know for sure, but this might also have been the Ollin.

In addition to making the case for Ollin as a grassroots concept of otherwise, in this book I further contend that a study of otherwise calls for an Otherwise Anthropology: an immersion within liberatory movement that infuses and, hopefully, transforms key aspects of anthropology itself (McTighe and Raschig 2019). The bread-and-butter method of cultural anthropology, participant observation, blends involvement in a sociocultural setting with analytical awareness. Generations of activist anthropologists have put their research in service to antiracist, decolonizing, or other liberatory political projects, though often without examining the ways anthropology as a discipline perpetuates liberal and colonial trappings, and itself must be transformed (Berry et al. 2017; Jobson 2020). Those who strive to do anthropology differently must be vigilant against (white) saviorism, inadvertently "racist anti-racism" (Baker 2021), empty allyship (Gomberg-Muñoz 2018), and persistent "liberal suppositions" (Jobson 2020). As Ruth Gomberg-Muñoz argues in "The Complicit Anthropologist," a move from allyship to accompliceship "demands that we take an unambiguous stance in a struggle that already envelops us, and that we leverage and sacrifice relative protection, access, and prestige in service to the subversion of oppressive systems" (2018, 36). Accompliceship entails becoming part of a community "that is fighting to build a more equal world" (36). As we will see, my initial participant observation in the healing collectives fostered a deepening of complicity into collectivity, an ethical and methodological mode of engagement in building substantive relations of mutuality amid relentless and racially inequitable structural violence. This has bloomed into a long-term feminist and fugitive commitment to "making shit crack off" together, in Shi's phrasing—to making something happen, prioritizing material action and shared scheming and dreaming, through means that may flout or subvert liberal academic norms (Rosas 2019; Berry et al. 2017).

This commitment emerged through relationships. While living in Salinas, I became well acquainted with people who worked in community organizations and local government, as well as residents who were generally unaffiliated with any particular group. Over the years, I have conducted semistructured interviews with approximately thirty-five people, some of whom were community organization staff, civil servants, locals, elders from the Chicanx-Indigenous spiritual community in Central and Northern California, or members of the healing collectives.[8] These relationships were kindled through my involvement in a variety of settings, especially during my initial year of doctoral fieldwork: a parents' program at a local continuation high school in Salinas; a DACA and U visa clinic in Watsonville; United Farm Workers (UFW) outreach in the fields of the Salinas Valley; an immigrant detention center visitation program in Contra Costa County; and a wide variety of one-off community events, *teatro* (Chicano critical consciousness theater) workshops and performances, and meetings and trainings with nonprofit, city, and county groups.[9]

I continued to do participant observation in many of these settings even as I became increasingly caught up in the healing collectives, which I found magnetic in their vibrancy, warmth, and critical consciousness. As members of the collectives let me tag along to many of their *encuentros* (encounters with other groups), circles, and road trips, they also put me to work in leveraging my privileges; for example, Shi made me a co-facilitator of La Colectiva de Mujeres, a role that largely provided material and administrative support to the group; Juan and Daniel were constantly enlisting me to provide public comment at county meetings, which was prefaced with mention of my "credentials" as a PhD candidate from a foreign university. I was happy to be useful to their project and didn't take this for granted. After an *encuentro* between an early formation of MILPA and peace activists in Monterey, debriefing as a group at a nearby Chili's restaurant, Daniel told me, "It means something to roll with us. I don't let just anybody into my car. Welcome to the family." After years living thousands of miles from my actual family, this invitation to belong and be part of a collective liberatory project was immensely meaningful to me, and I have taken seriously that *hermana* (sister) status and the accountability and care it entails. On numerous occasions, some members of the healing collective have made sure I behaved honorably and safely at ceremonies, or helped me feel protected in situations where I may have been vulnerable. They have also leveled with me about the privileges from which I benefit, and pushed me to be more up-front and reflexive about being a white woman writing about Chicanx lives. To be transparent about all of this is important, and I foreground my ongoing commitment to cultural healing in Salinas to maintain fidelity to the ways the people in this text have called me into intimate and active relation as a fellow member of the collectives. An Otherwise Anthropology is built through relationships that are materially and pragmatically engaged—cultivated over time through experience, effort, experimentation, and accountability—and sometimes also love.

After a year of doctoral research, I kept in contact with key interlocutors and returned for short visits to Salinas once or twice per year while finishing my dissertation abroad. I moved back to California in fall 2018, excited to be in renewed proximity to these friends and their projects. At this time I was living a three-hour drive north in Sacramento, and key members of the collectives and I intentionally built out ways of working and thinking together: redirecting grant money to interlocutors-turned-colleagues, starting new circles, compiling critical and public-facing archives, and coauthoring papers that forwarded movement goals, among other endeavors. We also just visited each other, hung out and got food or drinks, went to the beach, and occasionally did ceremony. Years on from the heyday of the police homicides and community healing circles, some friends from the collectives were doing well and excelling in their lives and careers, while others were experiencing scarcity, housing insecurity, loss, chronic illness, and stress. I was deeply cognizant of the ways I had benefited from this research over the years while others, especially among the Mujeres, had become unmoored from this network of mutuality; they had been abandoned not only by the state but also by the philanthropic organizations that were purportedly supporting them. I aimed to disrupt the ways my academic work was reproducing and profiting from this abandonment, and divert and generate social and material capital to some of the people featured in this text. Ethnographic research is not philanthropy, but, as I hope parts of this book demonstrate, its resources can be leveraged and redirected into marginalized communities in an effort to mitigate and offset the extractivism and exploitation that seems baked into academic knowledge production. As Stefano Harney and Fred Moten write, "The only possible relationship to the American university today" (2013, 26) is one of theft and fugitivity, an imperative I align with intersectional feminist commitment.[10]

This fugitive and feminist approach has theoretical implications, adding layers to the anthropology of potentiality (Zigon 2019; Mattingly 2018), a strand of the discipline that explores continental phenomenology for insight into the ontological and ethical dimensions of surprisingly radical social movements. Jarrett Zigon, leading some of this work on potentiality, has written extensively about detecting otherwise shifts through "critical hermeneutic" strategies. Critical hermeneutics calls us to "think, imagine, creatively experiment, and articulate the emergence of possibilities along with the worlds we find ourselves in" (Zigon 2018, 20). With this method, the anthropologist analytically "discloses" the novel moments of openness and shift that may be unremarkable to outsiders. These shifts may also be inarticulable to insiders, like the drug user activists Zigon works with, who often continue to invoke facile liberal discourses of rights or unity despite their actions effecting much more radical disruptions to ways of being and responding to each other.

Can such critical hermeneutic disclosure of potentiality take place during ethnographic research in collaboration and co-thinking with interlocutors themselves, rather than in its post facto analysis and writing up? Drawing on Xicana, Native, and Black liberatory literatures that have deeply concerned themselves with potentiality and the search for new modalities of change, I aim to emphasize and demonstrate an embodied methodology of potentiality: rooting the detection and analysis of otherwise in the affective qualia of bodies-in-proximity and bodies-in-a-world, "tarrying" with the intensity and materiality of shared practice to live into emergent possibilities (Crawley 2016). Ethnographic disclosure of potentiality can, and should, happen in the mix with others during fieldwork itself, as well as thereafter, in continuing dialogue and relation with interlocutors. This necessarily involves the anthropologist's accountability to intersectional and incommensurable differences in experience and privilege that have differently shaped those bodies that share space through ethnography—what Berry and colleagues (2017) articulate as the "gendered racial positionalities" that "inflect the research process" in ways not always acknowledged. It entails reckoning actively with our responsibilities to our interlocutors and each other in building equitable relations and "thick" solidarity (Shange and Liu 2019), supporting emancipatory projects in effective ways that challenge the ethical norms of academe. It means being intentional and collaborative in deciding what stories to share and how, and in making sense of interpretations that have real bearing on real lives, in real time. In so doing, we root our understandings of potentiality in bodily knowledges born of shared practice, engaging that which reforms our senses of relation and possibility (Anzaldúa 2015; Shotwell 2011). As I tracked the otherwise possibilities underway in Salinas, and the uplifting of obscured practices and understandings taking on liberatory qualities, it became clear that such tacit "enlargements" of consciousness are essential to transformative political projects (Shotwell 2011). They are also essential to a revised, liberatory purpose and value of anthropological knowledge: not to know more but to know differently, and in line with a community's political goals.

As a white, middle-class, transnational academic, I am wary of my potential misappropriation of any knowledge I forward in this text. Let me say from the outset that there are many aspects of what I write about here that I cannot and do not know because of my gender, race, and class positionality. I am uncomfortable with the fact that I, as a white woman, write about a movement of Chicanx-Indigenous cosmology, possibility, and love, and claim no right to it. I cede any authority I have to my interlocutors, who have trusted me with their experiences and teachings, and generously combed drafts of these chapters. Some key texts have come from interlocutors, like Juan, the founder of MILPA. In the context of our more recent collaborative research, he introduced me to Patrisia Gonzales's *Red Medicine* and a worn, bootleg PDF of Roberto Vargas's *Razalogia*, among other documents that have greatly enriched this book. That said, any mistakes or misinterpretations presented here are my own.

I have been granted *permiso* to gather and hold stories and support the movement's goals from my own position, its privileges, and its incapacities. And I have also been invited to sit together in circle, to walk together, to share medicine at times, to be in relation, to be an accomplice. These have been invitations to collectivity, accountability, fugitivity, not-so-fictive kinship, and other arrangements that have helped me to be, see, and know differently. I write to share this and meanwhile think about how it may inform anthropological efforts at building cross-racial and intersectional ethnographic coalitions, remaking our discipline as we contend with its ever-shifting neocolonial and extractive tendencies. At the core of this text is the beauty and potential of this community, which I am honored to share.

Tracking the Movement

This book attends to a movement that began long before those reading it were born; it will continue well past the publication cycle. It is important to remember that we are just picking up the arrows shot out by my interlocutors' ancestors, as Juan might say, leaving space in the teaching for your imagination and understanding to grow. While accounting for that longer and ongoing history, this text focuses on a period in Salinas from late 2013 through early 2023.

The first chapter offers a succinct outline of the sociohistorical context of cultural healing in Salinas, tracing the colonization and criminalization of Indigenous, *Mexicano,* and Chicanx residents of the region. These ongoing histories have strongly shaped the narratives of notoriety that have been used to characterize Salinas and its residents. Expanding on criminalization as a theoretical construct and its overlap with disposability (Cacho 2012; Giroux and Evans 2015), the chapter shows how members of the healing collectives refused these conditions as they sought to "occupy the narrative" about their home and themselves, using and expanding on the resources of health equity philanthropy. I attend to the creative, critical, and ceremonial work underway to dismantle deep-seated carceral logics and local institutions through the turn to cultural healing.

Next, I focus on the emergence of this healing movement, beginning chapter 2 with literal movement: a road trip by a small handful of collective members and me down to San Diego's Chicano Park. I attend to how the collectives creatively and strategically navigated the terrain of health philanthropy and cultural healing to challenge the proposed expansion of local carceral facilities. As this chapter will detail, the antecedents for their approach are found not strictly in the heart of Chicano Movement strategy itself—which has been widely critiqued as appropriating Indigenous identity at the expense and erasure of "contemporary Indian counterparts" (Saldaña-Portillo 2001, 405)—but in its aftershocks in subsequent decades in California. As the Chicano Movement gave way to the 1970s, a generation of activists graduated and got to work, bringing their political paradigm into professional practice (R. Vargas 1984; Acosta 2010; McKibben 2022). A lineage of Chicano activists turned mental health care professionals, community workers, and local politicians in the Central Coast region of California helped to create the conditions for cultural healing as a project of community uplift and well-being, supported by the rise of health foundations as major philanthropic players. As the subsequent generation of these activists-turned-professionals, members of MILPA and La Colectiva de Mujeres built on this project while making it their own, turning their intervention to carcerality while "getting close to" or entering into relation with the cultural and spiritual practices understood as ancestral. Tracking the collectives' exuberant and careful cultivation of a cultural healing praxis in their early stages of formation, as they engaged in struggle against the local juvenile hall expansion, reveals it as a critical method in a Chicanx-Indigenous approach to carceral abolition.

Subsequent chapters shift focus to La Colectiva de Mujeres. While initially united with MILPA with shared meetings and projects, the Colectiva was created in early 2014 to provide women on the East Side with their own space. It increasingly became independent from the other collective while still funded by Building Healthy Communities and The California Endowment. I became a part of the Colectiva early in its existence, urged by Juan to attend its *círculos* (healing circles) and "be with the women." I had never pursued friendships with other women exclusively, or imagined a shared set of experiences that I thought would be beneficially cultivated through "being women" together despite myriad other intersectional distinctions. In subsequent years, the collectives became more gender-expansive, but at the time Juan justified this split by referring to the work of healing: "The men have their own work to do, and so do the women."

While MILPA cultivated a multifaceted organization that has successfully intervened in state, county, and city policy and held leading roles in national conversations about racial equity, the Mujeres had a realness that was unconcerned with social change on an abstract level. Their bodies bore the bruises and burdens of "systems" and "institutions" every day, through their own lives and those of their kids, partners, family, and friends. The term that Shi often used to describe herself and many of the Mujeres, and that echoes throughout this book, is "raw." Rawness refers to the urgency of what they had been through and what they were ready to heal; it was unmistakable, without affectation or pretense. The Mujeres' approach aligned with Xicana feminist "theory in the flesh," where the "the physical realities of our lives . . . fuse to create a politic born out of necessity," a responsiveness to bodies as embodiments of ancestral and ongoing dispossession, and loci of collective potentiality (Moraga and Anzaldúa 1983, 23). However, this theory in the flesh did not always align with the TCE's philanthropic "theory of change."

The third chapter foregrounds the Mujeres' healing praxis as based in their twice-weekly circles. It interrogates the relationship between stress and possibility as shaped by Chicanx-Indigenous cultural healing. The bodies of low-income Chicana-Indigenous women are often sites of chronic racialized and gendered stress, as well as tremendous potentiality. Women in the Colectiva articulated chronic stresses as *cargas*, Spanish for burden, baggage, or charge. Unloading these stresses within the group, or *descargando*, led to actions mobilized as anticarceral activism. Attention to their sense of stress carried collectively as *cargas* builds on Black feminist understandings of stress as structured by racialized criminalization and state and carceral violence, while illuminating the materiality and potentiality of this embodiment in Chicana-Indigenous contexts. The strategies cultivated for healing in these conditions underscore that stress is a worldly phenomenon, requiring emergent coalitions addressing social and structural conditions rather than solely individual therapeutic remedy or resilience. I follow how the *cargas* of a Mujer named Esme were "picked up" by others in the Colectiva to launch a variety of world-building efforts. These actions may not have directly mitigated Esme's situation but were refracted into other social and structural transformations, demonstrating how cultural healing, as a praxis of possibility, can instigate a variety of shifts compelled by a deeply embodied, haptic sense of contingency and connection.

Chapter 4 argues for a homegirl *noble* (noble) femininity at the core of many of the Mujeres' ongoing intergenerational affiliations in and beyond local gangs. I ask, how do Chicana and *Mexicana* women who have been active in local gangs make sense of and build upon their experiences with gang affiliation? In contrast to literatures that seek and champion the "exits" or "recoveries" from gang affiliation, I take a relational ethics approach to explore the continuities and ambivalences of affiliation across generations through the intertwined lives and forms of care demonstrated by some members of the Colectiva, their friends, and their children. I track how some Mujeres carefully navigated and mobilized these relationships to maintain a sense of generational belonging and accomplishment for the work they "put in" as women in gangs, and realized a stewardship role in easing the lives of younger generations. Paying attention to the ways the Mujeres and their homegirls maintained these caring relations undermines the broad notion that gangs are primarily criminal organizations, and that gang membership is an inherently detrimental state that must be rejected, or from which one must recover, in order to participate fully in society. I show how a social shift away from preventative and violence-suppressing strategies, and toward a culturally affirmative paradigm, provided a welcoming and generative set of conditions for the continuity of ethical aspects of affiliation. By continuing to nurture these relationships, now inflected by the Colectiva and its cultural and ancestral teachings, the women cultivated a homegirl-turned-Mujer, chola-turned-*comadre* femininity that had long been growing, its roots in their youth, its bloom undetected.[11]

Chapter 5 centers the Mujeres' actions and affects in response to the police killings in Salinas in 2014. This was a fraught and factionalized period, as local and nonlocal groups attempted in various ways to organize residents and intervene on police brutality. In response to the homicides of four Latino men, the Mujeres made a series of very visible as well as more covert and intimate *movidas*, movements or actions (Espinoza, Blackwell, and Cotera 2018, 2) that asserted their roles as caregivers of community healing. Though the collective conversation just prior to these homicides aimed to affirm and make space for women's leadership, the Mujeres' actions were interpreted by some movement colleagues as "too rugged" and contradicting or endangering community strategies of cultural healing. Later, they were left out of official local accounts of resident action, in a parallel to how many Chicana feminists' interventions have been largely absent from or silenced in memorializations of the Chicano Civil Rights Movement (Blackwell 2011). Working closely with Shi and Pamela, I offer this alternative historiography to show how their actions were taken in adamant affirmation of Latinx life, with cultural healing at their core. In doing so, I open otherwise understandings of the change fought for in this period and acknowledge and honor what was dismissed. I show how the Mujeres' commitment to going *out there* and *walking together* remade the grounds of struggle, extending beyond the four police homicides of Chicano and Salvadoreño men to address urgent and embodied experiences of state violence and abandonment in the lives of those intimately impacted. This chapter is an inherently partial account of this period of police homicides, but its fragments refract bodies in collective movement and struggle, walking together when it felt like everything was falling apart. Drawing on Eve Kosofsky Sedgwick's "reparative read" (2003), I suggest here an Otherwise Anthropological way of reading that is oriented to taking up the provocations of transformative political projects. I hope that as you read the words on these pages, they pierce you like a *grito*, or a shiny point of obsidian, refracting something more.[12]

I underscore the critical importance of affirming rugged or raw femininity and building spaces and socialities of its cultivation in the sixth and final chapter. The ethnography featured here picks up five years after the initial period of police homicides, when Shi and I both returned to California and decided to start holding healing space again. When another police homicide occurred in March 2019, this time of a young woman named Brenda Mendoza who was mentally ill and experiencing homelessness, it confirmed the necessity of carving out space for women to heal and be playful or unruly away from the disciplinary and punitive technologies of the state and health philanthropy. Brenda's life and death were emblematic of the compounding challenges facing low-income women of color in the region, with its housing costs skyrocketing, in part, after a decade of philanthropic investment. Compelled to respond to Brenda's murder, and without philanthropic funding, Shi and I redirected an ethnographic research grant to be able to hold a space of abundance. In these new circles, held at a methadone clinic among Chicana and *Mexicana* women largely experiencing addiction and housing insecurity, the work of healing as well as the healing possibilities of play could be practiced and shared. Participants in these circles engaged in a playful and ribald mode, in experiments with freedom and relationality that capacitated the *confianza* (trust and familiarity) to excavate and remediate painful experiences. Focusing on this experimentation, this chapter speaks to the gendered and classed limitations placed on cultural healing when it is professionalized in philanthropic contexts. It further explores the more radical possibilities of fugitive anthropological engagement in support of spaces of nourishment and play, in contexts of state and institutional lethality.

The conclusion draws together the myriad strands of anticarceral action enabled through cultural healing efforts in Salinas to emphasize the multifaceted and grassroots work that braids distinct campaigns into a transformative movement. Alongside MILPA's more public anticarceral work and achievements in the region, I recenter ongoing relations among the Mujeres and consider how their trajectories continue to be shaped by carcerality as well as cultural healing. Sharing scenes from a memorial circle to mourn a deceased Mujer in late 2022, I emphasize that this otherwise project may not fully overcome entrenched structures of power, but it has made clear relational impacts that continue to remake the world for those intimately involved. I consider what an Otherwise Anthropological commitment looks like in the face of these ongoing struggles and disparities.

Back Together

In early 2014, after a Colectiva circle but before the police homicides that would direct our lives in the coming months, Shi and I held one of our long debriefs in the ever-darkening parking lot behind the BreadBox. Arms crossed and holding our bags of supplies, we stood next to my car. After circle, we typically worked through what some of the Mujeres had shared, and what we thought would be good to talk about in the next circle. This time, Shi told me about a dream she had had that weekend.

"We were together in a past life, doing this work," she said, going on to describe the dream involving both of us and an elder who was also part of the Colectiva at that time. In the dream we were shadowy but discernible, late-stage Aztec, working together in another moment of the same struggle: what was now a fight against the expansion of the local juvenile hall, more abstractly the criminalization of *Mexicano*, Chicanx, and Latinx residents of Salinas, and soon acutely against racialized police violence, was meanwhile also the ongoing struggle against colonialism and genocide.

"We were working together on something but, like, it didn't get complete," she said. "Now we're back together trying to do it again."

I was both excited and terrified by what Shi was telling me. Excited to be accepted by this powerful and sensitive woman after having randomly shown up in her midst. Terrified because I took seriously her idea that we were together in a past life and immediately began to reckon with what this meant. Was my presence in Salinas part of a broader metaphysical transformation, not the result of my research design? Was it something about my patrilineal Spanish heritage? How were my ancestors complicit in colonialism? How was I? How did these intergenerational complicities and entanglements shape my accountability to this emerging movement?

In dreaming this and telling me about it, Shi was calling me in to a struggle with stakes much deeper in time than was immediately evident. To Shi, it was not entirely random that I ended up doing my doctoral fieldwork in Salinas. Our connection had already been established on some other level we couldn't fully know or understand, but which we could embrace and live into. These were the stakes of cultural healing: nothing less than the broad sweep from colonialism to carcerality that had variably impacted us, but which nevertheless involved us both. We were going to continue the work our ancestors had prepared for us. This was the Ollin.

1

Occupying the Narrative

From Criminalization to Cultural Healing

Refusing Oppression

In the classroom of a Salinas community college, a *maestra* (respected teacher) took a bright green feather and wafted copal smoke over a plastic cup of water. After a short prayer in Nahuatl and English, she sent the cup around the *círculo* to be collectively sipped by the array of women and men present. Some young and others considered elders, most were members of the healing collectives, and all were Salinas residents.

The ceremonial gesture formally opened day one of the Academia Ollin, a youth healing and critical consciousness program organized by MILPA in 2014. I use it to open this chapter as well. When I write here about criminalization and disposability, I want readers to remember this moment with water. *Stay close to the water*, as my friends would say. The blessings of togetherness, and of water and its medicine, are at the core of the work to build otherwise and, as they put it, "occupy the narrative" of Salinas.

Situating Salinas

"California is a story. California is many stories," Deborah A. Miranda writes in *Bad Indians: A Tribal Memoir* (2013). Her memoir is a critical reassemblage of state history from the experiences of her Ohlone Costanoan Esselen ancestors in what is now Carmel, about twenty miles west from Salinas on the Pacific coast. Miranda's work reveals the rich lives of her relatives as they came to intersect with the Carmel Mission; marginalized or left out of state history, their restored stories offer important counterpoints to settler power. She provokes the question:

Who gets to tell the stories or craft the narratives that determine how a people and a place are known or knowable?

In this chapter, I trace some of the historical and socioeconomic dynamics of the Central Coast of California to demonstrate how generations of settler colonialism, racialized and exclusionary immigration policies, civic disinvestment, and carceral capture have shaped the conditions of life in Salinas and the state. California's economic prowess has been contingent on industrialized agriculture and mass incarceration, both of which have roots in settler colonial labor formations and rely on a steady number of bodies conveniently rendered "surplus" (Gilmore 2007).[1] What was formerly "uncivilized" and requiring colonization became criminalized and disposable in a durative and dehumanizing system of racial capitalism, rooted in local economies such as in the Salinas region. Moving from this historical context into the specificities of contemporary Salinas, I show how these conditions fostered narratives of notoriety of the city and its working-class inhabitants. These narratives provided clear domains for intervention, which members of the healing collectives sought to refuse and co-opt, "occupying" and reorienting these damaging discourses through the turn to cultural healing.

The terrain now named as Monterey Bay and the Salinas Valley have long been home to Ohlone peoples known as Awaswas, Mutsun, Rumsen, Chalon; and to the Esselen and Salinan peoples.[2] The diverse and at times majestic region is abundant with marine, coastal, and sylvan resources and has been tended since time immemorial. In December 1602, the Spanish soldier, merchant, and explorer Sebastian Vizcaíno and his crew, making their way north along the coastline, landed at the village of Achasta, unilaterally renamed by them as Monterey (Akins and Bauer 2021, 42). Local populations tried to compel them to leave the coast, in part through temporarily retreating to the interior themselves (42). More than a century later, in the late 1760s and early 1770s, the Spanish returned as Jesuit missionaries, establishing the Carmel, Soledad, Santa Cruz, and San Juan Bautista Missions in the region as well as the Presidio at Monterey. These settlers sickened, disciplined, displaced, enslaved, or exiled many Indigenous inhabitants in a vast campaign of dehumanization waged in the name of saving souls (D. A. Miranda 2013).

The region formed a key ground of settler power, with Monterey serving as the political and religious capital of Mexican California until 1846.

The Spanish, and then the Anglos, victors of the Mexican-American War (1846–48) who took over the landscape and means of production, accumulated profit and political and epistemic power in what would become the modern state of California. A few miles inland from coastal Monterey, in what became established as a highly productive agricultural landscape, individuals of multiple racial, ethnic, and national identities converged to turn Salinas into "the poster child for nineteenth-century city-building" in the region and the nascent state of California (McKibben 2022, 23). However, those of Mexican and Indigenous origin (also known as Californios) were ultimately dispossessed of their land and racialized as inferior and criminal—despite the Treaty of Guadalupe, which was signed at the end of the Mexican-American War and was meant to guarantee the citizenship and property rights of Mexican citizens residing in the United States. The treaty was famously disregarded in practice (Escobar 1999, 8).

In the early 1930s, Salinas, sitting at a crossroads of state transportation infrastructure and power, became a magnet for dust bowl refugees and migrant laborers. Poor white populations from the Great Plains, also known as Okies, made their way to the fertile valley to work in the fields along with a mosaic of other racialized groups already doing this labor. As the United States entered World War II, conscripting male citizens to fight abroad, the Bracero Program was established to bring Mexican laborers to pick crops in America's fields, importing an estimated 4.5 million workers from 1943 to 1964 (Massey and Liang 1989). Advocates for the Bracero Program and this kind of targeted labor immigration stressed Mexican "docility," even as contradictory racialized narratives of juvenile delinquency prominent in cities like Los Angeles were criminalizing Mexican American Pachuco youth in the same period (Escobar 1999). Despite critiques of the Bracero Program from Mexican and US perspectives, and white xenophobia that aimed to keep these workers temporary, many braceros, as they were known, ended up settling and put down roots in the United States, including in the Salinas area. They used the guest worker program as a means of building other opportunities for careers in agriculture. These workers and their families largely settled in an unincorporated annex of Salinas known as the Alisal, which remains today a heavily working-class *Mexicano* and Chicanx area and the heart of the city, also called East Salinas or simply the East Side.

The braceros' settlement in Salinas tipped the demographic balance in the area toward an increasingly *Mexicano* and Mexican American labor force and population. With its large farmworker population, the region provided an important battleground for the United Farm Workers movement in the 1960s and 1970s. César Chávez and his UFW followers literally and figuratively set Salinas's fields on fire in the 1970s in the name of farmworker rights and protections, amid embattled worker-grower relations. Chávez was incarcerated—his only time locked up as a UFW leader—for twenty days at the old Monterey County Jail during a UFW-led lettuce boycott in 1970 that halted production for months in a region that produced most of the country's salad greens. His imprisonment in Salinas for the lettuce strikes and related actions, and the subsequent years of violence against UFW members in the city for their role in the struggle, offer an early glimpse of the role of police in maintaining labor and agricultural production in the region. Chávez's eventual release, ordered by the California Supreme Court, affirmed that boycotts were legal organizing strategies, paving the way for future radical methods of organizing that rework ideas of criminality. Even as the UFW's prominence as an activist organization decreased in the region after the mid-1970s, Chávez's approach to organizing, and the self-determination values at its core, gave rise to the impressive panoply of community-serving health and civic institutions in the region (Kohl-Arenas 2015; Seif 2008).

Salinas's proximity to a set of carceral and military institutions further underscores the region's centrality to shifting twentieth-century and twenty-first-century ideas about surveillance, incarceration, and justice in California—itself a bellwether of carcerality across the nation. Just down the Salinas Valley, Soledad State Prison (later renamed Soledad Correctional Training Facility) was designed in the 1940s as a "model prison" oriented to the virtue of hard labor (Yee 1973). It was the site of infamous prison riots in the 1970s and the deaths of George Jackson and two other inmates, icons of the Black Panther movement. The Naval Postgraduate Academy, a half-hour drive west of Salinas on the Monterey Peninsula, has been key in the development of counterinsurgency tactics, used not only in global military interventions but also in domestic policing strategies that target "street terrorism," a legal term for gang activity. While many California cities are home to gang organizations,

Salinas has an outsize notoriety as being rife with gangs and gangsters, a narrative that is arguably an attribute of its police force's early adoption of this military tactic and collaboration with federal street terrorism task forces. Gang affiliation here is relatively common, though far from total, with both Norteños (typically involving those who see themselves as Mexican American, and more common in Northern California) and Sureños (who tend to be more identified with Mexico, with a large base in Southern California) establishing a strong presence in this Central California region. In Salinas, these groups have been splintered into factions in the past few decades, destabilized by federal stings in the 1990s and the first decade of the twenty-first century that took out gang leadership only to see low-ranking "foot soldiers" take over and multiply rather than quit (Reynolds 2014).

Fundamentally, I want to stress that gang affiliation does not equate to criminal activity. Often, affiliation comes through cultural, geographic, and kinship ties and produces an array of prosocial and noncriminogenic impacts and outcomes (Mendoza-Denton 2008; Brotherton 2015). Attempting to shift the academic conversation toward an appreciation of the resistance qualities of gangs as "street organizations," David Brotherton and Luis Barrios characterized them as providing their members with a "resistant identity, an opportunity to be individually and collectively empowered, a voice to speak back to and challenge the dominant culture, a refuge from the stresses and strains of barrio or ghetto life and a spiritual enclave within which its own sacred rituals can be generated and practiced" (2004, 23). Similarly, as my friend Nathan put it as we drove up to do ceremony in Northern California with other members of the healing collectives, "A gang is just a group of people who refuse to be oppressed."

Today, Salinas is a growing city of approximately 165,000, though unofficial tallies place this number closer to 180,000, suggesting a significant undocumented population. It is prominently *Mexicano* and Chicanx. East Salinas is a particularly family-oriented and youthful place, home to hardworking *abuelitas* (grandmothers), beloved *paleteros* (people who sell ice cream and snacks from a mobile cart), cholos and chipsters (Chicano hipsters), youngish professionals who want to give back to their community, and elders who love to recount how they marched with César and the United Farm Workers in the 1960s.[3]

The census glosses over such details in listing Salinas as nearly 80 percent "Hispanic or Latino." More than a third of the city's population is foreign-born; about one-quarter is estimated to be undocumented; and approximately 14 percent of the population is considered to live in poverty (United States Census Bureau 2022). These are likely conservative, undercounted figures, excluding the swells in population that come during the harvest, most visible in the increased number of cars lining East Salinas neighborhood streets, or the prominence of people living unhoused, temporarily or permanently displaced by housing insecurity in this increasingly unaffordable region. Salinas has been named as one of the most expensive cities for housing in the country (Cimini 2020).[4]

Heavily industrialized fields of lettuce, strawberries, celery, broccoli, artichokes, and other crops form a perimeter around Salinas and extend south down the Salinas Valley. In this mild growing climate, there is work in or around the fields ten months a year. Some ninety thousand people in the region work in the fields, making an average annual income of $17,500, serving a farming industry valued at $8.5 billion (Villarejo and Wadsworth 2018). Even the high property values of this region, within striking distance of the Bay Area, cannot compete with the value of land for agriculture. Down the valley, unincorporated farmworker communities endure pesticide-contaminated water while their residents pick America's food. In uncanny juxtaposition to this entrenched structural poverty, a half-hour drive from Salinas, along a road that winds between rolling golden hills at the north end of the Santa Lucia mountains, will deliver you to überwealthy Monterey, Pebble Beach, and Carmel. Salinas thus straddles both abject poverty and extreme wealth, and Monterey County, with its significant disparities, encapsulates many of California's inequities: an agro-carceral economy that creates enormous wealth for some on the Black- and Brown-skinned backs of populations deemed exploitable, expendable, and criminalized (Gilmore 2007; Cacho 2012).

Made Criminal

Criminalized: made criminal. Criminalization, of both people and places, is the institutionalized and intersubjective assumption of inherent criminality along raced, classed, and gendered lines and spatialized in neighborhoods (Cacho 2012). It overlaps with disposability: a lived condition of being considered and treated as not mattering, as being expendable, producing an alienation that can discourage political solidarity and resistance (Giroux and Evans 2015). In Salinas, these logics result in suspicion and dehumanization, demonstrated in the vast city resources spent primarily on policing streets and schools; they creep into the imaginations of Brown kids who may learn early on to see themselves as destined for the juvenile hall perched on a hill above the local soccer complex. These logics surface in the words of the probation officer at a traffic stop who sneered at Yarri, "You'll be back," or Juana's palpable stress as her son faced down what was likely to be a very long sentence; they suffused other Salinas residents' judgment of some Mujeres as too "raw" to be taken seriously, making them feel like their struggles and the urgency of their pain disqualified them from being or belonging in the community. Logics of criminalization and disposability fueled the dismissal of shootings in Salinas as "just gangsters killing gangsters," leaving those cases cold, unsolved, by a police force that believed a season on the pro-police reality show *Live PD* would be good public relations for them (Duan 2016).

These logics shape painfully stigmatizing discursive narratives, evident in clickbait headlines that declare Salinas among "the least educated cities in America" (Dill 2014) or "the murder capital of California" (Magdaleno 2016). And these narratives also echoed through what some Salinas residents themselves were saying during my initial fieldwork in 2013–14, that residents needed to "look inside their families" and "speak out," exercising vigilance at home and telling police about what they have witnessed in order to achieve justice.[5] These were the narratives of notoriety that needed to be occupied and changed, as they shaped the ways Salinas residents saw themselves and each other.

The call to look inside one's family and turn on one's loved ones made Shi's stomach churn. It came out, loud and insistent, at a press conference she and I attended in 2014 with the theme "Living in Fear." The event featured a city councilor and the leader of a Christian group for mothers of murdered youth, organized informally outside of a rotunda in East Salinas's Closter Park, after three of that year's four police homicides. The twenty-five or so attendees had informally arranged themselves in a circle, but Shi and I held back; this was one circle we didn't want to be a part of. As the speakers exhorted the audience to not live in fear of police, and to take up the surveillance of the carceral state at home, Shi made small noises of disgust and refusal under her breath. At some point, she had to step away, and motioned for me to come with her. We walked back across the grass to her parked blue Mustang, which she leaned on, clearly anguished.

"Megan, they can't expect people to be connecting with police after all this shit has happened," she said, referencing the police homicides but also the community's much longer history of violence, surveillance, and dehumanization at the hands of state agents. "The police are not gonna be protecting the community. They're just not. That's the way it is."[6]

Stay close to the water and the sharing of blessings, amid that abandonment and this explication. Stay close to that connection.

At its core, Salinas is a place where things grow—lettuce, strawberries, cannabis; kinship, ideas, possibility. Residents of Salinas have developed their own ways of refusing and destabilizing the myriad forms of state and epistemic violence that had turned their city into a notorious place and rendered themselves criminalized by association, reframing those supposed deficits into new tools for novel action.

At times it felt like everyone I met in Salinas was engaged in some process of trying to "change the narrative," telling a different story about the city. Often, these revised narratives aimed to reveal the "good" amid the prevailing negative imagery of gang violence and grinding poverty. Many of these efforts trafficked in easily redemptive imaginaries: the straight A student coming from a poor farmworker family, the good but doomed kid who resisted the gang life but still got caught up. One documentary about the city, *The Salinas Project* (C. E. Brown 2014), epitomized this approach. Its description characterizes the four young people featured in the film as being "without resources, and sometimes undocumented," with a future that "is often uncertain," yet "their hope and resilience is abundant" (C. E. Brown 2023). The film's narrative upholds the neoliberal idea of individualistic resilience as what is required to transcend the challenges of everyday life in Salinas, and rests on the values of hope and hard work. While these four young people deserve to be celebrated, so too do the resources that do exist in this city and among its residents—resources that may not match existing liberal expectations or are misrecognized as deficits.

At the same time as *The Salinas Project* was developed and released, a more creative and radical reframing and rebuilding of criminalizing narratives and logics was also underway. It was driven by systems-impacted or formerly incarcerated women and men like Shi, Daniel, and Nathan and, perhaps surprisingly, funded by health equity philanthropy. How could such radical realizations take form in a philanthropic context, notoriously structured to neutralize any challenges to status quo understandings and power relations?

Health Equity and Cultural Healing

I first met members of the nascent healing collectives at a public hearing about the county's proposed juvenile hall expansion in late 2013. In a bright but windowless gymnasium, staid civil servants tried to put a positive spin on expanding this carceral facility for children. Poster boards with blueprints for the facility's potential new locations lined the walls, and while some people milled about examining them from a distance, a group of parents and youth stationed themselves around the perimeter of the seats and packed the speakers' line.

At this point, I was still finding my way in my fieldwork. I had met some friendly and interesting people but didn't feel like I had found solid ground, and my initial attempt to conduct ethnography with a local health promotion organization was not panning out. To placate my insecurity and keep busy, I was attending any and all programming in Salinas that seemed related to community health. Though the county government likely tried to bury this public hearing, it was being heavily promoted by community organizations to encourage residents, those most likely to be impacted by this juvenile hall, to show up and realize they could have a say. These organizations framed the event (improbably, to my fresh-to-the-field mind) in terms of health. I was noticing the phrase "Health Happens Here" all around town, on billboards and flyers for events, reflecting a massive influx of funding from The California Endowment, the philanthropic offshoot of insurance giant Blue Cross and a major funder of health equity projects in the state. "Health Happens Here" was a catchy, alliterative slogan for the healthification of a variety of social problems, and was both active and ambiguous: How exactly does health "happen"? It seemed to me at the time that criminal justice and health were separate domains—surely, incarceration was horrible for bodies and led to dire health outcomes. But I did not yet grasp how health equity could offer a critical framework that, as others would later point out to me, could "give cover to what we're doing"—abolish carceral systems and dismantle logics of racialized criminalization, bit by bit.

People who would soon feel like family were quietly organizing against the juvenile hall expansion and were present at that public hearing. In the audience, I listened to the woman I would get to know as Shi as she stood at the podium, eyes downcast as she described what her severely epileptic son had been through with probation, routinely testing dirty for the medical cannabis prescribed by his doctors. I spotted a couple of men whose stylish attire stood out among the sea of Cali Bear hoodies among residents, and suits among the civil servants. To my surprise, the two men approached me toward the end of the event, shaking me out of my assumption of invisibility. In Salinas, Shi told me later, there are always eyes on you. You are always being seen.

"Hey there! I'm Daniel," the shorter one, his outfit complete with a bow tie, said to introduce himself while extending his hand. "This is my brother, Juan," he added, gesturing to the taller man who was wearing a distinctive and, I thought, very cool felt bowler hat. I shook both their hands and introduced myself.

"Are you a journalist?" Daniel asked.

"Not exactly," I replied, as I explained my unusual situation as a PhD student from the University of Amsterdam. They asked how I ended up in Salinas, and I said it was a long story.

Luckily, there would be time for long stories. As we exchanged contact information, they said they would reach out to me to do more *conocimiento*. At the time, I took this for granted as meaning "getting to know each other" but have come to appreciate *conocimiento* as a relational knowledge practice at the core of the healing collectives' praxis of change—getting to know each other; sharing space, experiences, and dreams; and building a movement through and upon those relations. Juan and Daniel were just starting up a collective they called MILPA and were looking for folks to join what Juan called "the movement, the new social justice of healing."

Among those trying to build otherwise in Salinas, a discourse of health was growing in relevance and possibility. *Health*, in all its broad polyvalence, had become a critical and capacious framework for understanding and addressing Salinas's social conditions for a variety of stakeholders. As we will see, it may have been *too* capacious in some ways and deeply limited in others, able to hold contradictory aims and disciplinary constraints all at once. For example, county law enforcement problematized crime and gang violence as a public health problem, reiterating a key tenet of violence prevention and suppression strategies active across the country and in the region since the first decade of the twenty-first century.[7] These strategies gave police greater ability to act on suspicions and intervene, preemptively, in school zones and communities, contributing to the carceralization of schools and the criminalization of *Mexicano* and Chicanx youth. But discourses of health were also mobilized by liberal philanthropists to problematize the structural conditions of local poverty through quantitative data on resident life outcomes. Using these data, they argued for and funded more streetlamps, park improvements, community biking events, and other infrastructures of wellness broadly aligned with liberal notions of health. They also, at times, made space for more radical notions such as those forwarded by the healing collectives.

East Salinas was one of fourteen sites statewide selected for long-term funding by The California Endowment through its Building Healthy Communities initiative, with a ten-year engagement begun in 2009. The California Endowment funded grassroots projects that addressed and built health equity, contributing significant resources to improve the social determinants of health in sites of socioeconomic disparity along race, class, and geographic lines. From its health equity perspective, a key domain of social justice is bodies capable of achieving certain criteria of healthfulness: life expectancy; daily activity; access to fresh and healthy food; as well as "social-emotional wellbeing," or the ability to form friendships, build confidence and happiness, and become reflective. Investment by BHC in resident health equity funded and supported the initial emergence of the Salinas healing collectives, and over the years imparted training, vocabulary, and expectations that strongly shaped the collectives' impact in the community.

I consider health equity to be another narrative that the collectives further sought to occupy—that is, make use of while also making it their own. While it was less pernicious and violent than other prevailing narratives of criminalized notoriety or moralistic redemption, health equity was nevertheless limited, imposed, and at times disciplinary. Without specifying what exactly health equity could be or how it could be achieved, TCE gave space for radical projects while also maintaining the power to decide at what point something was no longer "healthy" and meriting support.

Uncovering a Path to Our Spirits: Cultural Healing

Among the community organizers and residents who form the focus of this ethnography, occupying the narrative of health equity while pivoting to *healing* opened up a fertile set of material, sensorial, and imaginative resources for pursuing forms of world-making that would provide more opportunity and affirmation to residents. Material or financial resources can, of course, be crucial in any underresourced community, with TCE and other health philanthropy organizations providing considerable funds for grassroots organizing in Salinas. These material resources are laced with conservatism and professionalization, obligations and norms that can neutralize radical projects (INCITE! Women of Color against Violence 2009; Kohl-Arenas 2015), yet they can also make it possible for many individuals to participate in them and be remunerated. As we will see, the professionalization of social movements attempted by philanthropy is not always complete and sometimes can help to sow radically affirmative projects and visions of liberation.

    For now, I want to draw attention to the resources that afforded novel imagination and experience of given social realities: the capacity to feel, acknowledge, and affirm that Salinas is not inherently the notorious or deprived place claimed by hegemonic narratives of disposability and deficit. The community's assets surface through what Shi earlier called "that cultural piece": the revelation and affirmation of residents' Mesoamerican Indigenous ancestry and *cultura*, and the value of their contemporary streetwise way of life, as a foundation for otherwise understanding and practice amid interlocking state-sanctioned campaigns dedicated to their criminalization and disposability. The California Endowment did not create or control *cultura*, but it did fund and facilitate access to it for some. And lifting up and living into this cultural patrimony, in the community as well as individual lives, was the work of cultural healing.

Without ethnographic attention, "healing" as it circulates in contemporary American political vernacular risks being dismissed as individualizing at best and empty and patronizing at worst, alongside routine invocations of "hopes and prayers." As Dian Million powerfully writes in *Therapeutic Nations* (2013), the twentieth-century trope of colonialism as "wounding" and the attendant turn to programs and narratives of healing in Indigenous communities in settler colonial contexts can easily slip into individualizing self-care at the expense of collective self-determination. These projects are formed in neoliberal conditions and may end up reinforcing those social and economic structures rather than undermining them or growing radical alternatives (Million 2013, 8).

But for the people featured in this text, cultural healing was not an empty or neoliberal gesture. Instead, it was a rich and generative set of practices and relationships blending Chicanx-Indigenous spirituality and anticarceral activism. It especially resonated among those who had been impacted by carceral systems, whether through their own experiences or those of their loved ones—those who experienced criminalization in its most insidious forms.

Healing practices were appealingly "familiar," as a Mujer named Eli put it, "because we lose it." She was referring to a common generational rift between Mexican grandparents, migrant parents, and American-born or American-raised kids, where ancestral cultural practices become subject to acculturation pressures in a new environment. In our interview, she recalled as a child watching her *abuelita* put herbs into a bucket of water to sprinkle around an accident-prone intersection near their house in East Salinas, not understanding the act or what it might do, but retaining the sense of its power with her decades later. The healing collectives, Eli said, were primarily for these American-born or American-raised Chicanx generations, and especially those whose lives unfolded in or adjacent to gangs and mass incarceration, opening up a form of reconnection with a part of themselves that had been buried but was still somehow familiar—and essential.

Alvaro, a young man incarcerated for much of his youth, described cultural healing to me as "uncovering a path to our spirits"—a path that had been covered over by centuries of dispossession and displacement, organized oppression and its daily indignities, and, for some, *la vida loca* of gang involvement as a form of survivance and solidarity inviting profound social sanction. The notion of "uncovering" stands in critical contrast to narratives of "gang recovery" (E. O. Flores 2013), which posit a therapeutic trajectory away from gang life and toward respectability, often through spiritual or religious frameworks. Cultural healing, here, does not require a movement unidirectionally away from "that street part of ourselves," as Alvaro put it, so much as an emphatic public revaluation of it: as something with distinctly positive attributes as well as something with deeper roots in systemic oppression, with a "timescale of genocide" (National Compadres Network 2012).

Palabras and *Palabra*

As subsequent chapters will continue to demonstrate, cultural healing became a widely shared, collective project and source of potentiality in Salinas as residents rallied against the juvenile hall expansion and wave of police brutality. These flash points laid bare the deep-seated carceral logics of criminalization and disposability that heavily shaped resident lives and futures. Re-membering and reframing *cultura* became a means of reworking these logics from their quotidian experience and embodiment, while also providing tools for organizing against carcerality. It was these vocabularies, practices, socialities, and affirmations that made their work to revise Salinas's narratives of notoriety so exciting and potentiated—not only changing the words but challenging the foundations of social life in this city.

"Megan—you feeling it today? Can you talk about occupying the narrative?" Juan asked me, as we collectively chilled on benches and picnic tables beneath a grove of trees on the UC Santa Cruz campus. He had invited me to join a group that was giving a presentation on MILPA's method and goals to an ethnic studies undergraduate class. We had not prepared in any specific way prior to arriving among the redwoods, but luckily the class we thought started at 2:30 actually began an hour later.

"I can try!" I replied, though I was anxious about being in a position to represent the group. I typically avoided public speaking at all costs, and as a white woman relatively new to the area I did not want to speak for the collective or take an opportunity away from someone else. However, as Juan explained, eight of us were there from MILPA, and each would take a piece of the presentation.

"Three things," he enumerated. "One, this generation has the opportunity more than ever to tell its own stories. Two, we are imparting a vocabulary and it is based on love and discipline. Three, *palabra*. All of this has to be done with *palabra*."

I scribbled down these thoughts into my yellow composition notebook, trying to capture his exact words. Juan was always dropping sharp phrases and crisp ideas.

"Maybe you can also say something about how we're challenging our language and thinking, not our principles," he added.

"Sure, yes," I replied, still jotting notes.

Perhaps sensing my nerves, he brought out his gourd rattle, a dried, hollowed-out squash with a long wooden handle and white beaded strands of leather hanging down. The gourd rattle is an important instrument in Native American Church ceremonial practice, and members of MILPA often brought theirs out to practice together during quiet moments.[8] With his elbow stabilized on his knee, Juan began to shake the rattle at a brisk tempo I recognized from the peyote songs he would play when we carpooled, and that were performed as prayer in ceremony. "The rattle focuses your thinking. The sound, those are your ideas. The rattle syncs up with your heart and mind and focuses it all together and when you shake it, it prepares you to speak."

He offered it to me to try. It felt at once energizing and grounding. A few of the youngsters rolling with MILPA that day gathered to try it as well.

"That's your heartbeat," Juan told us. "And the sound is channeling the elders. It syncs up with their ideas too. The knowledge comes through." His teaching linked the generation of words, literally *palabras*, with the ethical concept of *palabra*, having integrity in one's word and honor.

As the class started, the eight of us took turns presenting solo or in pairs, while the rest stood attentive and waiting at the side of the room. Rene, who had a degree in criminal justice, introduced the collective and its work around health equity, race, and justice. John, sharply dressed in a suit and with his hair in a long braid, discussed "the need for solidarity." Two youngsters outlined how MILPA was building an "intergenerational think tank," engaging in "critical resistance" and addressing "structuralized racialization." Each speaker held the gourd rattle as they presented, careful not to shake it around while gesturing, but to instead calmly hold it upright, like a strong, straight spine.

The "Occupying the Narrative" segment of the presentation was up after "The Canary in the Barrio." As they called me up, I set down my notebook as I took the rattle. I could not hold both at once. But also, if they trusted me to speak, I should trust myself, as well as trust the rattle and the elders to guide my thoughts. I tried to hit all the points listed on the PowerPoint projected behind me: *flor y canto*, sacred intersectionality, pedagogy of *palabra*, using a different style to tell another story about this people and place.[9] Occupying the narrative was about much more than words. It was in the praxis of cultural healing in everyday moments; staying close to the water, grounding with the rattle, leading with *palabra*, doing it together while mindful that the ancestors were with us. This was the movement, and we were moving with it.

2

Making the Movement of Healing

Navigating Paths to La Cultura

Going with the Medicine

"Shit, guys! We're gonna come back *all* medicined up from this trip!!" Juan said, smiling big. He craned his neck from the passenger seat to look back at Shi and me in the second row and the young brothers, known as AB and Batman, in the rear of the rented van. Rene drove, barreling down the coastal Highway 1.

We were somewhere between Morro Bay and Santa Barbara, en route to San Diego's Chicano Park with a few special stops along the way. After

Figure 2.1. Shi and the author offering *pirul* near Morro Bay, California. Photo by the author.

45

a week of meetings and before the next one could begin, we set out on a long, gorgeous weekend. The California Endowment was paying for our fuel, meals, and hotel rooms. Peyote songs played loud from a USB stick plugged into the stereo while Juan and Rene practiced their gourd rattle techniques and Nahuatl pronunciations. Dried corn husks soaked in a covered plastic container on the front dash, for a ceremonial purpose Juan hadn't yet explained to us. We were spotting eagles and pulling over to pick *romero* (rosemary) and *pirul*, plants used for *limpias* (spiritual cleansings).[1] We took dramatically posed photos next to cliffs that AB and Batman declared, in their youthful parlance, "Clean!!!" Shi was cracking up at the antics of the two teenagers, aspiring filmmakers involved with MILPA. The two of them had taken to calling me "Canada," a reference to my homeland, and peppering me with ironic questions about being Canadian. And in all this, Juan and I were drafting a letter at seventy miles per hour to a Monterey County supervisor, advancing MILPA's stance on the reduced bed count at the local juvenile hall, after remembering that it had to be sent out that day.

"Hey. I can't even believe this," Juan paused as we wrapped up the letter. "If we're fucking successful . . . it's that freaking *pirul*!"

Shi laughed, "All that lavender, *romero*!"

"All that medicine, hell yeah!"

"Hell yeah!" Shi reiterated.

Juan asked AB and Batman to start filming the moment, feeling it to be important. Over the noise in the van, he narrated the journey into Batman's phone: "OK, so, we're in the midst of a bunch of ruckus. We started out in Salinas with some somatic movement building." The instructor, who had come down from Oakland to lead the session, called it Tai-Chicano. We had spent an hour doing movements adapted from tai chi but reframed as Nahuatl cosmological figures like Quetzalcoatl, the plumed serpent, designed to help us tap into our embodied power in this movement for justice.

"Then we went out toward the land, planted some corn, went out to the sweat lodge, got grounded." We had done a *temezcal* (sweat lodge) ceremony at dusk in nearby Gilroy, and helped the uncle there with his planting, before setting out on the road.

"We picked up our sister, Shi," swinging back through Salinas on the way south; Shi hadn't wanted to sweat.

"From then on just trying to go with the medicine. Right now we're here, not only are we in the midst of a cross-site learning exchange, with Santa Ana and East Oakland [both sites also funded by TCE, the latter we had just met with two days before, and the other we would be visiting with on the way to San Diego], we're also in the midst of a heavy, combative campaign around influencing and designing the new juvenile hall construction in Monterey County. Right now, it's down to the last wire, we're riding the medicine, the Board of Supervisors is conducting a lot of stuff. I mean it's crazy, I'm feeling it, definitely. Megan's here with me, she's working on this!"

I jumped in about how we drafted the letter in the car, carefully framing the "asks" for the county supervisor to echo MILPA's demand for a reduced bed count in the juvenile hall and an updated institutional needs assessment, which would be funded by TCE. It would present data showing that juvenile crime and incarceration rates in Salinas and Monterey County were declining and that the facility's size should be adjusted accordingly. It was a critical moment in the campaign to shift the scope of the proposed *expansion* to a *reduction*, attempting to intervene not only on the design and size of the facility, but also in the logic of racialized criminalization at its core. I added, "We've seen so many beautiful things, like so many eagles, on this trip. We're taking all that energy and putting it into the work!"

"That's right," Juan continued. "And then we got the young lads right here. I'm very thankful that they're here, just because that's the next generation and they have a separate vision, so sometimes you gotta put in the work so they can benefit from it and also have fun with it. I hope they learn from it. And they can tell you a little bit about what they do."

Batman shifted the phone toward AB, next to him, as he talked about the film they were trying to make. "We try to add *cultura* to our films, and we try to express it the best way that we can. Every time we do a film we try to make a character stand out that is connected to MILPA in some way. Right?" he asked Batman, who paused awkwardly. Shi laughed loudly.

Batman gathered his thoughts before responding and turned the camera toward himself. He stated, "Every situation can be turned into a cultural movement. Very simply. And that's what we try to do. We try to not only change the idea of how we learn culture, but the idea of making a movement itself. You don't make a cultural movement by just sitting down and writing."

This chapter tracks how members of the nascent healing collectives "made" this cultural movement, building on but differentiating their vision and methods from the Chicano Civil Rights Movement of the 1960s and 1970s. As we will see, the Chicano Movement (also known as El Movimiento) was rooted in political claims to Indigenous ancestry, and its iconography and literature leaned heavily on selective tropes of Indigeneity. The movement has been heavily critiqued in subsequent years for this essentialization of Indigeneity for its activists' own purposes, effecting erasures of Native American and Indigenous lives and experiences. Acknowledging and working through these critiques, I will turn to the ways some Chicano Movement activists in California centered Indigenous epistemologies in their professional work, building novel institutions for the cultivation of cultural healing as a means of intervening on racialized dehumanization, community violence, and carcerality. Through individual case studies and ethnographic scenes that demonstrate the legacy of these Chicano activists-turned-professionals, we will see how members of the Salinas healing collectives were developing a novel approach to dismantling carceral institutions through strategic mobilization of health equity resources and discourses, and the "re-membering and reframing" of shared practices of cultural healing (Gonzales 2012).

As noted earlier, "culture," or *cultura*, here refers to the practices, teachings, and socialities understood as originating among Mesoamerican Indigenous ancestors and relations of people typically known today as Mexican American or Chicanx. Re-membering this *cultura* took shape throughout their daily lives and movement-building work in traditional and novel forms: from the *temezcal* under the stars the night before we set out on that road trip, to contorting our arms and stretching our legs during our Tai-Chicano session. The re-membering was in gathering and offering *hierbas* along the route and acknowledging the *pirul* and *romero* as making a difference with the juvenile hall bed reduction. It was in "going with the medicine," placing trust in these entities and allowing space for possibilities to emerge. The collectives were engaging this re-membering, and exploring its potentiality, as they set about dismantling local carceral structures with their own distinctive style.

The collectives' anticarceral work was also, importantly, funded and shaped by health philanthropy, adopting some of The California Endowment's language of health equity along with its financial resources. They made good use of TCE's resources to engage with concepts of health equity, gain access to opportunities for training in movement strategies and cultural healing curricula, and forward the latest data on carceral trends to influence the juvenile hall rebuilding. However, while funded by TCE, the "healing piece" was most powerful when the collectives translated health equity jargon into their own terms, experiences, and goals, specifically around juvenile and adult carceral systems and police brutality. This chapter establishes how the collectives drew on these cultural healing and health equity influences to articulate and activate an abolitionist vision for their community, day by day, circle by circle, chipping away at logics of carcerality and institutions of captivity.

El Movimiento and the Healing Piece

The realization of Indigenous ancestry was novel and powerfully appealing for many members of the healing collectives, who sought to learn more about and embrace the practices and relationships associated with their lineage. However, similar realizations were a prominent part of the Chicano Civil Rights Movement, a social and political project of the 1960s and early 1970s devoted to establishing Mexican American cultural autonomy, gaining civil rights and equal access to opportunities, and promoting empowerment and community development. While the Chicano Movement was deeply impactful in its time, an era of radical shifts in consciousness and power, its leaders faced critique in subsequent years for their perceived appropriations of Indigeneity. Surfacing some of this critique in this section, I want to stress that, as a white woman invited into this collective space as an anthropologist and collaborator, it is not my role or my intention to evaluate the Salinas healing collective members' re-membering of Indigeneity. Instead, I am tracing the context of this identification in a historical lineage, demonstrating its embodiment, and tracking its renewed potentiality. As we will see, despite these critiques of appropriation often leveled at the leaders of the Chicano Movement, the countless individuals it radicalized at the grassroots level took up its concepts, relations, and aspirations in a variety of ways that exceed any simplistic extractivist interpretation.

Chicanx and even *Mexicano* radical imaginations have long been oriented to a particularly compelling version of history: a set of vibrant and advanced Mesoamerican civilizations, a violent colonial encounter, the dramatic decline of the Aztec empire, and the oppression yet endurance of Indigenous ways of knowing and being (Alarcón 1997; Alberto 2016). The selective and often symbolic celebration of Indigeneity has deep roots in nineteenth-century Mexican nationalism. At that time, Mexican nationalists, who were largely elites in government and the arts, developed and valorized a sense of *mestizaje*, the mixture of Indigenous and European ancestry, as an identity that affirmed a glorious and unique past. At the same time, they did little to integrate or improve the lives of contemporary *indios* in Mexico, who were socially and economically marginalized (Saldaña-Portillo 2001). A century later and in the United States, these idealized tropes and aesthetics found new momentum as some Mexican Americans reevaluated their collective experiences alongside the African American civil rights movement and American Indian Movement, and upheld *mestizaje* as a biological inheritance (Haney-López 2004, 210). Chicano community leaders, artists, and authors like Luis Valdez and Corky Gonzalez "created a cultural reservoir through the selective elevation and celebration of an indigenous ancestry" as a "counternarrative" to the oppression experienced by Mexican Americans in the United States (Alberto 2016, 107). Like their Mexican nationalist predecessors, the twentieth-century Chicano Movement's "uses" of Indigeneity have been criticized as "recuperating" a lost past to legitimize their claims for civil rights, in the process potentially negating or reducing the existence of contemporary Indigenous groups (Saldaña-Portillo 2001, 413).[2] This has especially been the case in the US Southwest, claimed by Chicano Movement activists as Aztlán, an ancestral homeland—at the expense of the myriad Indigenous groups that have lived in, cultivated, and been forcefully displaced from these same territories.

Subsequent Chicana/Xicana feminist reevaluations of Indigenous tropes and figures, most famously in works like Gloria Anzaldúa's canonical *Borderlands/La Frontera*, addressed some of the masculinist glorification of this past, while inadvertently reifying its objectification.

Critics such as postcolonial theorist María Josefina Saldaña-Portillo singled out Anzaldúa in particular for seeming to employ reimagined Nahuatl figures, like Coyolxauhqui, or her own *prieta* (dark-skinned, Indigenous) identity as a "pastiche grab bag of Indian spiritual paraphernalia" (2001, 419). Anzaldúa responded to some of this critique in her later writings, noting that Chicanas needed to acknowledge and act against the enduring colonization of Natives, "forced on real bodies," while also working collectively to create a "new tribalism" that makes space for the many Indigeneities realized and claimed today as a form of shared survival (2009, 286–87). Conflict between Chicanx peoples and Native Americans, in academia and activism, is often rooted in this tension of "reclaimed versus lived Indigeneity" (Calderón and Urrieta 2019, 231).

These myriad critiques suggest that there are multiple genealogies of Indigeneity, and that "multiple colonialities" may be at work even in projects that claim to be liberatory or decolonizing (Blackwell, Boj Lopez, and Urrieta 2017; Alberto 2017).[3] Appropriations of Indigeneity as a set of symbols to be filled in opportunistically by political actors are colonial acts themselves that can reproduce invented notions of race as biological and inherent. As Robert Weide argues in *Divide and Conquer* (2022), political projects rooted in identity, including social movements and gangs, ultimately reify invented racial categories. This prevents the formation of solidarities across race or within class categories—solidarities, he argues, that would actually challenge racism, racial division, oppression, and inequality at their capitalist roots. However, this analysis does not preclude the potentially transformative world-building that can happen when an "identity" is lived into for more than recognition as such, instead fueling resurgence: centering Indigenous ways of knowing and relating, aimed at flourishing (Coulthard 2014; Betasamosake Simpson 2016). How people identifying as Chicano/a/x and Indigenous have actually embodied and practiced this identity, and the socialities and epistemologies associated with it, is an empirical and ethnographic question.

In parts of California, as Chicano Movement activists graduated with college degrees and went to work, they brought their radical imaginaries into professional practice. Seeking more than symbolic gains, these activists-turned-professionals intervened in some institutions to make them more *progente* (pro-people), as one account frames it (R. Vargas 1984), while creating new ones alongside them. As Roberto Vargas notes in *Razalogia*, named for the community learning and healing process described in the book itself, the professional fields and service areas that "implicitly assert that people are unable, without professional guidance, to teach their children, maintain their health, or even engage in mutually supportive communications" were particularly ripe for intervention (1984, 4).

In *Razalogia*, Vargas recalls his realization as a budding community health professional in the Bay Area in the early 1970s that his sense of health was greatly shaped by a sense of powerlessness (*no puedo*) and lack of value (*no valgo*). On this foundation, he articulates an important and transformative relation between health and the lived experience of possibility, power, and worth in the Chicanx community. As a corollary and corrective to the direct action of the Chicano Movement, people like Vargas were world-making, creating new paradigms and programs oriented to affirmation and healing to meet the "intimate needs" unaddressed through "promoting *huelgas* (strikes), walkouts, marches, demonstrations or going to college" (R. Vargas 1984, 61). Chicanx communities needed "not merely more professionals or services," not merely access to or inclusion in Eurocentric social institutions, "but an ideology and activism that [sought] radical change in our social systems" (16). Wider efforts to establish "a Chicano psychology" were born of this shared realization—a project that may have "primordialized" ethnic identity and reified racial categories (Santiago-Irizarry 2001, 4)—but so were a set of creative community-based institutions aimed at improving mental and physical health, and life outcomes, among underserved Chicanx populations.

Barrios Unidos and La Cultura Cura

Two such novel institutions set formative conditions for the Salinas healing collectives. One is Santa Cruz–based Barrios Unidos, initially created as a movement for community peace amid "warring" *Mexicano* and Chicano gang factions. The other is La Cultura Cura, a project to develop and circulate rites-of-passage curricula for Chicanx youth, especially those impacted by carceral systems. Both shared the fundamental concept of *cultura (es) cura*, culture heals or culture is the cure—namely, that "restoring cultural traditions and values to the people is the essential medicine needed to begin healing what ails the youth of America's *barrios*" (Acosta 2010, 7). Both made Indigenous cultural practices and spiritual expression the cornerstone of their approach, bringing Chicano Movement Indigenous aesthetics and identity claims into a more grounded praxis articulated as healing.

Barrios Unidos and La Cultura Cura, with their approach to community health and violence, were in a prime position to benefit from a state and national boom in "health conversion foundations." In the 1990s, as health systems shifted from nonprofit to for-profit, they were forced by law (and enticed by tax breaks) to create philanthropic endowments. These new endowments, like The California Wellness Foundation and The California Endowment, funded projects that worked on the upstream social determinants of health as a foil to their for-profit care-providing systems. As Otilio Quintero, an early leader of Barrios Unidos, noted about that time, "It was as if the community peace movement and the public health movement were two pieces of a puzzle waiting to find each other to become stronger and more complete" (Acosta 2010, 50). The assets of California health foundations "more than tripled during the 1990s," a result of real estate growth and the burgeoning dot-com era (Ferris and Graddy 2001, 2), and this enormous wealth funded more creative approaches to violence prevention and enabled projects like Barrios Unidos and La Cultura Cura to become durative community institutions. Ironically but unsurprisingly—as nonprofit and carceral systems have been noted as interlocking, complementary industrial complexes (INCITE! Women of Color against Violence 2009)—these newly fundable projects were unfolding alongside increasingly punitive laws, such as California's Three Strikes Law, passed in 1994.[4] Both major shifts would have significant impacts on the generation leading the cultural movement in Salinas, with the sentence-lengthening Three Strikes and other tough-on-crime laws sending some key members of the healing collectives to juvenile detention in the 1990s, and health foundations and healing organizations investing in the leadership of these same individuals in the first two decades of the twenty-first century.[5]

While key healing movement leaders like Juan and Didi came up through Barrios Unidos in the first decade of the twenty-first century,

La Cultura Cura was training a generation of civil servants in Monterey County. Miguel Ferreira was, decades earlier, a UFW organizer and Chicano Movement activist and had recently retired from upper-level management of the Monterey County Department of Behavioral Health. Over lunch at a Mexican diner in Salinas, Miguel explained to me how he helped to bring La Cultura Cura and its founder, Jerry Tello, to Salinas. The two men had met each other as college graduates in the 1970s in Southern California, working collaboratively to create "one of the first Latino-run mental health offices in the entire county of Los Angeles," according to Miguel. Three decades later, he was seeing the same patterns in Salinas and Monterey County: the population was largely Latinx, but individuals were hardly utilizing the county's mental health programs or services, which Miguel and others saw as designed for a mainstream white population.

Miguel invited Tello, who often was granted the honorific *maestro* as a respected teacher and leader of spiritual and cultural practices, on behalf of the Department of Behavioral Health to train the staff. This in itself was only possible because other Chicano activists-turned-professionals had already fought and litigated their way into positions of power in Monterey County (McKibben 2022, 297–99). La Cultura Cura's training and Maestro Tello's stories quickly made a strong impression among many staff participants. Subsequent training sessions attracted a range of staff from other county departments who, informally, were able to take up what they had learned in their own institutional spaces. They even found what Miguel called "an unlikely ally" in the probation department, which started training probation officers and staff to learn La Cultura Cura curricula to run in the juvenile hall. Miguel noticed that, as they completed this training, these probation officers were speaking differently about their work and the youth, displaying more empathy and attention to healing rather than punishment.

"This is what we thought would happen," Miguel said. "It changes the provider, and it changes how they interact with others, how they see themselves, and how they are able to then grow from that." Permeating the institutions themselves through individual county civil servants risked objectifying the *cultura* and codifying its expansive teachings. However, *cultura* evaded capture: as staff from the Department of Behavioral Health were tasked with logging their activity, they didn't know how to register that what they were doing was informed by the ideas and practices of cultural healing. They couldn't code for it in their accounting system. Eventually, as staff from a variety of agencies were trained, and county funding for La Cultura Cura workshops waned, they couldn't keep track of who was running curricula even as ideas and practices of healing were widespread, put into practice among those who did the day-to-day work of state institutions.

A few years later, in 2010, when Building Healthy Communities was established in East Salinas, TCE brought La Cultura Cura and the charismatic Maestro Tello back to train community organizations' staff in the paradigm as well as its curricula. These curricula—Joven Noble (Noble Youth) for young men, Xinachtli (Germinating Seed, in Nahuatl) for young women, and Cara y Corazón (Face and Heart) for parents—reframed behavioral "problems" as resulting not from individual deficits or flaws but from cultural and spiritual displacements, wrought by colonialism and carcerality. Though each curriculum had its own demographic focus and tailored activities, they shared a conceptual foundation that moved away from individual culpability, instead imparting a sense of structural vulnerability to be remedied through cultural healing and collective action. As Maestro Tello articulated it at a training I attended in 2014, these curricula shifted the question from "What did you do?" to "What happened to you, to make you lose your sacredness?"

Paths to La Cultura

Among members of the healing collectives, Maestro Tello's *dichos* (stories) made distinct impacts. They were one path, among others, to re-membering their ancestry, alongside realizations of their own worth and potential. As comes through in the following narratives from interviews with Tenoch and Yarri, early members of the healing collectives, the *maestro*'s teachings struck at core experiences of deficit they had long carried with them. Both were deeply shaped by carceral and white supremacist logics that devalued Mexican and Chicanx youth, as well as their own experiences with carceral systems. Hearing that their ancestry was beautiful, and being introduced to new practices associated with it, were pivotal events. This re-membering was less about an acclaimed identity than a set of ceremonial practices and a vibrant, welcoming form of kinship relation, which helped to make possible their ability to do the difficult work of confronting the carceral systems—juvenile halls and jails, overpolicing on neighborhood streets and in schools, the foster care system, among others—that had already wrought displacement and dispossession in their lives.

Tenoch

Tenoch was a father of four in his midthirties attending the local city college alongside construction work before he linked up with MILPA. He described himself to me as "obsessed with tearing down the prison-industrial complex," which I can confirm was accurate, as he showed up as a passionate and deeply informed abolitionist in all he did. He was the first to teach me about the Salinas Police Department's employment of counterintelligence techniques, a strategy of warfare developed for use in Afghanistan, on his generation (Raschig 2018).

In an interview conducted over iced tea on a Starbucks patio, Tenoch reflected on a seminar with Maestro Tello we both had attended the day before. He found that Tello's words "really touched home." The seminar made him think about what he had inherited from his relatives and what he wanted to pass down to his son and young daughters. As an early member of MILPA, he saw the collective addressing "the theme of self-hate" among youth in Salinas, which he could relate to, most overtly through experiences in his childhood with an uncle who upheld white supremacist views at home. This uncle would taunt young Tenoch with Clorox baths, threatening "to throw me in there to wash off m'dirt," as he put it, attempting to skip syllables of the painful slur. He saw that "internalized self-hate" was endemic in Salinas among those who looked like him. "Day in, day out, that oppression can make us go crazy . . . at the slightest provocation I could blow up because of that internalized self-hate."

With MILPA, he felt, "we are setting the record straight. Saying that no matter what you look like, who you are, you are somebody and there's a purpose here for you. . . . You are somebody and you need to be proud of that." As he told it, not having an affirmative sense of one's identity and purpose was rooted in that pervasive racist logic, associating ethnicity with criminality—but also intergenerational experiences of colonial displacement and not having a sense of one's roots. He brought up his wife's grandmother in Mexico, who raised her kids to speak Purépecha, even as other family members would "demonize it" and call her crazy. "Coming from south of the border, we hold onto those, like, macroaggressions and microaggressions, as we go on in life. We always acknowledge it but we don't even wanna talk about it. So I now think that like the growing trend is, people are like, eff it. This is who I am, I need to be proud about myself, I need to feel good about myself, these are all my ethnicities. When you're not ashamed of who you are anymore, then you can heal."

He continued to tell me his family history, of grandparents forced out of their home under threat of violence near the border of Guatemala,

> where they were called Rarámuri. . . . And we left our Indigenous roots, in fear of violence. And so, how that intergenerational trauma has affected my family, to this point, in reading all about, like, negative stuff, and having no real identity, you know, to this land, or to this economy, or to this nation, that creates a self-identity crisis. It creates depression. It creates instability. So far that you, um, you act out, you act out in different ways, you lash out, you feel like you're not good enough, you feel like, shit, *all I am is a problem. My damn ancestors, you know, they were so much of a problem, I don't wanna be like them.* That creates havoc within your growing up. So when you're talking about it, beginning to understand it, it's part of healing. And if you can check that box that says I am Mexican *and* I am Chicano, I would love for one to say "I am Chicano, but with Indigenous roots to this land."

Yarri

Yarri, twenty years old and experiencing housing insecurity with her toddler daughter when she started attending La Colectiva de Mujeres circles in early 2014, was initially struck by how welcoming and friendly the women were. They saw something in her that she didn't yet recognize in herself. She felt the same sense of investment at her first sweat lodge, when she was strongly encouraged to "keep the fire," to build and maintain the sacred fire that heats the rocks brought into the lodge. The role is an honor and a physical and spiritual challenge—it's hot, the rocks are heavy, and one has to remain attuned to the fire to tend it over many hours. At first she thought, "It's not gonna happen, it's too hot, I don't want to." Then, she recalled, "I was like, OK, people that I care about are in there, and I did it with a lot of patience, it was super-hot, and then, um, I prayed on the rocks, for the wood to fall where it should fall and how it should fall, and it actually worked. I feel like I did really good." At her first tepee ceremony, a dusk-to-dawn gathering, she admitted to being hung over and didn't really start to feel "the healing" yet, until she got more committed to the process. That commitment came in a Xinachtli activity about setting boundaries that drew on a teaching about *chimales*, the Nahuatl word for shields. Describing that activity as a "breakthrough," Yarri reflected on how she had always made herself available to her loved ones, doing whatever they wanted, but envisioning her *chimal* made her realize she needed to work with that idea of a shield to protect and honor herself.

She described hearing Maestro Tello talk, explaining, "He speaks so beautiful. He would make me cry for like five minutes and then he'd crack a joke, and I'd forget about it, he is such a beautiful speaker." With TCE funding, Yarri was able to be trained as a facilitator of Xinachtli, attending a three-day workshop in San Jose. She noticed that there were probation officers in the same workshop. Thinking back to her experiences with her probation officer as a teenager, she enjoyed the fact that they had to humble themselves in front of the medicine too, "like we're all here and we're all even." It was with the teachings in Xinachtli that "I decided like, OK, I'm gonna change this and I'm gonna change that. It wasn't like them asking you what's wrong in your life, it was more like they're teaching us this stuff, and I'm thinking about it, and I'm like, OK, maybe I should change this, I should do this, I should do that." Teachings, such as about the grandmother figure of Malinalli, and the female Moon Dance performers who honor their feminine lineage and power, pushed Yarri to reframe the shame she was taught about her menstruating body as a young woman. She was eager to teach her daughter otherwise: to value and honor her body and celebrate its abilities. She embraced Danza Azteca, a ceremonial form of dance rooted in Aztec cultural traditions, to feel more of the power and beauty of the movements, even if she hadn't learned all the teachings about them quite yet.

Yarri also mentioned some incidents in which she and the other Mujeres were being judged as "not Native American enough" or "not taking care of the teachings." After the Mujeres held a ceremony with a local *maestra*, a respected female teacher and leader of ceremony, who brought out a *chanunpa* pipe of the Lakota tradition, Yarri overheard another elder saying that the Mujeres weren't ready to be near that strong medicine: "I think that kind of judgment is not OK, you know? Just having that ego, like, 'you guys are not fully Native American.' We do come from that." That same elder also apparently said that "there's no need to protest," which Yarri interpreted as a critique of the direct action against police homicides that many Mujeres in the Colectiva were engaged in at the time. Yarri disagreed that their acts of protest or raw anger disqualified them from ceremony or getting close to medicine; in the Colectiva, she saw how ceremony and medicine made it possible for the Mujeres to work toward the world they dreamed of. The protest was part of their broader work, every day building otherwise for each other and their community. "I think that if I didn't have the Colectiva I don't know how I would have done it"—found housing, gone to school, gained stability for her daughter, and got close to the medicine—"because a lot of the support that I had was with Shi and Pamela and the women, and being able to let go of things in ceremony."

* * *

Tenoch and Yarri, among others in the collectives, found resonance with the teachings and medicine while engaged in work to address and dismantle carceral systems and logics. They both began as interns for the collectives, receiving a decent if temporary stipend from TCE to keep pursuing cultural healing and a greater sense of belonging and affirmative identity, while also developing professional skills. These internships led them to attend La Cultura Cura trainings in addition to meetings and projects devoted to justice reform. Each narrated their path to me with a strong sense of transformation and aspiration for themselves and for subsequent generations.

Though unique, Tenoch's and Yarri's narratives have much in common with those of other early members of the collectives, who were making sense of their Indigeneity and the ways they had been impacted by carceral systems alongside each other, and putting the teachings into the context of their lives and community. The next section examines how this collective process of articulation was influenced by the institutionalization of cultural healing as well as health equity philanthropy, as members of the collectives produced a grassroots take on the relationship between carcerality and health in Salinas. This radical understanding—getting to the root of their understandings of self, community, bodily and spiritual wellness, and possibility—was cultivated in circle and spread in other spaces of power through their advocacy and activism.

"Safety Now Would Mean Healing"

Seeking a fresh approach to improving the lives of Salinas residents, rather than recycling the tropes of poverty and resilience that often suffuse nonprofit endeavors, early members of MILPA sought not individualized "bootstrap" but "rootstrap" thinking: an appreciation and understanding of their ancestry and culture (their roots) as a form of collective power, combined with structural critique. This slight semantic shift, with its subversion of neoliberal individualism, and minted in a "brown paper" cowritten by Juan and funded by TCE, itself exemplifies the clever subterfuge of nonprofit resources both epistemic and financial (National Compadres Network 2012). As one healing activist noted in late 2013, invoking "health equity" in their activism "gives us cover from police and politicians."

Such acts may be critiqued—and in fact they were during this time of the healing collectives' emergence, among some residents of Salinas who refused to use "the master's tools" in this struggle. But members of the collectives were engaged in creative and opportunistic repurposing of these epistemic and financial resources to grow a project of cultural healing that could stand up to the carceral systems and logics that shaped their lives.

This creative work unfolded across a hefty weekly slate of meetings. Once I joined MILPA, attending everything I could with the enthusiasm of a doctoral student flush with time and energy during fieldwork, my days became dense with constant commutes zigzagging across Salinas. Each day's schedule had many of us moving from the juvenile hall to the county chambers, to the Building Healthy Communities office to meet with regional management and other community groups' leadership, to lively coworking sessions at Viva Espresso (voted "the best place to meet a revolutionary" by *Monterey County Weekly* in 2014), and often in the evenings to a *círculo*.

Círculos were unlike conventional meetings. They were in their own category of gathering, often grounding us in the early evening "after work," after long days, even as they were an integral part of "the work." Before the Colectiva began running its own women's circles, and in the early days of MILPA's formation, critical consciousness circles were a space for many of us to build *conocimiento* (knowledge and familiarity) and *confianza* (relational trust), debrief on the day, and build toward the next. They were crucial sites in the development of shared knowledge and a vocabulary of health equity rooted in the specificities of Salinas, akin to the collective knowledge practices described in the book *Razalogia* (R. Vargas 1984). Though hardly the only place where we could "get close to the medicine," *círculo* was perhaps where many became acquainted with it. In these spaces, members of the collectives were making sense of health equity in terms of their own lived experiences and spiritual commitments, as well as the group's political goals. Attention to this negotiation shows how the scope of health equity and its strategic deployment in terms of healing provided a safe framework to do the deeper abolitionist work of undoing and dismantling carceral logics and systems.

At one such *círculo* in late 2013, I arrived at the BreadBox community center just before 5:30 p.m., greeting Juan at the door. "You're in the right place!" he said, welcoming me inside. I made the rounds, hugging those I knew and shaking the hands of those new to the circle. There were three new young men there that day in addition to those who formed MILPA's core (Juan, Daniel, and Rene), other community organizers and teachers, Shi, an elder *maestra* named Elena, a journalist from the county paper, and myself. I was concerned to see Daniel agitated about something; you can't hide your vibes in a circle. I tried to parse his mood from across the altar that we encircled. Shi sat down next to me and offered a sweet orange aromatherapy lotion from her purse.

"This has really been calming me down a lot today," she said, rubbing the lotion onto her hands. I squeezed some into my palm, still aware of Daniel but shifting attention to Shi and chatting about her day.

Juan opened the circle with a blessing, offering sage to the four directions. We passed the bundle of medicine around the circle for each of us to wave the smoke over ourselves to refresh us and remove negative energy from the day. Juan then introduced the theme of the *círculo*, community health, as part of a discussion on the healing-informed curriculum some MILPA members were trying to build. Though they ran La Cultura Cura curricula like Joven Noble and Xinachtli, they wanted to develop their own framework of teachings, ancestral and contemporary parables that corresponded closely to local conditions in Salinas. Since there were a few new youngsters in the circle as well as the journalist, Juan decided we should first explain what he called the MILPA get-down.

First, he said, "We are all the cofounders of MILPA. You can call yourself a cofounder! I mean, this has been cofounded a long time ago." He backtracked slightly to invoke a teaching that rooted the healing collective in his ancestors' efforts, likened to arrows shot out to land afar. "But we're just, like . . . We're picking up those arrows." What was happening in that moment was just a flash of a longer set of shifts, the low and slow rumble of the Ollin. There was a much deeper history to this, but we were continuing the work in a unique moment. Juan had a gift for helping us feel these moments as profoundly historical, like we were part of something much larger and more powerful than we realized.

He then outlined MILPA's approach to the problems impacting *Mexicano* and Chicanx populations by lifting up the practices and perspectives of their ancestors. He spoke in terms of teachings from elders of the Chicano Movement and Native American Church, weaving in health equity jargon. As he spoke, he occasionally transcribed key terms on a mobile white board:

Círculo
Critical consciousness
Cultural valores (values)
Moral conduct
Integrate teachings into modern lifestyle
Tradition
Pedagogy
Scholarship
Movimiento

Maestra Elena jumped in to support him as he discussed MILPA's purpose and jotted down these key terms. Elena had been involved in the Native American Church for decades and marched with César Chávez. She was excited about her role as an elder in this burgeoning collective. She announced to the circle, "We are making history here. We have lost touch with our ancestral values, and here we are getting in touch again and making them useful." Elena used the collective first person to draw continuity from much of the group in front of her to their myriad ancestors, who would have belonged to various Indigenous groups in what is now Mexico and the US Southwest—the journalist was South Asian and I was white, but everyone else was Mexican American.

Continuing, Elena noted that "we used to have a male-female balance in leadership," and that MILPA had to work again to build gender equity and elder respect in light of centuries of colonization and patriarchal relations. "The way I see it, we are just bringing it back to the family. What we are creating here is something that's going to last for a long time."

Juan continued to write on the whiteboard while Elena spoke, adding an index of health equity jargon:

Farming/nutrition/green work
Environmental racism + toxins
Life outcomes
Social-emotional toxins (trauma)

Juan then explained why we arranged ourselves in a circle: the setup evoked a Medicine Wheel, an understanding of health as a balance of spiritual, physical, emotional, and mental components. The core teaching of coming to a circle like this was both giving attention to one's own individual well-being while becoming mindful of others' experience and the context of structural oppression.

With this, Juan began to shift the conversation to how we needed to think about "health" in Salinas as going beyond not being physically injured or sick. We also had to make sure we didn't focus on, as he put it, "that individual responsibility shit, hell nah. None of that 'parents' fault' shit." Here, he was referencing a common narrative used to explain the prevalence of gang membership and violence in Salinas: the parents of gang-involved or systems-impacted youth were farmworkers, out working in the fields well before sunrise and coming home exhausted, unable to provide the care that their kids needed to avoid getting caught up in gangs. It was a durative narrative that upheld the seemingly positive value that farmworkers were hardworking, but it nevertheless forwarded the racist and paternalistic notion that they were unreliable or unfit parents, providing insufficient care that caused a social problem.

So, if health was not merely an individual concern or the exclusive purview or fault of elders or parents, we needed to understand the role of racialized oppression on bodies. Around the circle, folks started to chime in with examples of how this oppression was manifest. In broad oppositional terms as Maestra Elena had already established, most described the Mexican American population in Salinas and its ancestors back to an idealized pre-Columbian era as "us" and "them" as a composite subject of colonizers, industrialized agriculture, and capitalist enterprise.

"They made us fat—they put GMOs in our food! Our tortillas used to be made of *maíz* and now it's all GMO corn!"

"Cooking oil was introduced by Europeans. Our diet was water-based, it was healthy."

"Living here is a public health issue. We gotta tap into our ancestral diet. My *abuelitos* [grandparents] always grew their own food; there were always some *nopales* [cactus paddles] growing or a *chayote* [thin-skinned gourd] vine around somewhere." Indeed, these subsistence gardens, named *milpas*, inspired MILPA's name and purpose.

"They made us lazy—shit, they got rid of the pyramids, we used to clean those things every day!" This was a joke, but it harmonized with the indignation going around the circle.

"There's so much fast food, with all its hormones and crap. That's kind of the same as spiritual colonialism."

Juan responded to this, bringing in more jargon and context from his additional years of training with Barrios Unidos and The California Endowment. "What you're talking about is health literacy—this is a huge thing nationally right now with the Affordable Care Act," which was set to expand considerably in early 2014. "It's huge. But we have to talk about it in different ways to make it relevant for people in the community."

Someone brought up the Mexican American health paradox, which held that Mexicans living in the United States had excellent long-term health outcomes despite generally being poorer, less educated, and medically underserved relative to white populations. These were all factors that should have diminished health outcomes among this population, with a vague notion of cultural ties, faith, and family values often posited as the reason for this good health.

Charlie, a playwright, clarified that in the wake of the North American Free Trade Agreement (NAFTA), implemented in 1994, and its numerous negative consequences for Mexicans' health and well-being, Mexico is more obese than the United States per capita. Folks around the circle were blurting out their take on whether or not this "paradox" still held.

"It's getting crazy in here!" Juan said, excitedly. He tried to steer us back to the curriculum and what it should include.

"We have to reclaim *nuestra cultura, nuestra historia, nuestra salud*," Elena added, referring to "our culture, our history, our health."

Diego, a high school teacher, suggested we start with the relatable question "What did you eat today?" and then unpack that food's conditions of production and its relative nutrition.

Jose, a musician, brought the discussion back to the conceptual level by commenting, "It's like a genocide with our food; but we should also talk about PTSD and fear from *la migra* [immigration enforcement] and the police."

Charlie insisted we ground this discussion in NAFTA and the damage it caused to Mexican families, economics, and foodways. Diego shifted the focus again, saying that "food is one thing, but the more pressing cause of the decline in our health is through being second-class citizens. What about the microstresses? Just gunning it all the time to the next stop sign?"

Juan wrote "acculturation-related stress" on the whiteboard while Diego spoke, again aligning the particulars of life in Salinas with TCE-approved health equity jargon.

The conversation turned to the "gutted" food garden at César Chávez Elementary School and other changes that some had noticed around the city. Daniel, who had remained uncharacteristically subdued for much of the circle, finally spoke up. He had driven by the youth center on Circle Drive, a satellite location of the county juvenile hall for long-term incarceration. The youth center sat at the perimeter of a low-income housing development named Acosta Plaza, known as "AP." These apartments had plummeted in value in the 1990s as local homicide rates soared, and buyers from outside of Salinas had bought them up. Now, landlords charged high rents but claimed no responsibility for maintaining clean and safe apartments, amenities, or public space. Acosta Plaza had been the scene of a few high-profile homicides and had a reputation for violence. It was being actively organized by various community groups advocating for city, county, and private investment in its infrastructure.

"It was like a little Pelican Bay back there," Daniel complained, comparing the youth center to a maximum-security state prison in Northern California where many Norteño leaders were incarcerated after antigang task force sweeps of the city. This unsettling realization seemed to be the source of his agitation that day. He continued, noting the way AP's garages and balconies were also gated and fenced: "It's like they're jailed up in their own houses!"

At this, Shi jumped in. Three or four years ago there was a hearing about the safety of the Youth Center, she recalled. "And they were stressing the community's safety in terms of that fence and gate. The city's idea of safety was the gate . . . like, what?"

Most folks around the circle shook their heads and expressed disgust at the idea that the youth themselves were a threat to the neighborhood. What about the safety or well-being of the young people housed there, isolated from their loved ones? Or the safety of the community from the police itself? There were murmurs about the police in East Salinas and growing up fearing and distrusting them, and how that wore on residents' bodies over time.

Diego summed it up: if that hearing were held today, the conversation would be different. Safety would mean thinking about those who were terrorized by that carceral institution in their midst, who bore the psychic and physical violence of police presence. Safety, now, would entail change to the facility (or, better yet, its closure) and to police (or, better yet, their abolition).

"Safety now would mean healing," Shi added.

Juan smiled contentedly, leaning back in his chair, and said, "This is a place for just *cariño*," referring to care or love. Quieting down, we offered a little more medicine as a collective to close the circle. We packed up the altar, and each of us went home.

The conversation's movement through health and colonialism and NAFTA, to a food garden, to an overly surveilled and terrorizing space in their midst underscored the expansive and situated sense of health being cultivated in *círculo*. Whether translated into TCE jargon as "acculturation-related stress" or layman's terms like "gunning it . . . to the next stop sign," the lively conversation demonstrated a nuanced and shared understanding of the harsh incursions of police and the carceral system into daily life and on peoples' bodies and well-being. The approach that MILPA took to health equity and cultural healing was fundamentally shaped by this understanding, and the need to dismantle carceral systems and underlying logics of racialized criminalization if "health" was going to "happen here" in this community, per BHC's slogan.

Some members of the healing collectives took these liberatory understandings of cultural healing and carceral oppression, developed together and in a sacralized configuration of a circle with medicine at its center, into other areas of their lives. For those whose schedules were full of meetings about the juvenile hall expansion—with the Board of Supervisors and the city council, with TCE and BHC management and community leadership, with the Community Corrections Partnership alongside the diverse and mostly elderly peace activists of the Monterey Peninsula—these understandings fueled their interventions. At the core of this epistemic shift was an affirmation that they were sacred, in defiance of the logics and systems of colonial, criminal, and even capitalist capture that had shaped their lives. As the next section demonstrates, the way to build this out in the world was both to influence and diminish the carceral institutions that impacted their community, and to spread the understanding that *Mexicano*, Chicanx, and Latinx youth deserved otherwise.

Revolution

On April 9, 2014, Juan sent an email to members of MILPA and La Colectiva de Mujeres:

> Urgent,
> Tomorrow is judgment day for the juvenile hall. . . . We are requesting your support if possible tomorrow to either speak or just show up. If time permits please join us at 9:00 am at Action Council of Monterey County at 295 Main St. Suite #3 for a pre-BOS mtg.
> Please I am asking for your support. . . . Note if we are missing anything.
> Best,
> Juan
> If you need a ride please call and we will try and arrange your pick up.

Juan's email put into lean terms the strategy that both MILPA and La Colectiva de Mujeres had prepared in anticipation of the county budget meeting the next day. Shi and I had called and texted members of the Colectiva, inviting them to join an intended critical mass at that meeting. We hoped to have a few of the women speak about their children's experiences at the juvenile hall. Third on the agenda, cloaked in procedural terms, was "Approving the Change in Scope, Cost and Schedule for the New Juvenile Hall Project." This specifically referred to a vote on decreasing the bed count from 150 to 120, thus reducing the juvenile hall rather than expanding it, as had long been the stated goal of the county. Juan's email and our preparation for this meeting made it feel like a historical fulcrum, a critical moment in an emerging movement.

The morning of "judgment day for the juvenile hall," members of MILPA and La Colectiva de Mujeres lingered in the dappled shade in front of the county Board of Supervisors chambers. Shi had brought Juana and their old friend, Lisa, also known by her *placaso* (gang-given nickname) as Gata, or its playful translation, Kitty Cat. The three women had known each other since their teens when they were all affiliated as Sureñas. Gata spread out on a concrete bench, resplendent in the warm sun; her partner was locked up, and she worried about protecting her son from a similar outcome, but she was primarily there to support from the sidelines. Shi and I focused on talking to Juana about what she would say in the meeting. Juana's *placaso* was Sleepy; she was quiet and reserved and not especially forthcoming with her opinions in public settings. But her son had been in and out of the juvenile hall for years, and Shi had compelled her to share their experiences in testimony to the Board of Supervisors at this meeting. We tried to guide her toward talking points, such as how opportunities for cultural healing could have diverted her son from recidivating, and how painful it was for both of them, and her other kids, for him to be constantly separated from them. Juana fidgeted nervously with her sunglasses and sweater as we jotted notes for her on a piece of paper about the need for healing and a health-centered approach to juvenile justice. Around us, members of MILPA and other BHC groups passed around a bundle of sage for a quick premeeting grounding and blessing. We took a group photo and then went inside.

In a small boardroom rather than the Board of Supervisors' wood-trimmed public chambers, the budget committee meeting was called to order. Two supervisors, Lou Calcagno and Fernando Armenta, presided along with a host of civil servants, seated at long tables arranged in a square, while the public sat in stacking chairs to one side. When the time came for the third agenda item, a slew of audience members stood up to give comments on the change of scope decision. Colectiva and MILPA members worked through the preprepared asks—the request to remain open to further reductions in scope; the urgency of a new needs assessment to make a data-driven decision; and the possibility of revisiting the scope and making space for BHC involvement in the juvenile hall's design process, integrating movable partitions and more flexible spaces.

Juana stood up, with Shi at her side, to read the statement we had helped her prepare. With Shi's hand on Juana's shoulder, both women quietly cried as Juana outlined her son's experience at the juvenile hall and the feeling she had that he was capable of something different, yet kept getting pulled back in. There were so many moments in his life when other interventions could have been made to prevent him from entering or reentering the system, and when he could have instead been able to process what he'd been through and heal.

After public comment, Supervisor Calcagno decided to weigh in. Although it was all but decided that the county would approve the reduced scope, his remarks centered aggressively on how the proposed changes to the facility would be giving "a first-class ride to the people outside of society who don't want to follow its rules." He doubled down by predicting that the juvenile hall would have to expand in the next ten years and that this reduction was a mistake. His words assessed *Mexicano*, Chicanx, and Latinx youth in the region as inherently criminal, destined for incarceration, regardless of any potential interventions or changes in carceral policy. Pamela, also present in the audience, caught my eye, looking enraged at his words. Others around me shifted in their seats. Calcagno had made no meaningful consideration of current best practices in juvenile justice, local and statewide rates of juvenile incarceration trending way downward, or the possibility of change for those who were already systems-impacted. Instead, he relied on racist and tough-on-crime tropes.

Supervisor Armenta replied firmly to his colleague's diatribe. Armenta had a personal history of activism with the Chicano Movement and three decades of civil service in the region, and was deeply involved in the long-term project of growing the local Latinx community's political clout and representation. He noted with appreciation the work done by MILPA and other BHC groups to provide healing-based alternatives to detention, and he disagreed with Calcagno's assertion that the facility would need to expand. Instead, he said, it was incumbent on the county to heed the efforts and calls of the community and work together to steer youth away from the facility and the juvenile system. In his measured way, he was refusing Calcagno's reiteration of racialized criminalization and instead echoed the lexicon of health and healing.

Juan, seated in front of me, leaned over to his right slightly and wrote discreetly in Joaquin's notebook: *Revolution*, in red pen. They each gave a subtle, conspiratorial nod.

The scope of change for the reduced bed count was approved by the budget committee. We left the meeting feeling triumphant, though still buzzing about Calcagno's words. Some of us went for lunch at Mountain Mike's to celebrate and debrief, carpooling to the pizza spot a few blocks away. The air was zesty as Juana, Gata, and Shi sat sharing a pitcher of beer on one side of the table and Daniel and others from MILPA and supportive county staff stood around with their slices. We celebrated the win and cheered for Supervisor Armenta, while dismissing Calcagno's relevance. The idea of *Mexicano*, Chicanx, and Latinx youth criminality still circulated, but slowly and from multiple angles, residents and leaders of Salinas were eroding it, surfacing a framework of cultural healing instead.

In Collectivity

Wilding out in a full van driving to Chicano Park; unpacking the "little Pelican Bay" on the East Side of Salinas in *círculo*; sharing medicine and testimony on judgment day for the juvenile hall: in moments like these and countless others, the cultural movement was built. Teachings, medicine, and being together gave rise to otherwise perspectives on entrenched carceral logics and institutions, keying the work of movement-building as sacred, and imparting a sense of belonging in a historical and collective pursuit of possibility. And—as I hope this chapter has conveyed—this was an exuberant time, rife with youthful energy and the electric, revelatory sense of transformation. Revolution was scented with *romero* and written in red pen. We all rode together.

I have argued that members of the collectives re-membered their ancestral *cultura* through everyday acts of ceremony woven into the conscious cultivation of a framework of cultural healing, rather than simple or appropriative claims to identity at the expense of others' lived Indigeneity. Through the efforts of activists-turned-professionals who centered key understandings and practices of cultural healing in their work, and in alignment with growing philanthropic capital oriented to public health, these teachings could find their way to a new generation eager to shift paradigms and build otherwise. Imparting teachings and medicine through curricula run in therapeutic and rehabilitative settings, and ceremony, rendered these understandings, practices, and relations available for revising deep understandings of self and collective, addressing colonial-carceral dispossessions at their roots.

The sense of oneself as sacred, valued, and capable rather than culpable made deep impacts on some members of the collectives. Addressing internalized criminalization through cultural healing was an integral part in the struggle against carcerality, making it possible to address its logics and work to diminish and dismantle its key institutions. Though it was work on the self, it was largely done together, and with medicine. The Colectiva and MILPA were *collectives* in the truest sense, filled with individuals who were taking time to become intentionally in relation to each other. Abolitionist Mariame Kaba writes that being part of a collective "helps to not only imagine new worlds, but also to imagine ourselves differently" (2021, 4); nothing actually otherwise could be built without individual dispositions and social relations changing as well.

3

Cargas Coming Down

Chronic Stress and New Possibilities in the Women's Healing Circle

Recover Every Day

"It's not just what you go through, it's how you recover every day," Pamela once told Juana and me while we circled up outside the Monterey County juvenile hall, set back from an arterial road between Salinas's North and East Sides. It was midsummer 2014. Juana's son was awaiting sentencing for an attempted robbery charge. Soon she would have to pass through security and enter his hearing. I lit a small bundle of sage and passed it to Juana on my left; she breathed it in with vigor. This shared saging opened our ritual of *descargando*, a moment to articulate and unload the affective burdens that weighed on us in order to move through the world otherwise. We called these loads *cargas*: a Spanish triangulation of burden, baggage, and charge, in the sense of both something weighty and something for which one is tasked with caring.

"I need all the sage!" Juana laughed, but sadly. "I'm so stressed. Oh my God, I need the healing." Her son Vincent had just finished his last parole period, and she was concerned this sentence would be disproportionately heavy. Juana was a regular attendee of the Colectiva's healing circles and occasionally made it to county meetings related to the group's juvenile justice reform work. She was often distracted, prone to laughter at the edge of deep worry. Her drive in all of this was the prospect of losing her eldest son to the carceral system for what felt like it could be forever this time.

Pamela and I nodded, feeling Juana's *cargas* tense our own bodies in the cool morning air. For us, as dedicated members of the Colectiva, cultural healing was increasingly shaping our lives, relationships, and daily practices of endurance. The spiritual and political syncretism of healing resonated among women in the Colectiva who sought relief for a variety of chronic stressors. In their rounded shoulders, hypertensive blood, sore knees and swollen ankles, or vigilant agita, many held in their bodies the stress of their children's and their own susceptibility to colonial and carceral logics and structures: the disposability at the heart of racialized criminalization, rooted in settler colonial dispossession. In our healing circles, rituals of *descargando* to unload the weight of stress catalyzed new relational practices to mitigate it. In the process, they and I came to realize the insidious proliferation and embodied impacts of state-led or state-sanctioned degradation that many experienced individually. Together, we sought otherwise: other affirmative possibilities for their kids and themselves beyond the narrow scope of criminalization. Sending sage smoke all around our bodies in elaborate swirls and unloading our *cargas* to each other, at each circle we hoped to leave feeling lighter, ready to move.

This chapter centers the Mujeres' practice of *descargando* and its role in fostering a grassroots feminist collective dedicated to mitigating the worldly conditions of each other's stress. *Descargando* can be understood as an "idiom of distress," a particular expression of stress and attendant suffering shaped by sociocultural and economic conditions, at the intersection of race or ethnicity, class, and gender. However, we will see not only how this stress is articulated but also how it is embodied and shared across subjects, who further cultivate a commitment to addressing it through cultural healing praxis. Paying attention to how *cargas* are "carried" and "unloaded" among the Mujeres, we will see how the embodied work of *descargando* made further coalition-building and world-building possible in Salinas.

Many women in the Colectiva held tremendous pain as well as potentiality in their bodies, "weathered" as they were by a relentlessly stressful world (Sharpe 2017): as low-income women of color, carrying the intergenerational trauma of their ancestors, with children often caught up in the carceral system, in a time and place where quick-to-shoot police faced little accountability. Such weathering takes a toll. The chronic stress of anticipating and experiencing racial discrimination, such as criminalization, founds an unthinkable, possibly infinite variety of poor health outcomes. Biomedicine calls the impacts of this chronic stress "allostatic load," but the Mujeres, in the context of healing, articulate it in terms of *cargas*. Similarly, biomedical terms will not carry understandings of stress as a social phenomenon very far. Instead, I follow Emily Mendenhall (2012) and Sarah Horton (2016, 98), who note that ethnographic narratives and accounts can "radically contextualize" the relationship between socioeconomic conditions, social idioms, and physical distress in their accounts of the relationship between chronic stress, diabetes, and hypertension among Mexican and Mexican American farmworkers. I support this ethnographic analysis through perspectives borne of Black, Xicana, and Native feminists on the impacts of racialized stress remedied through embodied relational practices of care. The strategies cultivated for healing in these conditions underscore that stress is a worldly phenomenon, requiring emergent coalitions that address social and structural conditions rather than solely individual therapeutic remedy or resilience.

Black feminist scholars have rendered racialized and gendered stress as prominent aspects of contemporary Black women's experiences in the United States and elsewhere, expanding on medical metaphors to encompass the political dimensions of these experiences (Sharpe 2017; Smith 2016; Rankine 2014). Christen A. Smith, borrowing the biomedical term, called these socially determined health outcomes "sequelae," "morbid infections" occurring as a gendered corollary to more overt and direct state violence in her transnational work with Black mothers of children murdered by police (2016, 31). As Cynthia Colen et al. note, the impact of children's negative experiences on their mothers, and even the anticipation of potential such experiences, can be "relentless psychosocial stressors . . . implicated in the worst possible health outcomes and sustained racial inequalities in wellbeing" (2019, 476). While this is especially so for African American mothers, and the scope of anti-Blackness must be recognized as singular, many Latina mothers and caregivers must also maintain an energy-depleting "steady state of race-related hypervigilance," a "hyperarousal" which overstimulates and wears on the body (478).

Attention to the Mujeres' sense of stress carried collectively as *cargas* builds on Black feminist understandings of stress as structured by racialized criminalization and carceral violence, while illuminating the materiality and potentiality of this embodiment as a decolonizing praxis in Chicana-Indigenous contexts. It reveals the "felt" convergence of colonial and carceral logics in the Mujeres' bodies as a way of knowing (Million 2009). In a variety of Latin American and South American medical traditions, women's bodies are often seen as particularly susceptible to the manifestations of social disequilibrium, with emotional experience materializing in illness. Political and economic destabilization, the pain and trauma of family migration, and other broad structural conditions are understood to manifest in embodied conditions like uterine prolapse (Smith-Oka 2014), diabetes (Gálvez 2020), or, with mothers' bodies and fluids as vectors, infant debility (Tapias 2006). Xicana feminist "theory in the flesh" extends and builds political action from these etiologies, whereby "the physical realities of our lives . . . fuse to create a politic born out of necessity," an urgent responsivity to bodies as embodiments of ancestral and ongoing dispossession, and loci of collective potentiality (Moraga and Anzaldúa 1983, 23). Similarly, Native feminists note the "social-spiritual enactment" of women's embodied rite-of-passage practices as "responsible" for world-sustaining (Risling Baldy 2018), linking embodied ceremonial practices to worldly conditions. These far-reaching understandings hang together in the Colectiva to shape healing as at once ancestral and radical, a rich and urgent source of possibility to counter entrenched colonial and carceral logics and their quotidian stressful manifestations—their kids' apparent disposability, and their mothers' resulting pain.

Pamela put her hand on Juana's shoulder and said, "Think of my son and what happened to him. I'm here in your life so Vincent doesn't end up like Chris." Pamela had recently lost her son, Chris, when he was killed shortly after his release from jail in another county. He had not received treatment for his mental illness while he was incarcerated. Pamela was grieving but, as she put it with reference to her embodied endurance, "still standing." She made ways to heal through the Colectiva's circles, not only by unloading her own *cargas* but also by taking on those of others to prevent them from experiencing the same pain. This included being the first to arrive and last to leave at protests against local police killings, advocating at county and state levels to divert funding to community mental health resources instead of public safety (i.e., police), and performing insistent acts of care for women in situations potentially analogous to her own, like Juana. They had only known each other for a few months, but the contingencies of their sons' situations seemed strikingly close. What had been for Pamela's son could yet be otherwise for Juana's.

Knowing Pamela's commitment to preventing others from going through the same pain she had experienced, Juana had invited her to her son's hearing. Juana called me that morning for a ride there, knowing equally that as the student who always had plenty of time as well as "research funds" for gas money and snacks, I would be eager to go with her. I was. She seemed so anxious, and I wanted her to be more clearheaded and feel supported as she entered her son's hearing.

This chapter further illuminates the thick sense of feminist solidarity developed through *descargando*, which strongly shaped my Otherwise Anthropology ethical stance and methodological approach. Although I was not impacted by colonial and carceral systems in the same ways as women like Juana and Pamela and their kids, in the Colectiva I came to see how these systems and logics shape, or deform, all of our lives—that "this shit is killing you too, however much more softly," to borrow a phrase from Stefano Harney and Fred Moten (2013, 10). As a fellow Mujer, albeit one embodying a different set of life experiences, I was expected to pick up and hold onto others' *cargas* too as we together eked out everyday abolitionist relations of presence and practices of mutuality. This meant mobilizing the contingency of our experiences, leveraging my own privileges, and, along with others in the group, doing something else with the embodied understandings of violence and possibility that they catalyzed. Sometimes this "something else" has taken the form of material support and mutual aid directed at interlocutors, and sometimes it has been through theoretical and methodological interventions that target academic practice.

Maya J. Berry and her colleagues (2017), writing as a collective of women of color and queer anthropologists, urge activist anthropologists to recognize and account for the ways our positionalities and privileges shape how we are able to engage in ethnographic research. They argue that centering our bodies in our methodologies, and being accountable to the dynamics of our disparate positionalities vis-à-vis our interlocutors, can disrupt persistent heteropatriarchal, positivist, and colonial norms of knowledge production—that is, the standard practice of presenting oneself as a neutral and unencumbered ethnographer who can learn anything from anyone, and "penetrate" and "evacuate" the field or its relationships at will, answering only to a desire for knowledge. The coauthors call for a fugitive anthropology that incorporates knowledge praxis that works from these embodiments, thereby unsettling and transforming the way anthropologists are engaged throughout the research process. Taking up their call, I thus consider *descargando* as a core ethicomethodological praxis, at the heart of my anthropological commitment to building otherwise together in whatever forms that takes, amid relentless weathering by deep, durative, and disproportionately inequitable systems of oppression.

The sage came back to me, and I blew on its embers to make more smoke, aiming to ease the *cargas* surfacing in this parking lot *círculo*. The guards watched us from the door of the juvenile hall. We let the sage burn out, and entered the building together.

A Space for Raw Women

The Colectiva was founded in the final weeks of 2013 when, after being asked for months by Building Healthy Communities managers to start a healing group for women on the East Side, Shi finally accepted the role of facilitator. Although she had been trained in La Cultura Cura programs over the years, this new role required Shi to adapt her sense of self as capable of leadership and deserving of the opportunity. She knew that women in this community needed access to cultural healing, but she wasn't sure of the direction it would take; the group was not intended to follow a set curriculum. She tested the waters by first holding informal gatherings, *convivias* (translated to me as potlucks) at her apartment, inviting some of her old friends. The *convivias* were energizing events, and initial participants wanted to bring along more women they knew. Within a couple of weeks, Shi relocated these gatherings of women to a larger space at the BreadBox community center and relaunched them as weekly healing circles of La Colectiva de Mujeres. Before long, the group was meeting twice per week by popular demand.

Even with her work and lived experience, these circles felt novel and profound to Shi, a blessing in her life. In her career, she had largely worked with youth, so it felt different to work with adult women. Just a few weeks after the Colectiva's launch, she told me, earnestly, "I've never had so many good things happen to me before, to be in the company of women who are embracing one another. There's never been a space [on the East Side of Salinas] where women, *raw* women, could just *talk*." "Raw" women, in Shi's view, were those like her, who had come of age as the first female members of local Sureño and Norteño gangs in the 1980s and 1990s. She described that time as a "past life," when she and others would *descargaban* mostly through "sadness or self-destruction— tears of wanting to give up, fade away, escape awhile." The ability now to "just talk" and "feel safe in a *círculo*" felt radical. While the circles centered those Shi called raw, they also made space for "professional" women, a term she used to gloss those who had been through higher education or worked long-term jobs in county or community spaces. While Shi briefly considered splitting the group into dedicated raw and professional spaces, Mujeres across these categories connected in circle, sharing some experiences while realizing their differences as generative resources.

The circles opened a powerful organizing space to make change in contemporary conditions for each other and for future generations. Though most Mujeres had experience with community- or faith-based self-improvement programs, or mandated correctional programs, the Colectiva's healing circles smelled, sounded, and felt different, mixing the streetwise ethics and aesthetics, women-centered teachings, and sacred medicines of Xicanisma, a distinctly feminist, radical, and spiritually grounded movement of Mexican American women (Castillo 2014). Xicana spirituality is epistemic, embodied, and cosmological, a way of understanding one another's position in the world, shaped by and moving with the experiences of ancestors (Moraga and Anzaldúa 1983; Facio and Lara 2014). As an act of self-determination that generates a sense of control over "what makes us feel whole, what brings us tranquility, strength, nerve to face the countless . . . obstacles in the path on our journey toward being fulfilled human beings" (Castillo 2014, 160), it is fundamentally political. The Mujeres' cultural healing praxis was founded in these powerful understandings of how illness and stress are deeply political, racialized, and intergenerational in scope. This mix—of spirituality, the affirmation of women's embodied knowledge, and solidarity in the name of self-determination—was a capacious combination for collectively excavating stressful experiences of all kinds, with a particular emphasis on those wrought by proximity to the carceral system.

These understandings multiplied the stakes of *descargando*, as an individual embodied practice making collective impacts across generations.

Indeed, though having time to "just talk" was an important affordance of these gatherings, as noted by Shi, healing practices cultivated in circle extended beyond narration of experiences. *Cargas* "coming down" in the Colectiva's circles were seen to be heritable and sickening if not addressed or "picked up" by each other or the medicine, in commonly used terminology. In addition to those developed in real time, some *cargas* came from ancestral experiences of dispossession, "carried" to children and impacting their lives, weighing on them. As Shi would often repeat, "We're out there healing for those who couldn't or can't." These are more than metaphors. The reception of *cargas* is an embodied praxis built on the visceral realization of contingency and possibility: how what could have been for one may yet be otherwise for each other.

* * *

In the following, I will track how the *cargas* of a Mujer named Esme were taken up by the group over a series of healing circles to launch an array of projects that attempted to mitigate her stress and its structural conditions. What is shared is incredibly painful and, I warn readers, features child loss. I do not write about this lightly. I have carefully chosen and framed this example as it evokes the deeply embodied and multifaceted impacts of carceral systems and logics on the women of the Colectiva, as well as the resultant efforts of the group's by-any-means-necessary action and support. I ask readers to follow the thread of the collective praxis of potentiality underway rather than dwell in Esme's *cargas* themselves, or fixate on a sense of her suffering. The impacts of this *descargando* were not linear or directly healing of Esme's stress, but they should be understood as part of a fugitive feminist struggle to counter carceral dehumanization and its embodied sequelae through building otherwise in Salinas.

One evening in early 2014, members of the Colectiva unhurriedly arrived to circle. I unstacked plastic chairs while others grabbed snacks and put photos or small objects on an altar at the center of the room. As we chatted casually and took seats, leaving one chair open symbolically for those who couldn't join us, I noticed Esme was absent again. Esme was a friendly but reserved *Mexicana* with weary eyes and strong legs.

She was an avid walker who had worked for two decades in the *lechuga* (lettuce) and *fresa* (strawberry) fields while raising four kids. Shi opened the circle by honoring the four sacred directions and sent a bundle of sage and cedar around the group to her left. We each waved the smoke four times toward different parts of our bodies, standing in a quiet ritual that turned the group's focus toward the altar and our bodies, away from the day's grind.

"So, I just want to let you all know that Esme isn't here again, and it's because she got some news from her doctor," Shi said with gravity as the rest of us sat peaceful from the saging. Esme's doctor suspected she had a kind of reproductive cancer, and they were pursuing treatment immediately. Rarely did such a serious biomedical concern come up in the circle, though Shi and other *maestras* had shared that women carry their *cargas* in their reproductive organs and that, without healing work, serious health concerns would manifest there. Shi asked the rest of us to bring Esme some basics such as milk and tortillas, if we could, and to pray for her.

After the *círculo*, Shi and I debriefed in the parking lot. I asked about Esme, and Shi told me with distress how she had visited her at home, adding details that she had not mentioned to the group. The pantry was empty, the kids were home from school. Esme was nauseous from her treatment. And yet, she insisted on talking about something she had heard another woman say in circle a couple of weeks earlier during a round of *descargando*. June, a white "professional" woman in the group, had disclosed an experience of sexual harassment. This *carga* deeply resonated with Esme. "Something similar happened to them both," as Shi put it. It struck Esme that June had been through something devastating but had been able to articulate it to others and seemingly move forward, unburdened. It afforded Esme's imagining of what could happen if she shared more with this group, and she asked if she could tell her story to the Colectiva. Shi agreed to give her extra space at the next circle to share.

The next afternoon, Shi, Rosa, Didi—a Mujer and facilitator of other La Cultura Cura healing circles—and I had a meeting scheduled to talk over some of the plans for the Colectiva, as a proto–"leadership committee" for the group. Rosa was a facilitator employed by BHC to work with its funded projects in Salinas, corral their ideas, and help them to build power. Shi had brought Esme to the meeting as well. We met at La Plaza Bakery, a beloved local spot for pan dulce (sweet breads) and tortas (sandwiches), pushing two square tables together to make enough room for everyone, our phones and notebooks, and whatever treats we had each ordered. Someone brought a few sprigs of dried sage and placed them on the table. Rosa opened the meeting, describing it as "packed tight," and asked that we do a lightning round of check-ins, two minutes or less per person. I took fifteen seconds to say how my morning had been. Didi took the full two minutes. Esme, next around the table, began to share what had transpired for her that morning, before bursting into tears; her *cuñada* (sister-in-law) was also her landlord and was expecting the rent, which Esme couldn't pay. She was starting to feel unable to care for her kids, with a terrible sense of dread. She continued to share about her years of domestic abuse from an ex, and how she had been *callada por miedo*, literally shut up or quieted by fear, for years, but now felt an urgency to let it out.

We all paid close attention to Esme's *cargas*, nodding and offering small sounds of support and dismay as she went on for nearly an hour. Nobody stopped her, and as she closed off her check-in, Rosa sighed, creating a space of silence for Esme's *cargas* to land. In Spanish, she thanked her, reaching out to touch her arm. This was exactly the purpose of the Colectiva, she reminded us—to create spaces for women to talk about what they went through, and for others to hear it and build from it.

Esme returned the following week to circle, bringing along a small pinewood box. It held the remains of her eldest son, Andrés. It would have been Andrés's sixteenth birthday had he not been struck by a stray bullet in a period of retributive gang violence earlier that year. This was an accident of proximity barely investigated by police, though it was no secret in the community who was behind it.[1] Taped to the edge of the box was a black-and-white photo of him, crumpled from months of hugs, smoothed by affectionate tending. Esme did not put the box on the altar but kept what remained of her son's body in her arms or at her side.

With distinct heaviness already in the air, Shi noted at the beginning of the circle that the plan this day would be a little different. She passed the *palabra* to Esme, attempting a question-and-answer format to support her. In less than ten minutes, the structure had been abandoned. Esme bawled while telling us about her son as a slew of other *cargas* came down: an abusive spouse, her extortive landlord *cuñada*, being sexually assaulted as a child in Michoacán, and now this cancer diagnosis. Fifteen or so women were there that day as Esme put her *cargas* in front of us and the medicine.

Shi dabbed at her tears and carefully lit even more sage to help carry away the *cargas* coming down. Some parts of what Esme had shared resonated with her deeply, as Shi had been a first responder called to the scene of Esme's son's death and had also experienced gender-based violence. "I really feel this, because it's something I've been through too, I know what it's like to be violated and have your closest family reject you for it. . . . OK, Esme, we are going to stop the *descargando* now," her voice quickening, "and if we could each go around the circle and say something positive to Esme about your reflections on her story, just try to generate some positive *vibras* [vibes] for her."

Esme seemed spent while listening to the women, most of whom began to respond to particular aspects of her *cargas* and articulate how they would mobilize that response into other actions. Josefina, usually reticent to speak, said, "I've been through that, too," and decided she would be more open about her own story of childhood abuse, realizing the importance of raising awareness about these experiences for others to know they are not alone or at fault. Kesia, who worked at a local nonprofit, said she would help Esme find loopholes to get better medical coverage. I told her I would be there to honor her son and help her get to any appointments I could. Yesi said, simply, that she was sorry for what Esme had experienced. Pamela immediately pushed back, enflamed by what she perceived as the inadequacy of offering only an apology, a symbolic gesture, in a situation where there was in fact something to be done.

"Sorry doesn't cut it. I'm uncomfortable with just a sorry when you don't know this experience," Pamela said, causing raised eyebrows around the circle. She brought up the accidental death of her infant daughter two decades earlier, and the struggle to endure after such deep tragedy. She reiterated a commitment she had made to supporting single and homeless mothers through backpack drives and local advocacy. Pamela asked Esme to bring a picture of her son to put on the altar at the center of our *círculo*. She would bring a photo of her daughter, too, so they could be together and with us. Esme nodded, but didn't say anything more. We were learning to accommodate Pamela's intensity as borne of her experience and integral to how she cared, though it had led some to dismiss her in other community spaces as "too much."

Shi closed off the round of responses and suggested we shift to a creative activity, producing "road maps of our lives" with markers, stickers, and colored paper. Tentatively, we eased into the activity and quiet, informal conversations about our intended or desired life trajectories. Esme remained quiet and kept to herself through the rest of the *círculo*. I wondered if we should have given her more space, but during our usual parking lot debrief afterward, Shi noted that she could sense Esme was exhausted and others like Pamela and herself were becoming overloaded. She sought to create a lighter mood and orientation to the future in the group before dispersing. We would have more time to figure out how best to move with what we had taken on in circle.

The closing ritual of this and every *círculo* was a round of "I-appreciations." Someone would volunteer to start us off, standing and squaring up with the woman to their left, looking into her eyes and saying, "I appreciate you." It was hard not to laugh when delivering and receiving this earnest gesture. With a hug and a reciprocal "I appreciate you, too," the original appreciator would move on to the next woman on the left, with the appreciatee following thereafter, and each woman hugged, hugging, chuckling warmly, and directly appreciating the next.

Touch and Transformation

Esme's *descargando* of stressors including but exceeding her medical diagnosis, described as she held her son's ashes, was a catalyst for the Colectiva. The group was, at that point, a fresh experiment in care among women who were just building their relationships together, realizing and developing a language for the interlocking systems that impacted their lives, and figuring out what cultural healing might entail. Esme's *cargas*, palpable and multifaceted, were the "*gasolina* for our fires, exactly why we're doing what we're doing," according to Didi as she reflected on that circle the next day. *Descargando* was not just one person letting go of stresses through their articulation, but an imperative on the rest of us to pick up and address those burdens as we could. It opened onto the transformative potentiality of holding others' stresses, as well as the tremendous work this could and would take.

Understandably, some Mujeres—like Yesi—felt unable or unwilling to carry others' *cargas* in light of their own, and eventually took distance from the group. As a Mujer who did not face the same racialized and gendered stress as most others in the Colectiva, and who had the eagerness of an anthropology grad student seeking to learn about others' lives, I did have capacity for the process of *descargando*. Like others in the group, I learned to feel comfortable disclosing intimate *cargas* I carried, taking the opportunity to make sense of hurt inflicted by a toxic boyfriend or the loneliness of my academic trajectory. I learned to be present to the discomfort of witnessing and taking on others' often profoundly painful experiences, and to make space for the heaviness I felt afterward. I felt it was an honor and privilege to have developed the *confianza* to be in that relation, which sharpened into a vigilant commitment to support the Mujeres in ways material—leveraging my free time, transportation, and research budget—and epistemological. I swore to never reduce these stresses and stories to theories of violence or *communitas*, but to hold tight to how the circle felt and what it compelled, and stay with that soma to understand how it moved and potentiated our bodies and lives, and the role of such embodied praxis in otherwise social transformation.

The visceral realization of what could have been, in one's own or another's life, "intrudes on bodies," as Liane Carlson notes in her account of contingency in models of history (2019, 34). Though linked to systematic oppressions and structural in myriad ways, the facts of the Mujeres' stress were not an inevitable production of history, but marked by unknowable contingencies, twists of fate, stray bullets, crossed paths, and particular family histories, traumas, and medicines. There were stark contingencies that made our lives different as well as remarkable ones that brought us together to be in relation. As described by Carlson, "To be struck, truly struck, by the contingency of a problem can mean the total transformation of spatial and emotional geography" (37), arguing that this encounter happens not through cognitive faculties but through the body and its sense of touch, or hapticality. The body's vulnerability to contingency is what makes possible the constantly shifting relationship between our bodies and the world. This haptic force is at work when *cargas* are picked up and held, and perceived contingencies in what has been and could be catalyze new action.

In *The Undercommons*, Stefano Harney and Fred Moten characterize hapticality as "the capacity to feel through others, for others to feel through you, for you to feel them feeling you," where these feelings open onto rearranged, unregulated, and radically potentiated relations, a novel commons of mutuality (2013, 98). Building on their work, Rizvana Bradley argues that haptics are a "visceral register of experience and a vital zone of experimentation," opening onto otherwise formations (2015, 129). Encountering and holding *cargas* can be potentially transformative of relations and incite new world-making efforts, as we will see in the following section. Esme's *cargas* may have weighed differently on each of us but nevertheless called us into coalition that could support her, memorialize and honor her son, and launch projects to diminish each other's stress. In their varied and experimental forms, the outcomes were not known ahead of time, but we can see how these actions affirmed Chicanx-Indigenous lives, worked against carceral structures and logics, and built otherwise possibilities for connection and joy.

Turning *Cargas* into Action

An energy for new projects was evident at another *círculo* a few weeks deeper into the spring of 2014, in the colorful home of Rosa's *suegra* (mother-in-law). Rooted in what was unloaded during *descargando*, members of the Colectiva were pursuing further actions in the community. Circled up on couches and the floor, enjoying potluck fare, we passed a gourd rattle during *descargando* and punctuated our check-ins with mariachi flourishes. When it came to Juana, she shared that she "was nervous, but felt really good after" going to speak at the Board of Supervisors meeting the previous week, providing testimony about her son's experience in the juvenile hall that the county was trying to expand, as discussed in chapter 2. "Next time I'll prepare a little more," she said, "now that I kinda know how it goes." Pamela gave us more details about what transpired at that meeting so that all would be informed about the juvenile hall reduction effort. Didi cried, seemingly at the relief of being able to make it to circle, to which Pamela responded, "See, we don't even need to talk about anything in particular. Just being here is the medicine!"

At this circle, we worked toward creative and possible avenues for supporting and celebrating each other. Esme wasn't there, but we strategized about what we could do for her as she faced the anniversary of Andrés's death. We would show up to his church memorial and keep bringing her food. We arranged carpools to attend a sweat lodge ceremony and scheduled ourselves to show up to meetings related to the juvenile hall rebuilding and outreach for Proposition 47, the state carceral reform initiative that would reduce certain felonies to misdemeanors and enable many locals to reclassify or expunge their criminal records in California. We laid the groundwork for a series of workshops called "Voice of the Voiceless," to equip the Mujeres with tools for publicly telling "our stories" as a blend of art and advocacy. This was organizing in an organic mode, while we filled our bellies on a sunny afternoon in a warm, glowing house, on one of the supposedly most dangerous streets in East Salinas.

Some of these efforts crystallized into distinct anticarceral structural changes at state and local levels. Proposition 47 passed, making it possible for many Salinas residents to build lives no longer overshadowed by their former convictions, and to access better employment and housing. The juvenile hall was rebuilt with a greatly reduced number of beds.[2] But most of the residents' transformations were intimate, relational, otherwise shifts: friendships like Juana and Pamela's that integrated mutual aid and advocacy; Dolores's burgeoning career as an advocate and *maestra*; courage and resources to leave an abusive spouse; teachings that disclosed new perspectives on ongoing struggles and renewed energy to keep going. There were projects to deliver paper flowers to homeless mothers and backpacks filled with school supplies to their kids, in ardently feminist efforts to counter both dehumanization and material scarcity. These and myriad other hard-fought and earnest endeavors have contributed to improving the lives of *Mexicano*, Chicanx, and Latinx residents in Salinas, though they have not ceased interrelated phenomena of carceral dispossession, state violence, or chronic stress and its sequelae. The *cargas* keep coming down, in a nonlinear process, and in their own time.

Many of the Mujeres were offered opportunities to get closer to La Cultura Cura philosophy and curricula, which should be counted among the transformations sparked by the Colectiva that insist on their own time and are not always evident. A few weeks after the potluck *círculo*, Esme and I attended a La Cultura Cura "base training" led by Maestro Jerry Tello, in which the fundamentals of the project's philosophy were imparted in an afternoon session. Esme walked to the BreadBox, where I picked her up, and as we drove across the city we listened to the dulcet vocals of Mexican indie artist Carla Morrison and chatted. Approaching the former ranch house where the training was held, she remarked that she had walked by its tall, imposing gates for sixteen years and had always wanted to go inside. She was in a good mood, feeling strong, and looking forward to the training, even though it would be conducted primarily in English. Most of the audience members were staff of the various nonprofits or county departments in Salinas that drew on the La Cultura Cura paradigm or ran its curricula, and Esme was thus the rare attendee who was considered *gente*, simply a resident from the community.

We were directed to sit in the front of a two-row, semicircle arrangement of chairs, up close to a long folding table set up as an altar. A skin drum, a textile square of the Virgen de Guadalupe, two tiny plum-colored moccasins, and a *palabra* piece sat atop a striped wool blanket. A monitor mounted on the wall behind the altar showed a sun-streaked sky reflected by the sea, with the image overlaid by the words "Transformational Healing, La Cultura Cura." Maestro Tello, in a black shirt with "PALABRA" written in white letters on the back, began by introducing himself, saying it was an honor to be with us. Didi quietly translated to Esme as the *maestro* acknowledged all the relations we were bringing into the room too. "Everywhere we go, we bring our ancestors with us," he said, conjuring a vision of our grandparents crowding the corners of the old ranch house. Later, to close the training, he softly beat the skin drum as he asked us to just listen and feel our grandfathers and grandmothers next to us, supporting us. The tender drumming reverberated like a heartbeat.

It was both powerful and wearying. Though the training largely had the audience in a listening role, the *maestro*'s stories and rhetorical questions were so intimate that they cut to the core, touching deep-seated wounds and provoking strong affective and embodied responses. Being opened to transformation takes energy; transforming takes time. Esme told Shi and me that she enjoyed the training, but afterward we did not often see her in circle. Her cancer cleared, but Andrés's death weighed on her, and she became isolated and escaped into addiction.

After a period living in an informal encampment in central Salinas, she entered residential addiction care. But as she shared with me years later, she worked on becoming sober and stable, with seeds of the Colectiva's woman-centered support growing into a close relationship with her now-adult daughter.

While she appreciated the space to *descarga* her stresses and be heard, affirmed, and cared for by the other Mujeres, and to get closer to the medicine and cultural healing philosophy, the embodied pain of her son's death was not easily unloaded, nor was she sure if she wanted to do so. Shi told me that, after that intense circle with her son's ashes, Esme had told Shi that she felt, even saw, her son in the room with us, and her daughter had glimpsed him in the bathroom mirror. The group was too loud, and she couldn't hear or talk to him; she fell silent and frozen, even as she wanted to escape. Hearing about this version of the circle devastated and confused me: she experienced everyone's attention and care as overwhelming, preventing her from connecting with her son. But did something about the encounter bring him back, kindling that sense of proximity and touch between mother and child?

Healing, Not Therapy

"What do you do for women in that situation, seriously?" Shi asked me, rhetorically, as we reflected on the circles and Esme years later. "It was so emotional for me, too. I just couldn't hold it down no more. *She brought her son's ashes to the group*, Megan. That still makes me cry." Shi underlined the limitations of remedying racialized stress in terms of individual recoveries or straightforward structural change, as if the multifactorial conditions of what Esme or others embodied could be easily remedied through care, direct action, or advocacy.

"I don't even know," I replied. "But it reminds me of what you said before circle that day: this is a group for healing, not therapy." The Colectiva was a *collective*; those who experienced healing or benefited from the Colectiva's work to reduce the conditions of stress and affirm Chicanx-Indigenous life may not have been the original holders of the *carga* that sparked the group's efforts. Instead, it was through the Mujeres' ongoing commitments to each other's well-being, daily refusals of disposability, in whatever form it takes, that bodies were able to keep moving with integrity, self-respect and mutual respect, and realization of their potential to build otherwise and heal. This work came organically but was neither easy, smooth, nor direct. It should be understood as world-building even if its potentiality has been contested, its resources scuttled, its enactments fragmented, protracted, or wildly diverse.

Early on in the Colectiva's existence, when some of the women and I still attended the weekly critical consciousness *círculo* run by MILPA on Wednesday nights, one of the male members of MILPA was talking up the new women-only offshoot. "And who knows what the women are going to do, when they get organized," he concluded, encouragingly, "but we know it's going to be great."

The line stayed with me at that time and has for years; its mix of support and paternalism, cheer and neglect, still feels like a gut punch, a painful misunderstanding of the group's intense magic. The Mujeres were already doing the work of cultural healing in being together, bringing the medicine, and building a circle. They mitigated each other's experiences and conditions of chronic stress through a framework of cultural healing and feminist coalition, building otherwise in urgent responsiveness to each other. In working closely with women and families impacted by carceral systems, the Colectiva prepared the ground for further change to be enacted and built, for moments of shift to be realized and articulated as the Ollin. As Rosa had put it at that meeting at La Plaza Bakery after Esme's long *descargando*, women's stories were our key resources—or, more accurately, making a safe space for women to tell, hear, and move with those stories was our core strategy for change. In that way, she added, "We are not just demanding rights but cultivating community, doing transformative work in how social change actually happens."

Much of the time, this work was not flashy, and perhaps it was easily mistaken for "just talk" in the diminished sense of women's idle chatter or gossip. Perhaps I have inadvertently reproduced this patronizing idea, in arguing that what the Mujeres did needs to be recognized as *more than* talk, focusing instead on the embodied transfer of *cargas* and their transformation into action. However, I have aimed to show the embodied realities of chronic stress and its collective mitigation, through cultural healing praxis in its many dimensions as material reparation, care in the context of contingency, and haptic copresence. In this chapter and throughout this book, I have amplified aspects of that approach into the heart of an ethnographic ethicomethodology. This feminist-fugitive commitment has grown because of what is incommensurable between Shi and me, and other Mujeres, embracing the contingency of being in each other's lives despite our vast differences as somehow fated, for whatever reason. Otherwise world-building must be traced in this materiality, in the ways it grows from love and refusal, and the everyday embodied work of abolition from the grassroots.

4

Homegirl *Noble*

Relational Ethics across Affiliated Generations

How do Chicana-Indigenous women make sense of and build on their experiences with gang affiliation over subsequent years and decades? In contrast to literatures that seek and champion the "exits" or "recoveries" from gang affiliation (Valdez 2007; E. O. Flores 2013, 2016), this chapter explores the continuities, ambivalences, and possibilities of gang affiliation across generations through the relationships of some homegirls in the Colectiva, their friends, and their children.[1] It shows how a shift toward a culturally affirmative praxis, in contrast to moralizing or violence-suppressing strategies that further criminalize and stigmatize gang involvement, provides a welcoming and generative set of conditions for the continuity of some ethical and relational aspects of affiliation present in these women's lives. A "cultural healing" praxis, as imparted through the Colectiva, is aligned with and expands upon these relational ethics (Zigon 2021), making possible the achievement of what I call here a "homegirl *noble*" femininity. *Noble* can be quickly translated as "noble," but in this context it coalesces a richer set of meanings, as discussed toward the end of the chapter. Scant ethnographic attention has been paid to Chicana girls' and women's experiences of gang affiliation (M. Miranda 2003; Mendoza-Denton 2008), and even less to the ways affiliation shapes their lives over the long term beyond criminogenic tropes (Moore 1991).[2] This chapter demonstrates how these relational ethics remain fundamental and generative to those who have been affiliated, despite institutional and societal exhortations to reject that part of themselves in order to live a rehabilitated and "respectable" life.

La Vida Loca

It was late morning on a weekday, and Shi had asked me to come meet her at Yesi's. The son of a couple old friends of theirs had been killed a few days earlier, and they were gathering to mourn his loss and visit the grieving parents.

As I reached Yesi's house on the East Side of Salinas, I found Shi standing out front at the window of a huge, lifted pickup truck, chatting with a woman in the driver's seat. She looked to be of the same "generation" as Shi, someone who had come up in local gang life in the 1990s. I had seen photos of Shi from that time: big, teased-up hair, white tank top and baggy blue Pendleton shirt, baggy jeans on her skinny frame, dark lipliner, eyebrows arched, looking *chingona* (badass). These days she wore dresses and cardigans, often with sandals and sunglasses, still *chingona* but a little different. She always wore blue tones or black, never red, in keeping with her Sureña roots. Her friend had a casual bun in her hair and wore a dark blue work uniform over inked arms.

I parked my Prius across from the truck. My little hybrid was given the nickname "gangster Prius" by my healing collective friends because of its black-tinted windows and supersilent ability to creep up on bystanders. It was a joke, since I had no gang experience whatsoever and a Prius could truly never be that cool, but it was an inclusive and approving tease for my otherwise out-of-place car and self on the East Salinas streets.

As I joined the two women on the street, Shi introduced us. "This is my friend Megan, she's from Amsterdam. She's a part of the Colectiva. And this is my friend, Sad Girl, Sara."

"Hi, Sara," I said, as we waved hello. Shi's inclusion of the name "Sad Girl" confirmed that their friendship went deep into homegirl history. Sad Girl was Sara's *placaso*, her gang nickname from those earlier days, referring to some prominent trait she'd had. Shi's *placaso* had been Shy Girl, naming her tendency of shying away from the spotlight. More than just indicating affiliation, these names condensed relational histories and asserted belonging (Pina-Cabral 2015).

They continued their conversation about their friends' son, Julian, who had recently been killed in Greenfield, an agricultural town down the valley. Shi was trying to determine what people knew about it. It didn't seem like details were widely known, beyond that he had been shot on a Wednesday and taken off life support on Saturday. It happened in Greenfas (the local Spanglish slang term for Greenfield), even though Julian lived in Salinas and had only been there to pick up his girlfriend. It didn't seem to be gang-related, since Julian wasn't affiliated, as far as they knew, though the person who shot him was a Northerner, or Norteño. The conflict was probably a "crime of passion," they agreed, something to do with his girlfriend.

"It's so sad," Sara said. "It's probably gonna get written up as gang-related anyways just because they fit the profile and one of them was a Norteño." They "fit the profile" because they were young, brown, and male, and one used a gun. Pausing, Sara added, "But at least then he'll get gang enhancements and the family will get some justice." Gang enhancements were additional sentences piled on to parole violations or new convictions, relating the infraction, often tenuously, to gang affiliation and thereby multiplying its severity.

Shi weighed this. They both knew a lot about the practical workings of the criminal justice system from their generational experiences, witnessing friends, partners, cousins, and kids get picked up and locked up over the years, or themselves serving time.

"Well, yeah," she replied. "But there are other things, like if it's gang-related or even if the victim was on probation, the DA won't give them anything," wouldn't offer them any support. The victim and his family would be on their own, abandoned to their grief, considered disposable as a result of any involvement whatsoever in gangs. There was little justice for Julian's life to be found through the judicial system.

Shi continued, "It fuckin' sucks, dude. If something happened to either of us they'd probably call it gang-related, too. They'd see the dots on our fingers *y ya*, that's it."

The three-dot tattoos on their fingers were a reference to *la vida loca*, the *locura* (craziness) and *desmadre* (chaos) of Chicanx gang life. The tattoos had faded and blurred, but they remained indelible, as did the experience they represented. Sara's and Shi's lives didn't seem that *loca* anymore; both worked full-time jobs and lived low-profile lives oriented toward their families. However, they continued to embody important traces of that affiliation: ink, names, memories, relationships. Even if they did not actively participate in gang life in the same ways they did as youngsters, they had not exited it entirely—nor did they seek to. Instead, they maintained a sense of generational belonging and accomplishment for the work they "put in" as women in gangs, even as that work had been largely unrecognized by others. Further, they pursued a stewardship role in guiding and easing the lives of younger generations, sharing the privileges they had accrued for their work. They carefully navigated and mobilized relationships with others of their generation, and their kids, in a way that suggests the affirmative and generative relational ethics of gang affiliation among some Chicana-Indigenous and *Mexicana* women.

The term "relational ethics," as Zigon (2021) notes, refers to practices and dispositions shaped and conditioned through being in relation with others in a particular context, rather than corresponding to overarching, predetermined, and/or codified societal moralities. Similarly, feminist philosophers have theorized an ethics of care, with "care" indicating practices that work on relations and worlds, unmoored from particular cultural connotations of care as sympathetic or warm (Tronto 1995). Practices considered ethical in a relational or care framework are responsive to one another among those who share certain conditions of life, in contrast with practices that adhere instead to legal frameworks or criminal codes, a priori religious doctrine, or other outwardly defined and top-down moralistic approaches to social life (Zigon 2008). There is nothing inherently "feminine" in care or relational ethics, though unique ethical formations often arise at the intersections of gender, race, and class, and autonomy and independence are more typically coded (and valorized) as part of the performance of masculinities (Bettie 2014).

In an example of how gender performativity is bound up with ethical projects in relation to gang life, Edward Orozco Flores (2013) argues that a reorientation of masculinity through religious practices is fundamental to Chicano men's efforts to exit gangs. In his ethnography *God's Gangs*, Flores writes of "barrio masculinity" of either "deviant" or "reformed" varieties to refer to the performances of gender among Chicano/Latino men who either adhere to, or have since rejected, gang lifestyles. Focusing on those who take up a reformed barrio masculinity as part of their "gang recovery" (2013, 10), he argues that rooting their manhood in domesticity rather than gang activities is essential in their pursuit of redemption for the pain they caused their own families (13). Despite mentions that much of gang involvement is nonviolent and a reaction to racism and oppression, in framing this exit through renegotiated masculinity as a process of "recovery," Flores reifies a sense of gang experience as pathological and deviant, a state from which normality must be returned to or regained in the pursuit of predetermined virtue. In focusing exclusively on masculinity, his ethnography further begs the question of how a "barrio femininity" might shape or be shaped by longer-term relationships with the gang or one's affiliates.

In this chapter I attend to the enduring relational ethics among women like Shi and Sara, and their implications for a maturing femininity among members of La Colectiva de Mujeres and their friends. A relational ethics approach that centers an intersectional femininity, and that is grounded in ethnography, aims to humanize and complicate the study of women in gangs. Recent generations of critical gang studies and cultural criminologists have also sought to shift the fundamental conversations on gangs away from pathology, delinquency, and risk (Brotherton 2015; Weide 2022). However, these tendencies remain prominent in a context where societal and academic understandings of gang membership remain abundantly individualized, criminalized, masculinized, and overdetermined by violence, as is clear from both law enforcement and religious approaches to gang desistance. The implications of these reductive and racist, classist, and sexist perspectives filter down to people like Shi and Sara, and others like them in Salinas and elsewhere, who were inundated with the message that gang involvement guaranteed one's disposability by state and social institutions. In refusal of that message, and related demands to "exit" or "recover from" gang life, this chapter shows how these women "stayed solid" with each other. They maintained their *placasos*, continued to banter in the argot of gang life, and continuously renegotiated their relations through forms of care steeped in gang sociality. In doing so, they generated new possibilities for their own ethical standing through these relations with each other, as well as both prior and subsequent generations.

Paying attention to the ways the Mujeres and their homegirls continued to nurture their relations with each other refutes the broad notion that gangs are primarily criminal organizations, and that gang membership is an inherently detrimental state that one must reject or recover from in order to participate fully in society. It is important to note that women like Shi and Yesi were ambivalent about the more actively gang-involved time of their lives; they recognized the ways it hurt them and others. Similarly, I do not aim to romanticize gang affiliation, but rather look to how its sociality is rendered generative, in particular through its alignment with cultural healing. As we will see, the Colectiva opened space to acknowledge, affirm, and maintain some aspects of gang affiliation, making it possible to rekindle old friendships, make sense of inherited family trauma, and smooth the path for the next generation. Influenced by the Colectiva's cultural healing practices and teachings on intergenerational trauma and what it meant to be a "noble" woman, members of the group cultivated a raw, homegirl-turned-Mujer, chola-turned-*comadre* femininity that had long been growing, its roots in their youth, its bloom undetected.

Gang Girls Grown Up

Yesi eventually came out of her house and joined us at Sara's truck. Their friend Eva, Julian's mom, wasn't home yet, but Yesi knew that her daughter Serena was there "con un chingo de niños" (with a bunch of kids), and we could talk with her while waiting for her mother to get back. We piled into Sara's truck to drive half a block and around the corner to their apartment building. I didn't want to take the front seat, but Yesi and Shi had already arranged themselves in the back. Yesi joked, "If we get shot at, they'll hit you first!" Everyone chuckled. I laughed too, but nervously, never really sure what possibility those kinds of jokes held.

Serena greeted us at the top of the apartment complex stairs with a Chihuahua at her side and a cluster of kids playing behind her. The two-year-old was hers, but the rest of the children were neighbors. She looked tired as she led us into the sparsely furnished space. A small altar had been set up next to her mattress on the floor, where she sat now as we all found spots in a semicircle around her. The altar had photos of Julian, his hat and mobile phone, and a piece of paper with the words "We love you Julian . . . always and forever" written in bubble letters. Calmly, Serena gave us the rundown of what happened, showing us photos of her brother. Her father, Gordo (a *placaso*), was taking Julian's death heavily, she said. He had been working hard to keep his son protected. Even though Julian wasn't in a gang, Gordo was letting others from his generation know that his son was *his*, and thus the rightful inheritor of Gordo's hard-earned credibility.

Eva was doing the same thing. "She has always been so strong," Sara said about Eva. She'd heard of other moments when their son got surrounded and Eva would jump in to say, "If you're going to kill my son, you're going to kill me," and they would all back off. Others of that older generation should have informed their kids that Julian was not to be harmed. Unfortunately, Julian had been shot in nearby Greenfield, which was beyond Gordo and Eva's territory. Yesi, Sara, and Shi agreed there was nothing they could have done to protect their son there.

The conversation turned to Serena, who was dating someone affiliated. "Where's your man at?" Shi asked her. He was locked up down by San Diego. He had been sentenced to seventeen years, but this had recently been reduced to fifteen. He had been incarcerated for a year already, last seeing their son when he was three months old. Serena added that he had been in "the hole" since December, using a euphemism for a solitary confinement unit, and unable to make a phone call for months. Sara asked if they were going to stay together, sparking a long discussion about being in a relationship with someone locked up for so long. The older generation of homegirls had all been in that situation. They knew too well the amazing, rarefied feeling of getting a letter or phone call from an incarcerated partner, but also the deep disappointment of realizing that, even upon release, they often still had "that prison mentality."

Yesi was most concerned about this, elaborating to Serena, "When he gets out, he's gonna be looking over his shoulder, and you're gonna be in a different place, like you've finished your school, have a job . . . and what is he gonna be doing?"

Shi and Yesi began to share teachings shaped by both their gang days and the Colectiva: about being a strong *mujer* for one's kids, and about loving your man while he is locked up but also appreciating that distance from him and recognizing one's own strength and capability accordingly. Serena should rely on him for some support, they told her, but not put herself or her kids at risk to do too much gang-related business for him on the outside. It was a careful balance that she would have to figure out herself, but they wanted to impart their experience to the daughter of a homegirl, for whom they felt responsible.

Yesi, especially, seemed concerned that Serena and her child should avoid the same painful experiences she had while "coming up" as a young woman. Now living a low-key life with her three kids and two granddaughters, Yesi didn't quite remember everything she had been through, but the parts she could recall were enough to compel her to do what she could to prevent her daughters and other young women from getting too deep into that life—or at the very least to be intentional about what they got out of it. As always, she was laughing, but also casting her eyes downward, as she described how she had taken the fall and served time for the actions of more than one boyfriend. Like other girls and women, Yesi bore the brunt of "survival strategies" being criminalized (J. Flores 2016, 9). However, Yesi also learned that she could steal from the men who abused her, thereby finding a way to come out of a violent encounter on top and ahead. "How do you think I got my house?" she asked us all rhetorically and with a wry grin. "I *worked* for it!" She did have a very nice house, a bungalow on the East Side that was more spacious and comfortable than the other Mujeres' homes I had visited.

Criminological and sociological research on gang affiliation has largely focused on boys, men, and masculinity, with heteronormative assumptions (Panfil and Peterson 2015). Girls and women are often positioned as accessories, auxiliaries, or objects to the males, exploitable and expendable (Reynolds 2014), performing a "deviant femininity" (J. Flores 2016), and overdetermined by sexual violence and risky behavior (Valdez 2007).[3] This research does little to trouble the tropes of gangs as a social problem or explore the possibilities of gender performance on girls' or women's own terms. Marie "Keta" Miranda's (2003) ethnographic work with Chicana gang members in Oakland, California, by contrast, emphasizes the centrality of women's friendship and solidarity among the youth in a female-only gang in her study. And Norma Mendoza-Denton's ethnography *Homegirls* (2008) provides a critical alternative to masculinized and sexualized perspectives, focusing on the cultural and linguistic dynamics of high school–aged Chicanas who are gang-involved in the South Bay Area of California. These young women created and sustained a semiotically rich and ethically complex world for themselves, with intricate attention to makeup and clothing as part of the self-fashioning praxis of strong, protective, *macha* femininity. Girls like T-Rex (a *placaso* for Mendoza-Denton's key interlocutor) were proudly "down" for their gang and their families, and not only showed off but developed this strength through how they dressed, made themselves up, and carried their bodies as they walked, and through numerous other ways they practiced solidarity and uplift. I like to think that Mendoza-Denton's homegirl interlocutors, who were living in San Jose, an hour's drive north of Salinas, in roughly the same period women like Shi and Yesi were coming up, shared an ethical framework with many of the Mujeres—and that the Mujeres are akin to the homegirls a couple of decades further on, still holding it down.

The Salinas homegirls, now older, had navigated the challenges of entering new life phases and career and family responsibilities, while never formally exiting the gang. They adapted the way they dressed, made themselves up, and moved through the world, but not with goals of redemption or establishing irrevocable distance from gangs. Shi, for example, shifted to fit-and-flare blue and black dresses and cardigans, and she had some tattoos removed while adding others and keeping them on full display. She could be spotted zooming through town in a striking blue Mustang. There was no mistaking the Sureña coordinates to anyone aware of the Chicanx gang semiotics of color. Yesi had ditched her "sexy chola" look and now proudly maintained "my own eyebrows," making a distinction with the thin drawn-on arches so critical to the chola aesthetic. These modifications in self-presentation were not drastic makeovers but subtle embodied shifts that still performed the women's generationality and ongoing sense of belonging.

When I first met these Mujeres in the context of the healing circle, I assumed that they wanted to be radically different, to be transformed in the process of healing in a way that entailed letting go of their pasts. Instead, it became clear to me that the Colectiva was an appealing space for many of them precisely because they could continue to live out some of the practices and dispositions they already considered ethical, as cultivated through their gang affiliation. They could rekindle friendships that had been formative in the past, drawing and building on that shared history in new ways. Yesi, for example, joined the Colectiva upon Shi's invitation, despite being dubious as to "what colorful fuckin' characters would show up there." She wanted to "back up" an old friend with whom she "hadn't actually conversated" in years. After attending a few times, she was excited to realize that now she and Shi could be "official friends, without, like, using each other for money, for drugs, or to fight somebody. Like, just official friends where I'm just gonna call you because I'm lonely, no drama or anything. It's so awesome."

The Colectiva's nonjudgmental and even affirmative approach to gang life offered support to participants by stabilizing and enriching their lives without refusing the fundamental ethical context of their social world. Shi, similarly, held tight to "the way I was brought up" and its continuity with her current way of being. She had been part of the formation of a new-generation Sureño *cliqua* when she was in middle school, alongside her brother and his "road dog" friend. They have always, and will always, back each other up. She insisted that "this is the way that I believe in stuff, and no one's gonna change my mind because I have never been taught different. This is my life, and I can't look at it differently. I really can't. This is just life, this is our life." While there were certainly detrimental aspects of gang affiliation, there were also significant benefits and assets. Reflecting on the immediate impact of cultural healing and the Colectiva in her life, Shi added, "I always lived by the same core values, then and now, the same as in our group when I was banging [i.e., active in gang life], but now they are being used a little differently." In the Colectiva, these women created and held a space through which to continue living out those core values and relations of integrity, without having to court the physical or existential dangers of a hard disavowal of gang life.

Not Exit, but Credit

Such disavowal is often called gang exit or desistance in sociological literature, and is without question considered good or positive (Carson and Vecchio 2015). It is typically situated alongside aging and life course shifts: having kids, getting married, and other turning points and "hooks for change" (J. Flores 2016). But while those stages of life can have an impact on gang affiliation, they do not always entail or justify a hard exit. In carefully probing the question of gang exit with some of the Mujeres, it was clear that exit was an extreme risk to take for oneself and one's kids; if you exited the gang, you could easily be "greenlighted," meaning targeted for violence or death. You would have to move far from Salinas to exit without penalty, severing yourself from nearly all relations, and even then, there was no guarantee that you or your loved ones would not experience sanction or violence. When I asked Shi if it was easier for women to leave the gang life when they had kids, she swiftly refuted that possibility. She noted, "If they have kids or not, they're still gonna get killed . . . there are girls that get murdered too, they all had kids. It doesn't matter if you're a female or whatever. Cold blooded, honestly, I think they kill you even colder if you're a woman, just to make a point. You're equal as a man, basically you're equal. It don't fuckin' matter."

Having children altered the affiliation of these Mujeres, but not because of a strict desire to shield them entirely or escape from all gang life. This was an unlikely scenario in a community where affiliation came through families and residential blocks and was often deeply "pedestrianized," a matter of sociality and belonging rather than criminality (Mendoza-Denton 2008). Instead, their intention was for their children to inherit the privileges and protections that came from their earlier affiliation and ongoing relation with others. Just as Gordo and Eva mobilized their reputations in an attempt to protect their son, the women wanted to be able to call on those connections and the authority that came through their experiences; in Yesi's words, others should know that "these are our kids, don't fuck with them." They considered themselves OGs, "original gangsters," as some of the first women down for their gangs in this area, and thus deserving of respect that would shield their children too. Shi likened it to a system of credit, with the younger generation getting an "automatic open door" thanks to work her generation put in to fight other gangs to show that they shouldn't be messed with. Exiting the gang would negate these privileges accrued through their hard work. This system echoes the reciprocity ethics of debt and obligation Laurence Ralph (2014) notes in gang sociality in Eastwood, Chicago, but through a currency of care rather than violence, vengeance, and injury.

Instead of exiting, these women developed ways to lie low while still being present, and keeping in good relation with others who were able to vouch for their enduring credibility. If they were not in direct contact, they kept tabs on each other through those they did encounter, and in the process positioned themselves as still in good standing. Upon introduction to others from the East Side, I would often hear them coolly asking some variation of the inquiry, "Oh, do you still know such-and-such, Sleepy or Gordo or Green Eyes or Giggles, who stays by Mae Street?" Naming someone with credibility to index their own relational solidarity, often with *placasos*, they were always seeking common connections, emplacement, and a little information. At the same time, they would let just enough about themselves and their whereabouts be known too.

The importance of being in relation with others still more actively affiliated did entail some risks, hence the need to find a careful balance.

Another Mujer, Mia or Payasa (her *placaso*), described experiencing unwanted attention and vulnerability when her older brother became a "dropout," exiting gang life for a period of three years. "People were always questioning me," she said, especially as she was working for a community organization that implemented *cultura*-based programming. That organization was funded by federal anti-gang programs and collaborating with law enforcement, and thus was widely mistrusted in the community. Mia kept it real with youth in her caseload, open about her affiliation. "I never told them, *fuck gangs*, because I already knew you can't talk like that. I would just tell them the consequences." Still, she knew she was being questioned by others, since her brother "was a dropout and I was working for this rat organization, so people in the community were all, *where's she at?*"

Dating a high-ranking gang member who was locked up in Pelican Bay State Prison at that time, Mia kept a low profile in the community while mobilizing her incarcerated partner to vouch for her and help her "rebuild her credit," thus also keeping her kids safe. Though she was initially part of a different gang than her man, his status and ability to still participate in street life and power relations, even from the only supermax prison in California, was influential enough to protect her family from serious risk in various moments. Her man, like the partners or brothers of other Mujeres, was locked up in Operation Garlic Press, a federal sting operation that concluded in 2009. A string of operations like this were made possible in part through antiterrorism laws passed in the wake of the terrorist attacks of 9/11 (see Raschig 2018, 11; Reynolds 2014). Numerous men of their generation were caught up in those dragnets, leaving a vacuum of power at the street level that made space for new generations to come up and claim a space for themselves. Yet their incarceration did not prevent many of them from being active and calling shots on the streets, staying in relation, and providing protection to loved ones in Salinas and elsewhere.

Naming and Inheriting the Past

This transferable, intergenerational system of credit, secured through one's own actions as well as the ability to stay in good relation with others, harmonized with some of the *cultura*-based teachings disclosed in La Colectiva de Mujeres, MILPA, and other healing spaces in Salinas. The healing collectives opened important institutional space and resources to continue and elaborate these relations, among both women and men, providing an appealing spiritual and political alternative to Christian institutions of gang recovery. Many, if not all, of the "raw" Mujeres had been subject to some institutionalized efforts at their reform predicated on the criminalization of their belonging to a gang, whether mandated or voluntary, secular or religious. Programs that aim to suppress and prevent gang affiliation through a moralistic focus on stigmatizing gangs and rehabilitating the individual are inherently limited and often alienating, and literature that champions the exits ignores the dangers that hard refusals of gang life can entail.

By contrast, the healing collectives prioritized the relational ethics of gang affiliation centered in intergenerational solidarity and support, aligning this ethos with the symbols, rites, and social roles of Chicanx Indigeneity. As with other community-oriented programs designed for those at a maturing stage of their gang affiliation, religion and spirituality provided resources for reorienting gender roles (E. O. Flores 2013), but critically here without the patriarchal structures of more prominent churches with European origins. This is a significant reason why the Colectiva was so successful and felt historical to women like Shi at that time: the Colectiva affirmed that part of themselves and imparted a resonant, yet novel, framework for reviving their relations and practices of staying solid. It was a generative refusal of the logics and institutions of their criminalization and did not render their role as women secondary or subservient to men. The *cultura*-based approach offered ways to maintain the integrity of gang sociality and care while thickening it through novel spiritual and politicized practices that affirmed their role as women in this context.

For example, the practice of *descargando*, checking in one's *cargas* (baggage) and *regalos* (gifts), was seamlessly combined with many Mujeres' understandings of the credit system. *Descargando* extended this understanding of heritable experiences to include one's parents, grandparents, and ancestors deeper in time through a notion of inherited *cargas* or intergenerational trauma. In opening a paradigm for the intergenerational inheritance of experience not only forward with their children but also historically from their own forebears, the teachings quickly mapped onto their existing understanding of the credit system among those who were gang-affiliated. It thus gave some Mujeres new context to consider what they had been through, and why, while active in the gang. By reconsidering their own experiences as shaped in unknown ways by what their ancestors experienced, the Mujeres developed a novel understanding of the purpose and potentiality of their own healing for themselves, their ancestors, and their children alike. The deepened timeline of ancestral inheritance was a contrast to the temporal urgency of the present in *la vida loca*.

Reflecting on the more heavily gang-involved period of her life over numerous beers, late one evening at her apartment, Shi mused to me, "When I think about it now, it's like, we really didn't know why we were so hard, like, why we had to fight. I think I've come to realize now that there was some shit cracking off, like generations before. Some crazy trauma. And now I see the bigger picture and I think like, wow, that was some crazy shit that cracked off. Very unjust things that were before my time. I mean I don't know what that was. I can't solve it, but I . . . I knew, and a lot of people that were around me, we never asked that."

She was uncertain about the content of that "crazy trauma" that her ancestors and others around them had endured, but didn't question that it existed, and that she had been living it out. Over the years, she has shared her ideas about those traumas, in her frequent reflective and emotional moods. Shi had long had a difficult relationship with her mom, who was often quiet and restrained with her love, and disappeared for long periods of Shi's youth. Slowly, she learned about her mom's early experiences with sexual assault and kidnapping, always via others' hints and recollections. Her mom, now deceased, can't speak to those periods, and never mentioned them, so Shi lives with that uncertainty and possibility. Whenever she is struggling, she continues to question what else might have happened to her mom that she might have inherited.

Further back, she wonders about her paternal grandmother, whose name she was given at birth: Vicenta. She hated that name as a kid, she told me. And while her father would sometimes tell her stories of her grandmother Vicenta as a beautiful princess, he would also condemn her as a *puta* (whore) and a *bruja* (witch) who cursed their family.

"Why would he name me after someone like that, someone he hated?" she asked me once. Shi's continued if adapted use of her *placaso* Shy Girl, rather than her given name, thus reflects deeper concerns about intergenerational identity and her female ancestors' suffering. And as she increasingly uses a modified version of her given name when venturing into new contexts, she is continuing to build her sense of who she is in relation to her female ancestors in particular. While realizing she embodies some of their hardships, she has built her life differently as well and "gone out there" with the gang and the Colectiva to try to unload and transform some of those intergenerational *cargas*.

The Colectiva gave Shi a space to continue to work through these relational ethics and their bearing on her life, reworking her relationship with her past and her ancestors in light of her own actions over the years and in the present. I suggest this is a generative retemporalization akin to what Lisa Stevenson has called "belonging differently to time," opening a "possibility of building a different relationship to what is, what has been, and what may be" (2014, 136). Distinct from revivalism, belonging differently to time involves resituating oneself across different temporal and relational horizons and thereby interrogating the balance of experience and expectation, constraint and possibility. Similarly, and in a context of gang affiliation, Laurence Ralph notes how his Eastwood interlocutors mobilized an emergent, fertile sense of history to repurpose social injury, juxtaposing what has been with what could be in order to forward affirmative community projects and alternative futures for themselves and each other (2014, 16). This renegotiation of time and possibility is profoundly different from a more simplistic notion of recovery, which implies a necessary and healthy distance from the past in order to return to something "normal."

This renegotiation of one's belonging to the past to imagine and pursue different futures could take many different forms. Josefina, another Mujer in the Colectiva, felt a markedly contrasting relationship to her *placaso* and the past that it represented, as well as the deeper, ancestral heritage she felt to be deeply meaningful, if ambiguous. In terms of her recent history and her *placaso*, she was adamant that "that name was a negativity for me." In our years of friendship, I have never once heard her utter her *placaso*. "That name," she told me, "was my downfall, everything."

It wasn't just her own *placaso* that she couldn't stand; she found others' use of those names intolerable. Once, while giving Josefina a lift home from a healing circle, I carefully asked her if she could refrain from complaining about the other women's continued *placaso* use, since it violated the Colectiva Agreements, the collectively determined and stated ethos to be respectful with critique and not go behind each other's backs.[4] Shi, Yesi/Muñeca, and Lisa/Gata often joked and gently clowned on each other in the casual moments before and after circle, using their *placasos* and code-switching with select slang. Josefina had been complaining to other women in the circle about it, and I had been asked to intervene since I had a friendly relationship with her.

As I broached the topic, Josefina burst into frantic, angry tears about how hard it was to hear those names. They brought her right back to that time and all the things that she did, "all that shady shit" that she knew was wrong but she did anyway. She didn't want to expose her kid to it, she said; her twelve-year-old daughter Vanessa was often in the circle too and, like her mother, was very good at listening. During our rounds of *descargando*, Josefina often kept things vague and did not dig deep into past experiences. She had a firm belief in the need to "stop holding onto things from the past" to be able to keep going and not get stuck. As she put it, "When you wanna move on in your life and you wanna help other people, you needa let that shit go. You could be an example because you have that experience but don't carry it on . . . the secret in change is not to waste all your energy in fighting the old but focus instead on building the new."

Her approach was strongly shaped by her time with Victory Outreach, an evangelical Protestant church oriented to Chicanx and *Mexicano* populations seeking to leave gangs and quit addictions (E. O. Flores 2013; Sánchez Walsh 2001). Edward Orozco Flores (2013, 94) characterizes Victory Outreach's theology of gang recovery as built on moralistic "one-upmanship" and an oppositional stance to dominant society, a kind of "segregated redemption" that divides adherents from their broader world. Victory Outreach had a negative image among most women in the Colectiva for the church's vehement repudiation of gang life and, by association, many Mujeres' very way of being. Even though Josefina spoke highly of that church, she no longer attended its services and instead stayed with the Colectiva despite this significant conflict with Shi over their *placasos* and continued gang-inflected banter. She was compelled to keep attending the Colectiva in part because she wanted to learn more about "Aztec stuff," to which she already felt a deep sense of belonging. Josefina had been adopted from Mexico and knew that at least one of her birth parents was Yaqui, from the border region between what is now Arizona and Mexico. As she described various decontextualized but impactful encounters with Indigeneity over her life—like driving past a reservation with her family, spotting a tepee from the freeway—she asserted in an interview, "I'm Indian, and I wanna know more. I've always believed I'm more Indian than Mexican."

She mentioned this just as the Colectiva was starting the Xinachtli rites-of-passage program. Josefina was hardly known for her enthusiasm; her dominant mood was an "I'm cool off that" calculated distance. But she was all in for Xinachtli and was eager to learn more about what her ancestral Yaqui heritage might make possible for understanding her past, present, and future. She was especially excited for Xinachtli's closing ritual, a symbolic bridge crossing to join the ranks of *mujeres nobles*, noble women with *palabra* (integrity). "I just want to cross that bridge," she told me often. "I'm ready to cross that bridge."

Crossing the Bridge

While the Colectiva's twice-weekly circles featured rituals, topics, and teachings borrowed and adapted from Shi's training and experience in cultural healing, Xinachtli was a distinct curriculum meant for girls and young women along their path to adulthood. Along with the more prominent curriculum Joven Noble, translated in gender-neutral terms as Noble Youth but primarily oriented to boys and young men, Xinachtli was often run in juvenile halls and continuation schools. Its implementation required facilitator certification through La Cultura Cura, a Los Angeles–based organization that developed and supported Chicanx-Indigenous cultural healing endeavors in large part through these standardized curricula. In her career, Shi had facilitated Xinachtli many times for young women, and she decided that we should adjust and implement it for the Mujeres. Even though the women were already adults, many had not made that transition "in a good or healthy way," as she put it. She was referring especially to the raw women, those who had been gang-involved and thrust into substance abuse, incarceration, motherhood, and other challenges at an early age. She photocopied the Xinachtli handbook for me, with some pages upside down, and a statement on the front page not to reproduce any part of the curriculum without the expressed consent of the author. Shi, who had met the author, Sara Haskie, when being trained in the curriculum a few years earlier, said we would be fine. Since "nobody owns the teachings," we could pick and choose which of the creative and reflective activities from the curriculum we wanted to implement. The Mujeres would benefit from these teachings and the culminating rite of passage to realize themselves as noble women and be publicly honored as such.

Over seven weeks in the summer of 2014, members of La Colectiva de Mujeres spent their Monday evenings working through parts of the Xinachtli curriculum. This was an accelerated pace for a program designed to take three months. The curriculum gathered elements from a variety of traditions, combining motifs of Mexica (Nahuatl or Aztec, pronounced meh-SHEE-ca) material culture together with Native American Church spirituality and neoliberal work on the self. For example, the *chimal* (shield), divided into four quadrants reflecting Medicine Wheel holistic philosophy, was spun into a teaching on setting boundaries. As part of the *chimal* activity, the curriculum called for us to listen to and analyze Beyoncé's song "Irreplaceable." The *tortilla de mi vida* (tortilla of my life) activity combined a teaching on the centrality of *maíz* (corn) to Mexica lifeways, with a round tortilla divided into the four relationships that nourish us most, per the numerical motif of the Medicine Wheel's four quadrants and the four sacred directions. The codex activity involved a strip of paper folded into four sections on which we drew four key moments from our lives, in a nod to the Aztec codices, pictorial histories conveyed on long sheaths of paper, cloth, or deerskin. And a rain stick crafted out of mailing tubes and rice was designed to represent the straight, strong spine of the woman who walks tall; the stick, which made a relaxing rain sound that aligned with deep breathing strategies of relaxation, formed a centerpiece of one's at-home altar.

Inflected by idealized and easily digestible aspects of *cultura* and contemporary American self-improvement, these creative activities prompted reflective and intimate discussions among some of the Mujeres. Others, like Josefina, somewhat enjoyed the crafting but were not really understanding the purpose or the underlying philosophy.

When I asked her about her take on Xinachtli before the bridge-crossing ceremony, Josefina made a point of being unable to remember the names associated with the activities. "I wasn't there for the Kodak moment—whatever it's called," she told me in an interview at her home.

"The codex?" I offered back.

"Yeah. I wasn't there for that one and I wasn't there for the, what's it called . . . eechee . . ."

"*Chimal*? The shield?"

"I was there for the shield one. I dunno what Rosa did with my shield," she said, referencing one of the group's facilitators.

"She took it? I don't know where mine is either. What did you do for your shield?" I asked.

"I divided it into four. I put a cross on there. I dunno, I don't remember."

I persisted in asking about the impact of these activities. "Did the shield help you think about your own boundaries or anything like that?"

She yawned, replying, "I was there for the boundaries one, when we all heard that song. Why'd they pick that song?!"

I laughed, thinking of the Beyoncé song. "That's I think the one that goes with the curriculum, that's just what they always use. *To the left, to the left* . . . I thought it was a dance move but then she's like, *all your stuff in a box to the left*."

Josefina sniffed. I was a little surprised at how dismissive she was being about the activities I thought she was excited about, and I continued to probe, asking, "What about when we talked about being a noble woman? Did any of that land, does any of that make any sense to you, now that it's over?"

"I remember I asked you what the hell is a noble woman," she replied. "I mean, what does 'noble' mean?"

"I think it means something different to everybody, probably," I responded, vaguely, hoping not to overdetermine her sense of what it meant.

She paused and added, "Or maybe it's like wisdom, a lady with wisdom, a lady or someone that knows where they stand now."

Josefina's take on becoming a noble woman reflected her painful relationship to her past, as well as her firm belief that she had done a lot of reflective work in order to create distance from her time with the gang. As dismissive as she seemed of the Xinachtli activities, she was actively preparing dozens of paper flowers for the bridge ceremony and at numerous times during this interview mentioned wanting to cross the bridge. Her daughter would be attending, and Josefina was excited that the ceremony would be a public event. She wanted it acknowledged that she was a noble woman, a woman who knew where she stood. Though her manipulative and disruptive partner, Spider (a *placaso*), would not be there—he was suspicious of the Colectiva, disparaging the group as "a bunch of lesbians"—she hoped he would see the transformation in her, and that it would spur his own self-reflection and growth.

For myself, the days leading up to the bridge ceremony were a scramble. I was trying to support Shi's preparations, but with the accelerated pace of the adapted curriculum, most of our hastily made plans were falling through. Many Mujeres were eager to receive T-shirts with the Colectiva's name on the front, but the shirts would not be ready in time. There should be food, but there was no money for catering. Local *maestras* and a *maestro* were invited, as with the MILPA men, but we weren't sure who would actually attend, or what they would bring to add to the altar. And the *collares* (necklaces) that traditionally were conferred on Xinachtli bridge-crossers were delayed, as our jewelry maker couldn't source enough *ojo de venado* seed beads for them.[5] Shi and I tried to remind ourselves that the most important thing would be that the women would be there and would be able to cross a bridge, with women who had already crossed reaching out to them from the other side in support, ready to pull them over. They would be recognized and affirmed for who they were and what they had been through.

The bridge-crossing ceremony was held in the big room of the Bread-Box, the same community center building we used for our twice-weekly circles. We set up a small altar in front of the three carpeted steps that constituted a stage, with Josefina's colorful paper flowers lining the ledge. A small purple and black *falsa*, a woven Mexican blanket, served as a humble bridge in front of the altar, with a cluster of seats for the *comadres* and *maestras* waiting on the other side. An audience filed in and took seats facing the altar, as the women started showing up as well. They looked glossy, excited, and ready. Josefina and another Mujer, an African American woman named Cynthia, brought a container of cupcakes decorated with candy tape as little bridges, adding it to a table set up for snacks brought potluck-style. A *maestra* from a local Native American Church group, Suzy, insisted on offering copal as we waited for the ceremony to begin, "because copal is from where people here are from." While I was running around helping everyone get situated, I looked up frequently to see the copal smoke filling the silvery rafters of the multipurpose space, swirling slowly under the high ceiling. I imagined that the copal's blessings would linger here.

As the time came to begin, Shi took a mic and served as MC, launching straight into a brief history of the Colectiva and Xinachtli. Without providing much context about the ceremony itself, she asked the Mujeres to assemble on the left side of the bridge. One by one, she began by describing each participant rather than naming them outright, noting each woman's particular strengths: "This is a person who I met awhile ago, and from the very beginning I was in awe of how many different skills she had. And I admire her so much as a single mother. I want to call up Verenice."

Each woman would then sidle up to the bridge to be hugged by Shi and saged by Maestra Suzy. After pausing for a beat before walking over the *falsa*, the women crossed in different ways. Cynthia took up a stylized stride, pausing with her joints at right angles like a hieroglyph, giving the audience something extra to cheer about. June took off her shoes, as did I. Yarri draped her toddler daughter over her shoulder. Some, like Yesi, gazed quietly downward at the bridge, while others looked directly at the *comadres* on the other side. I think I saw Josefina close her eyes until she was over. Waiting on the other side to receive us was Lila, the program director of East Salinas Building Healthy Communities, holding a stack of certificates personalized for each participant, and Didi, with a bundle of *collares* draped over her forearm, which she and Lila had gathered for the group. Behind them sat the women who had already crossed.

After everyone had crossed the bridge, there was time for participants to make a public statement if they felt compelled. Surprisingly, Josefina came forward and stated, "I just wanna thank the group, and thank Shi, because I really appreciate this group. I've grown a lot in it even if it hasn't always been easy. Earlier, maybe, I came to it with more selfishness. But I appreciate the group for letting me go through it."

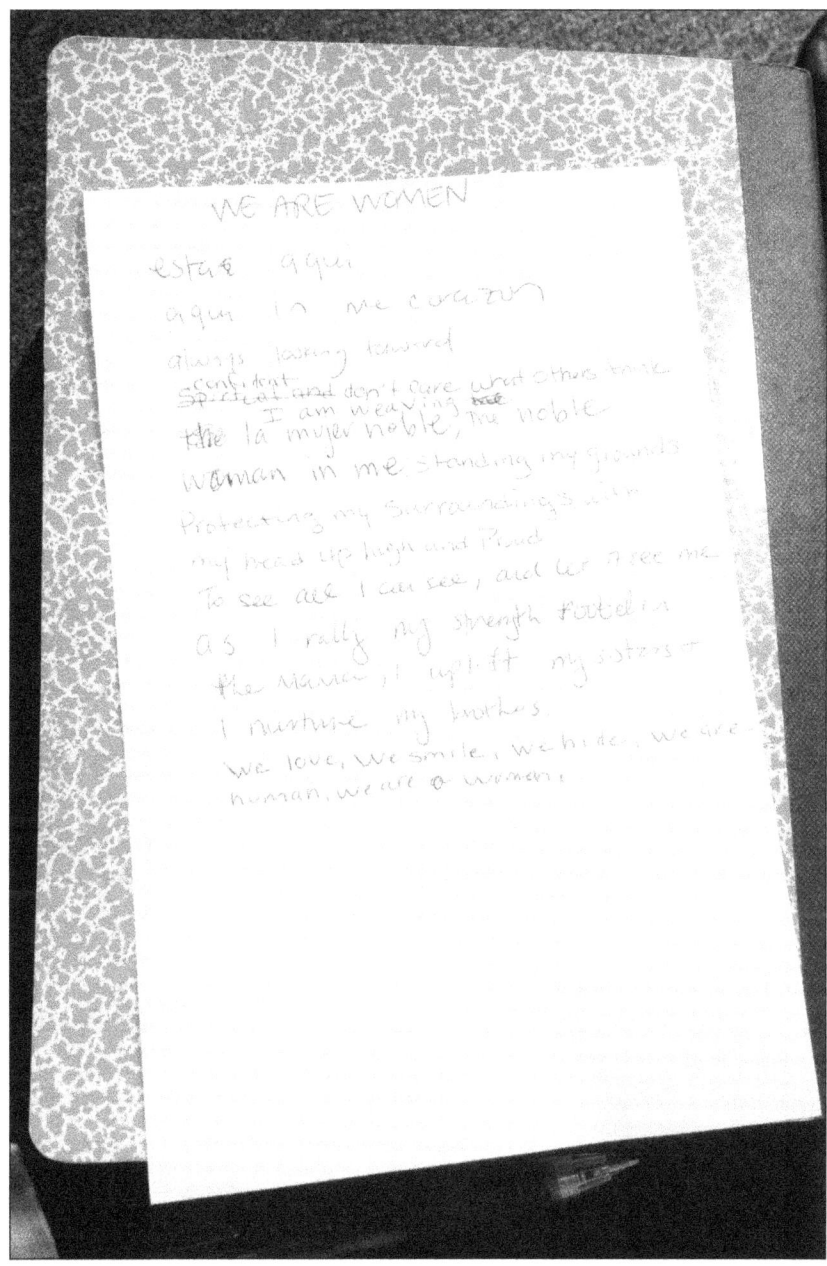

Figure 4.1. A poem cowritten by members of La Colectiva de Mujeres during a healing circle. Photo by the author.

The audience did not flinch at this statement, but many of the women, seated, raised their eyebrows at Josefina's earnest appreciation, knowing about her ongoing conflict with Shi over the *placasos*. Then, in another spontaneous moment, Josefina asked Shi if *she* was ready to cross the bridge. After pausing for a moment, Shi said yes—and set out over the *falsa*. I was stunned to see them momentarily overcome their conflict, for Josefina to offer that support to Shi, and for Shi to accept it.

Other Mujeres made statements of appreciation as well, directed toward each other rather than toward the crowd. Sensing this inward focus, the audience dissipated, with no formal ending to the ceremony. Eventually, it was just the women taking photos and group selfies on the stairs, absorbed in our postritual transformation, as a collective of *mujeres nobles* who acknowledged, accepted, and appreciated each other.

Becoming *Mujeres Nobles*

The terms that tend to characterize literature on gang life and desistance, like "exit" or "recovery," reinforce and reproduce a moralistic assumption that gang affiliation is irrevocably antisocial, deviant, and pathological. An approach grounded in the relational ethics of women's gang affiliation, seeking to grasp the situated ethical dimensions of life in that sphere over the long term, indicates alternative visions and possibilities. It discloses a homegirl *noble* femininity characterized by generational belonging, stewardship, and renewed solidarity. This was a way of being that women like Shi, Yesi, and Josefina had long cultivated, but for which they found enriching and generative resources with the Colectiva and cultural healing. In a bridge crossing meant as a culminating ritual, they celebrated this femininity not by leaving their pasts behind but by building different relationships to it. Rather than a regaining-of-"normal" recovery process, this praxis of cultural healing involved building on an enduring ethical foundation.

The ambivalence felt by many Mujeres regarding whether recognition for what they've been through and who they are is worthwhile or desirable, or how it might be achieved, is also noteworthy. The bridge-crossing ceremony that became an inwardly focused moment of mutual appreciation, never mind the audience, is one example of this ambivalence: we specifically held the ceremony in public, to the initial excitement of many Mujeres, yet the importance of this fell away in the process. This contrasts with the young women in Marie Miranda's study, who engaged heavily in the politics of their representation and, through a public service announcement project, attempted authorship of their own lives in a public sphere as they "refuse[d] to be othered" (2003, 72). The Mujeres participating in the bridge crossing were ultimately absorbed with each other rather than oriented to an audience. Like the "I-appreciations" ritual that closed every healing circle, with each woman looking another in the eye to say "I appreciate you" while leaning in for a hug, the bridge crossing was about acknowledging each other and affirming a collective transformation.

This ambivalence about recognition underscores a more radical stance at the core of this homegirl *noble* femininity: a refusal of the ethical norms and standards that would likely make an affirmative public recognition possible at all. What could recognition of their relational ethics look like, without sliding into spectacle or caricature, risking *misrecognition* in a discursive landscape cluttered by assumptions of gangs as inherently criminal and female gang members as sexualized hangers-on? Even beyond her original *placaso*, Shy Girl, I knew Shi as someone who did not seek the spotlight, who was deeply uncomfortable when subjected to any public gaze. In the years since our participation in the Colectiva, we reminisce often about our time not only in circle but also in protest and advocacy, with Shi musing about how incredible it was when "we were really *out there*," holding it down for other women in Salinas and their families, especially during the time of the police homicides. Shi considered that an extension of her lifelong service to her community, rooted in her time as an active Sureña but blooming into new dimensions and purpose. Whether visiting with old friends Gordo, Eva, and Serena in the wake of Julian's death, or attending to the Ruiz, Mejía, Hernández, or Alvarado families as they lost sons or brothers to police killings, as will be discussed extensively in the next chapter, being "out there" was not about being broadly seen or recognized by a public of strangers. Rather, it named a renewed service role that was only possible because of the credit she and others had already earned in this enduring ethical framework and were transforming into related but novel forms of care.

Rather than recognition by an imagined or broad public, Shi's reflections point toward acknowledgment of service and care in relation with others, earning a respect that was dislodged from respectability (Kendall 2020). Respectability would have required disavowal of the complex ethical formations found through gangs and alignment with codified law, liberal morality, and whitened norms of comportment (J. Flores 2016, 11). Respectability would likely be required for any public recognition, in a public sphere resistant to disruption of basic liberal tenets. For raw women like Shi in the Colectiva, the term *noble*, in Spanish and English, conjured a kind of respect in refusal of respectability. A *mujer noble* had *palabra* (integrity) regarding who she was and how she came up, and she trusted her rawness as an asset to herself and others, rather than treating it as a deficit or liability. They were emphatically not objects to or for anyone else. In bringing me, a white woman with no gang background, into that ethical framework—inviting me to join them in going "out there" to Serena's or to protest police brutality, joking about my lack of gangsterness as a form of inclusion, offering me their hands as I crossed the bridge as well—they underscored that maintaining relations and sharing their credit with others involved building new relationships and practices of care, too.

If any term from gang studies literature should continue to be relevant, it is perhaps "rehabilitation," albeit with alternative focus on worldbuilding: recognizing how gang life is understood in terms of service to and credit within a durative set of relations, tinkered with across generations among those whose ancestors have been dispossessed, oriented to stewardship of those coming up now or next. This alternative focus would be much more provocative, attending to how people conduct the everyday abolitionist work of refusing and transforming the carceral conditions of their oppression without fundamentally renouncing their loved ones or remaking themselves. Instead, such an approach would make space to see how they develop novel forms of care, presence, and affirmation from what is already available to them, and continue to hold it down while what "it" is continues to grow.

5

This Is Where We Walk Together

"Raw" Women's Movidas *amid Police Homicides*

FOR ANGEL, OSMAR, CARLOS, FRANK, CHRISTOPHER, LISA, GINA, AND RACHEL

Angel Ruiz

In early 2014, members of MILPA and the Colectiva, as well as similar groups around the state, were aware of the need to set up a solid foundation of gender equity in the emerging movement of cultural healing. This was, in part, an effort to repair some of the flaws of the notoriously masculinist Chicano Civil Rights Movement of the 1960s and 1970s and to address the latent machismo that haunted domestic and institutional relationships in this community. The contributions and interventions of Chicanas in the Chicano Movement have often been diminished, falsely claimed to be culpable for the Movement's decline, or left out of its history altogether (Blackwell 2011). Similar to what Shi described early in this book as "the healing piece," women's leadership could not simply be additive but would have to be transformative for all involved in contemporary movement praxis.

However, as will be shown, the overarching goal of gender equity did not always orient movement praxis in everyday or exceptional contexts, with notable divergences regarding what acceptable forms "women's leadership" could or should take. This became especially pronounced as the police homicides began and continued to occur in Salinas and some of the Mujeres became passionately engaged in community action and care. This chapter forwards an otherwise understanding of the Mujeres' powerful actions during this critical time, as the unfolding police homicides opened new spaces for community response and resident engagement, and new opportunities for the marginalization of women's leadership.

As winter shifted into spring that year, Rosa and others coordinated an *encuentro* between movement leaders from Salinas, Stockton, and Oakland, centered on the "leadership of the *mujer*." It would be an all-day event hosted by Fathers and Families, a Chicanx-Indigenous cultural healing organization based in Stockton, for a full slate of facilitated discussions and thematic activities. Late in the afternoon, the group would walk to a cinema in downtown Stockton to see a screening of the newly released film *César Chávez* and return for a talk by Dolores Huerta back at the Fathers and Families office. Like other Chicanas, Huerta had been critical to the founding and success of the United Farm Workers but only belatedly recognized and celebrated for her contributions.

I got the invitation a couple of days before the Friday departure, along with Shi and more than a few of the men involved with MILPA; there had been a bit of scrambling around who would be able to fit in the rented van, and who should get the opportunity to attend the event. Though we had seen the agenda, with its *teatro* and conversation prompts about the challenges of building gender equity in movement leadership, Shi and I didn't know what to expect from the day. We knew it would be very long and expected it would have its challenging moments, but we were optimistic and appreciated that there would be dedicated space to center women's experiences and visions in the work. The night before our early-morning departure, I wrote in my field notes, "Tomorrow is going to be intense. We are going to be talking about the leadership of the *mujer*. Let's see what goes down with so many men there . . . like, the van is going to be full of men."

A number of us hit the road at 7:00 a.m. in another rented white van, heading north-northeast to Stockton. After a quick collective round of *cargas* and *regalos* (baggage and gifts), we settled into quiet conversations. Shi and I sat next to each other, using the time to check in about the Colectiva's plans. Earlier that week, we had held a visioning session on *la consciencia* (the critical consciousness) of the Mujer, with a half dozen of us sitting in the patio of a Peet's coffee shop in the waning light of the early evening. Nobody ordered coffee or tea, but some had brought tamales, homemade salsa, and *gruesos* (thick tortilla chips) to share. As we ate, we built *conocimiento* and floated ideas for small projects and important *pláticas* (discussions), imagining what we could do together as a collective.

While going over some of those ideas, Shi asked if I had seen the news: the police had killed someone up by the new Wing Stop on North Main Street. It was a popular place, and I lived nearby. This was the first I'd heard about the incident.

"I knew the guy," she continued, her eyes wide open. "His name was Angel Ruiz. They said he was waving a fake gun around in the parking lot, and then they shot him. Eighteen times." He was probably having a mental health crisis, she added, looking baffled and deeply concerned that this seemed to justify his death in the eyes of the state.

She suggested that we, as the Colectiva, check in with his sister, whom she also used to know. We could support her and maybe she could join us in *círculo* to grieve and honor Angel. Meanwhile, Pamela was blowing up Shi's phone, sending a long string of texts with ideas about T-shirts for the group she wanted to have made. As Shi scrolled through these texts, I mentioned that Josefina had also been coming to me with the suggestion that we hold a mother-daughter circle. Pamela called Shi, and they started talking in real time about the shirts. As the van wended its way through the Pacheco Pass, I tuned into the conversation going on in the rows behind us, with Daniel and Jose joking about getting into fights when they were young. Daniel tried to loop me in—"Who did you bang with in Canada, Megan? Moose Lodge?!" as I turned around to laugh and roll my eyes at the good-natured clowning. The drive continued like this for the next hour and a half.

At the time, Angel Ruiz's murder at the hands of police seemed egregious, but anomalous, and our conversation about it was subsumed by the drive and the *encuentro* ahead. Little, if any, public action had yet occurred in the city to speak out against this homicide. Within two months, though, with the next two instances of police homicide of two recently arrived Salvadoreño men in this small city, the issue of police brutality exploded into everyday life on the East Side. As we have seen, police brutality became a critical site of intervention by the healing collectives, with the four separate police homicides of Latinos in five months in Salinas intensifying into a period of community reckoning with state violence and racialized criminalization. Like Shi, other Mujeres were deeply disturbed by the police homicides, responding immediately through an ethos of care. Some Mujeres became intensely and prominently active in demonstrations and protests, while also coming to circle and ceremony, and organizing with other women and relatives of the deceased. They were leading critical actions at the sidelines and frontlines.

"We prepared the space," as Pamela recalled to me, years later. "We made the altars and held the vigils . . . we helped the families feel that they were not alone, and to allow anything they were feeling to come out." In their copresence, the Mujeres opened a path for each other to keep going. They found strength in each other's ability to show up, as they insisted on the value of life in their community. She continued, "We made something out of nothing." Together and in the Colectiva's twice-weekly circles, many worked to process the ways their past traumas and deepest fears were being triggered, and in doing so they opened up new ways of fighting and enduring (Raschig 2017). They did not shy away from climate or crowds, smoky air, hunger and thirst, blisters and screams but worked from the pain they felt in their bones, so deeply in refusal of this state-sanctioned violence.

The Mujeres were crying out for all to hear—"just really fucking *gritando*," as Shi described it, just really shouting, crying, screaming, and attempting to call in those around them. "That was all the fucking pain we'd been carrying. We were the fucking *guerreras*, the warrior women." Like when Pamela screamed, twice, in the healing circle scene that opened this book, and when she screamed again over Zoom while we talked about it again years later, that *gritando* pierced and connected the Mujeres with others in Salinas who were experiencing the raw affect incited by police violence, beyond whatever words could convey. That *gritando* heralded a powerful approach to leadership among working-class, systems-impacted, and self-described raw women in this context: creating and holding a space together, whether on the sidewalk or in circle, where those in struggle and without other resources were safe to participate in the movement through voice, praxis, presence, or proximity.

It was a striking example of raw women's unflinching leadership at a time of widespread uncertainty and disagreement about how to respond, especially around how explicitly critical to be of the Salinas Police Department. The period of police homicides was identity-defining and purpose-setting for the Mujeres, though their emergent response to the homicides was at times ignored or critiqued as aggressive, emotional, and out of step with sanctioned strategy by those they considered allies. Their response provoked a pivotal schism from other Building Healthy Communities–funded groups, whose strategy hewed toward long-game relationship-building with state institutions of power.

The *encuentro* in Stockton, just after Angel Ruiz's death, foreshadowed this schism as it centered on gender equity in the movement. Through facilitated activities like "spectrum" questions, in which Rosa posed a statement and asked us all to position our bodies along an imagined spectrum to communicate "where we stood" on the issue, it became clear that there was a wide divergence in experiences and outlooks around whether women and men have the same opportunities and equal representation in each community, or whether women and men should be walking "together or apart" in this movement. As we unpacked these and other prompts together in a large circle, some of the women from Salinas and Stockton became very distressed, pushing back on how men were dominating a discussion that was supposed to be about women's leadership. Shi spoke up, noting that it was sometimes hard for her to be in circle together because the men's energy felt overwhelming and made her want to dissociate or escape. Still, she knew it was important to share that space with men, and she cried as she told a story about her sons' struggles and her difficulty witnessing it while nevertheless grasping the importance of doing so.

"These tears are also their tears," she said, "and the tears of all the men in my family who had their own trauma and can't or couldn't cry." She was explaining how the women were working to heal the men in their lives too, and that their strong affects had collective purpose and impact.

At this, Daniel, a few seats away, suggested we burn some sage to alleviate the pain that was surfacing.

Didi immediately snapped back at him from across the circle, "No, that's not the point of what we're expressing. We don't want to be told 'it's OK' and then be shut down."

In that moment, offering sage felt like an enclosure and dismissal of what many women were sharing and shouldering. In subsequent months, during the period of police homicides, those shouts, cries, and refusals to be anywhere but on the street with other residents or in circle with each other were criticized by some other movement leaders as "too rugged." Some outwardly complained or subtly suggested to me that the Mujeres' responses needed to be managed in order to "get to work" and participate in advocacy and activism that was more peaceful and strategic—as if I, considered less "raw" and more "professional," would convey or enforce that discipline. As I tried to keep a wide lens in my research and stay close to both the Mujeres and other BHC groups responding to police brutality at the time, Juan described me as a bridge walker, able to cross divides. This ability to bridge-walk only amplified my sense that the Mujeres were doing something remarkable but undervalued, and that their rawness was being mistaken as a liability.

Scaling up that dismissal, in the years since 2014, the Mujeres' response to the police homicides and their subsequent impacts in the community have been largely absent from BHC and TCE narratives of the impacts of their funded programs in Salinas. They are barely noted in the various reports issued by BHC or TCE over the years, with their name sometimes included but their actions left out or subsumed by their affiliations with other groups (see Valenzuela, Bradshaw, and Ortiz 2016). And while watching the East Salinas BHC ten-year anniversary event in the summer of 2020, a two-hour-long live retrospective on YouTube featuring photos and recaps of BHC's funded groups and their many successes and accomplishments, I noticed that La Colectiva de Mujeres was never mentioned. In a parallel with the way Chicana activists' work had been largely erased in the original Chicano Movement's history and imagination, the Mujeres and their contributions have been left out of much recent Salinas movement historiography.

When I told Shi about the Colectiva's absence from the BHC retrospective, she took a long pause before launching her refusal of that erasure:

> If people think they want to erase us, or us that we didn't have no voice, like, to me it's just like, yes, we did have a voice, we did have an impact. And the transformation that I've seen with all the women individually, like even with myself, with you, with everyone around us—you can't buy that, you can't get that anywhere else. What we witnessed and what we went through and what we saw, you're never gonna get that anywhere. That was a gift from Creator. And I will always honor that. I don't give a

fuck if they say we didn't do shit, or that we weren't good enough to even be put up on a fucking, like, PowerPoint. Well, you know what? We know. We fucking know in our hearts.

Recognition by BHC or others did not really matter; the impact of the Mujeres' voice and their transformation was all too evident to her in our bodies and relations. But as Shi stated a few moments later, "The thing that gets us angered" was not being acknowledged. "If they don't want to hear us scream, and they don't want to see us cry . . . you know what I mean? Acknowledge it, give us some space. Understand that we've also been through trauma, and we're also here, but no matter what you do, you're never going to be able to erase, like, our voice. Our voice is here to stay."

As a response to these erasures, and to acknowledge and honor what was dismissed, this chapter offers an otherwise understanding of the Mujeres' "rugged" world-making praxis and its transformations in that period of acute state violence and abandonment. Based on some of the Mujeres' narratives and my ethnographic participation in these events, I further a feminist and fugitive project of knowledge production in a context marked by marginalization, assembling a counterarchive to explore the potential for radical action found in a set of key moments. I am inspired by Maylei Blackwell's work in ¡Chicana Power! (2011) to "retrofit" Chicanas' actions and impacts to the archive of Chicano Movement history. Through careful oral history with members of Las Hijas de Cuauhtémoc, and in dialogue with other insurgent movement archives, Blackwell shows how Chicanas' efforts fueled multisited and localized struggles that coalesced into the wider, national movement. In *Chicana Movidas*, Dionne Espinoza, Maria Eugenia Cotera, and Maylei Blackwell further attend to Chicana activists' *movidas*, the "everyday labor and support as well as strategic and sometimes subversive interventions within movement spaces" (2018, 2). This focus on everyday and embodied labor, in less-visible sites of struggle, remaps the movement and transforms how it can be remembered and re-membered—not only memorialized on the page or in one's mind but also, like the re-membering of ancestral practices discussed throughout this book, rendered available as a "vital" resource "in creative political subjectivity" (Blackwell 2011, 11; Gonzales 2012).

Unlike interpretations of the Mujeres' actions as dangerously militant, naive, or inconsequential to the city's official history of cultural healing, this chapter offers accounts of how their multifaceted *movidas* enacted a broader anticarceral affirmation of life that made much further collective action possible—*movidas* that made "something out of nothing." It attends to how the Mujeres intervened in the spaces before, alongside, in between, and beyond the more public events of activism against state violence that unfolded around each man's death. It shows how their commitment to going *out there* and *walking together* remade the grounds of struggle, extending beyond the four police homicides of Chicano and Salvadoreño men to address urgent and embodied experiences of state violence and abandonment in the lives of those intimately impacted. This chapter thinks with works that treat bodies as archives, or, in Diana Taylor's (2003) terms, repertoires of embodied memory that surface in performance, orality, movement, dancing, and other acts "usually thought of as ephemeral, non-reproducible knowledge" (Blackwell 2011, 9). These insurgent approaches position an archive as a "link between past knowledge and future imagination" rather than a static repository of the past (Battaglia, Clarke, and Siegenthaler 2020).

I worked closely with Shi and Pamela throughout the drafting of this chapter. Their emphatic and impassioned commentaries surface in the text, in an attempt to convey their ongoing rage and insistence that what the Mujeres did mattered and that others should know about it, but that they also don't give a fuck (Shi's words) if people don't care to acknowledge it. These recollected actions and resurgent feelings suggest to me that there is still potentiality glinting in this time of struggle. We feel that things may yet be otherwise through our bodies, and must live into these senses to think and build the world differently (Crawley 2016). Plumbing the Mujeres' and my own memories, notes, photos, and recordings, writing this chapter was akin to assembling what Gayle Wald called an archive of affect (quoted in Thomas 2019, 6), tapping into an affective register prominent in that period that shaped their sense of possibility and justice. These affects are still palpable years later—still raw, not "cooked" by time—though they can be articulated otherwise, thanks to the radical and abolitionist projects in the meantime that have pushed the conversation from police brutality to carcerality (Shanahan and Kurti 2022; Maynard and Betasamosake Simpson 2022).

I invite readers into a way of reading and knowing that not only acknowledges the Mujeres' actions in this period of state violence but also hears their screams and feels the affect thereby provoked in whatever time and space it is read. This self-consciously embodied reading practice embraces the lively performativity of this knowledge rather than narrowing in on its facticity—what is provoked and grasped in the saying, in addition to what is being described. Eve Kosofsky Sedgwick called this the "reparative read," contrasting it with a more conventional "hermeneutics of suspicion" and critique (2003, 124). Similarly, Deborah Thomas, in her compiling of affective archives of human life in the wake of the plantation, offers the concept of "Witnessing 2.0" as an embodied and moral practice that "produces intimacies" and "reveals the ways we maintain the conjunctures of power within which we live" (2019, 2–3). Witnessing 2.0 implies a reading practice that attends to, and cares for, the potential complicities of inequality and carcerality between those depicted on the page and those reading about them, across time and space. An Otherwise Anthropology is enacted not only through research and writing praxis but also in cultivating ways of reading that can take up the epistemic and embodied challenges provoked through transformative political projects. This way of reading would also encourage those who—having read this far and feeling wary of sifting through more deaths and more endurance in their wake, wary of taking on rage or grief they may already be working to unload—should skip this chapter. Like the practice of *descargando*, those who can pick up these *cargas* and do something with them are invited to do so, and those who have had enough can let others do this lift.

Osmar Hernández

In the gray May days following the murder of Osmar Hernández, a lettuce picker, by a Salinas Police Department officer, a small but growing cadre of protesters stood at the edge of the supermarket parking lot, near where his life had been ended. He had waved his lettuce knife in the air after what was probably a rough day, coming off what was likely a rough period. He was far from home, El Salvador, as a newly arrived worker in the fields that surrounded Salinas. The protesters, now, waved their signs near the busy intersection, demanding drivers honk for justice. I drove by, fascinated by the spectacle of protesters in a city where most interesting things seemed to happen behind closed doors. I noticed a few signs that said, "Sin Justicia No Hay Respeto" (Without Justice There Is No Respect), in large black stenciled letters. As the light changed, I honked but kept going, with somewhere else to be, some other meeting to attend.

But when Shi passed the same group that same day, she stopped right away. She parked her blue Mustang to talk to the protesters and find out "what they were about." There was one person there she recognized instantly: Wera, her old homegirl.

It had been years since they had last seen each other, "in another life," back when they were both "gangbanging solid," or active in gangs, as Shi told it. Since then, Wera had dropped her *placaso*, her gang-given nickname meaning White Girl, and been reborn as Tara on the day she gave up alcohol. Both had fallen out of the active gang scene while never renouncing it; Tara had been in and out of jail while Shi had started working in the local gang-response infrastructure. But beyond recognizing Tara's blonde hair, pale skin, and sturdy gait, Shi further felt she recognized all that both had been through—all the deaths they had grown up and lived with that had to be abided, "taken like a G," like a gangster, in this youth homicide capital of California—as intricately involved in their respective decisions to stop at that initial protest to demonstrate against police murder and memorialize Osmar. Shi invited Tara to join us in the Colectiva, and she started attending the group's circles with the vigor of a woman who has so much to tell and so few who will listen.

One of Tara's first circles with the Colectiva was a short one, lasting a little less than an hour. An *asamblea pública* (public assembly) on police brutality was being held that evening at Closter Park, and Shi urged members of the group to walk over to attend after we had done a round of gifts and baggage. As Shi shared flyers for the *asamblea*, she and Tara told the group details about Hernández's death. The police had handcuffed him *after* he was already dead, *after* he had taken nine bullets. Some Mujeres responded angrily to this while others sat silent, their hands on their mouths or crossed in their laps. Next to Shi's chair was a stack of posters that she and her daughter had made for us to bring to Closter Park. On one side they had written "MILPA" in large letters, and on the other side, various statements against police brutality. At the time, though the Colectiva held its own space and vision, it was still considered a subgroup of MILPA.

We closed the circle and gathered our belongings. June, who lived in Monterey but worked in Salinas, asked me on the side if I thought it would be too dangerous for her to bring her adolescent son. I hadn't considered that it wouldn't be safe, trusting Shi to assess those risks for us. June and a few others decided not to join, while a small group of us headed out into the windy, cool early evening. All the women who attended, besides myself, were born-and-raised or long-term East Siders: Juana, Yesi, Tara, Esme, and Josefina. Those who had children brought them along.

A large crowd of *vecinos* (neighbors) was already clustered at the base of the park rotunda, and we found spots along the edges to hold up Shi's carefully crafted signs. Daniel and Ruben, a MILPA intern, showed up, too, and one of the organizers talked through a megaphone about Hernández's death, asserting that the police were targeting their community for "being Mexican." Daniel, surveying the scene, quietly told me that the Mujeres should not be holding up signs that said MILPA. He was unsure who had organized the event, or the tone it would take, and

Figure 5.1. *Asamblea pública* at Closter Park, with Salinas residents and members of La Colectiva de Mujeres. Photo by the author.

didn't want it to be mistaken as their own. There were preexisting political factions in Salinas that implicated those in power at the county level and in the city council, bodies that MILPA was trying to engage in their juvenile hall reduction efforts. He didn't want that relationship to be jeopardized. The Mujeres holding the signs didn't know about those entanglements of power, and those who did, like Shi, plainly did not care.

Asking for the megaphone, Daniel started to address the crowd, introducing himself. He then tucked it under his arm as he pulled a long branch of sage from the bundle in his jacket pocket and crouched down to try to light it. Four or five people offered hands, bodies, or posters around the medicine to shield it from the wind until it caught. Smoke billowed off of it in a long swoosh, out toward the open park. It was too windy for any of us to bless ourselves with it.

"We need to raise our voices on this issue," he told the crowd, "with respect, *con respeto*, because nobody is going to listen to us if we come in all raging." He said that the combination of being angry and being Brown could too easily make them targets, mentioning his brother who had been shot at numerous times by police, "just for smelling like *carne asada* [grilled beef]."

Various residents spoke up about fears for their children, their anger at the involved police being put on paid leave, and the lack of justice. In the array of statements and conversations that were forming, residents were coming to a collective understanding about what the homicide meant, while voicing a sense of uncertainty about how to proceed. As the *asamblea* ended and people started drifting away from the park to get on with their evenings at home, we took photos of the Mujeres holding signs. Then Shi collected the signs and placed them in the trunk of her Mustang for the next time we'd need them. It would be sooner than any of us expected.

Carlos Mejía

The next morning, as I was getting ready to meet Shi and Rosa to prepare for a visioning meeting with regional BHC leadership, I saw Yesi had posted on Facebook about someone being shot by police in front of her house on the East Side. There was nothing in the paper yet, but

I knew I'd find out more from the women soon; they always knew first. Arriving at the coffee shop for our meeting, Rosa immediately asked me if I'd heard what happened. We pieced together what we knew about it, debating whether to hold our meeting at all. We agreed that we would defer to Shi on what she wanted to do.

Shi arrived late, breathless, with the stack of white and hot pink poster boards in her arms and her huge phone in hand. Gata had dropped Shi off because she felt too upset by Yesi's news to drive. We decided to keep our meeting, and I would speak with Rosa while Shi would field calls with the Mujeres to try to figure out what was going on and what to do next. I was trying to focus on the visioning discussion, but the immediacy of Shi's conversations with Yesi and Gata was overwhelming. It felt like any vision we had for the group would have to be steeped somehow in what was happening right then. Shi kept popping back to our table and, in hushed voice, leaning in to tell us more details.

"They shot, the police shot, like, a *paisa* [recently arrived rural migrant] in front of Delicia's, that bakery up on Sanborn."

"Yesi lives right down the street from it. She lives where the police tape ends."

"Her daughter's friend has it on video."

Shi asked me to take her to Yesi's. Yesi said she had been in her front yard with her granddaughter when the two cops, in pursuit of Mejía, turned the corner onto her street. They had their guns drawn. Yesi immediately grabbed her granddaughter and ran inside, leaving her tricycle out on the lawn. She was scared the man or the cops would try to come onto her property or into her house. Now we stood outside, watching kids come home from school past the police tape, as men in ranchero hats sat on a fence as the police crew did cleanup. Yesi showed us the video her daughter's friend had taken of Carlos Mejía and the two police who pursued him. Mejía shuffled slowly, perhaps intoxicated, toward the bakery at the corner. The video was posted on the local paper's website, but Shi and I each filmed it with our own phones, creating backups, just in case it got scrubbed. The police had already confiscated the girl's phone with the original recording. Later, we stood around in Yesi's backyard, as if in wait for other action to become possible, touching the dry soil and talking about the garden she wanted to grow.

Figure 5.2. Watching and waiting, where the police tape ends. Photo by the author.

I woke up the next day to texts from Daniel, urging me to come to city hall, where there was a press conference being held by various community groups against this latest act of violence by the Salinas Police Department. As some of us circled up in the crowd between speakers, he accounted for Shi's absence. "So, Shi's not present, she's actually facilitating a process with yesterday's victim's family. She's jumping in, kind of like the looper, going from the first responder mode, to MILPA mode, to gangster mode. So our blessings are with her that she stays grounded, stays clearheaded."

He and a few others invited me to join them for lunch at a brewpub in North Salinas; it was our friend Joaquin's birthday. As we ordered, I texted Shi from our leather booth. "Where are you?" I wrote. "Do you want to join us for lunch?"

"No, im koo off dat," she wrote back. "Im at to the corner by Delicia's, Yesi and Juana are here too. We're having a vigil, come thru."

After a lunch that, to me, felt shamefully detached from the reality setting in across Salinas—two men had been murdered by members of the

Salinas Police Department within ten days of each other, and Angel Ruiz's murder months earlier made this a string of three—I drove over to Delicia's to join the Mujeres. I expected to see the three of them and their kids on the side of the bakery setting up the candles. Instead, all four corners of the intersection were packed with dozens of youth and residents holding signs—"Cops Gone Wild!" "Policias Corruptas Fuera!!"—and cars honking like crazy. I parked way down the block and set out to find the Mujeres. Shi and Tara were trying to keep the kids on the corners rather than in the streets, their fists raised high in the air, leading the chants. I ran into Yesi near the altar, cluttered with *velas* (devotional candles). She gave me a huge hug, telling me that the owner of Delicia's was bringing out free water, coffee and pan dulce. The rally had been announced on the radio and was steadily growing in numbers. People had their phones out, and the local news station was recording footage, with the crowd growing angrier as the afternoon turned to evening, and more and more cops showed up from Salinas and neighboring counties.

I texted Daniel and others to come through. They didn't.

Figure 5.3. Young protesters crossing the intersection in front of the bakery where Carlos Mejía was killed, as the rally grew. Photo by the author.

I reconvened with some of them later, just down the street from the rally, to plan a community healing circle with other BHC-funded groups as a response to the shootings. At that meeting, we arranged ourselves in a multilayered circle that kept getting jostled and expanded as more folks joined. Those present spoke in a clutter of war metaphors as we compiled a list of "battlefronts," scribbled on a whiteboard, trying to make sense of how to move:

> media + messaging
> politics + co-opting the struggle
> hearts and minds + building community
> identify and cultivating organic leadership—palabra

At the last point, I mentioned that it was a group of our Mujeres that had started the rally down the street, and that this was a great example of organic leadership among women and children. These women had *palabra* for their community and didn't hesitate to make themselves available and hold a space for collective solidarity. The BHC group wanted to organize something off the street, a community-wide circle and space for healing and dialogue. The Mujeres' organizing and presence, it seemed to me, could feed into the success of that event.

I texted Shi, "Are you coming to this meeting? We're planning a big community *círculo*."

Her response came a few minutes later. "No. I'm staying out here on the street."

A clear split was already in motion: the Mujeres were refusing to be anywhere but with other residents and community members. They were not interested in attending meetings and press conferences, in articulating a stance or planning a response. They were already responding in where they went, what they did, and with whom they connected. For some of the Mujeres, it was the reality of proximity and relation that made direct response the only option. Yesi lived down the street. Tara knew both Hernández and Mejía. And for Shi, the meetings were a waste of time, "all about the politics, but what about the community? I don't care about the politics. I want to be where my people are, where I am needed."

While BHC-funded groups planned and held a series of community healing circles with the name Palabra Comunitaria (Raschig 2018), a group of old-school Chicano Movement activists had planned a *marcha* through the streets. This group, branding themselves the May 1 Alliance, had a controversial city council member as their figurehead and were perhaps best known for their efforts to restore an East Salinas school board to local control after it had been taken over by the state for poor performance years prior. They had adopted the slogan "Respect Dignity Justice," stenciling it in English and Spanish onto countless heavy wooden signs with pointy stakes.

Shi wasn't involved in planning the *marcha*, but in preparation she invited the Mujeres to meet at Closter Park the day before and help make and decorate signs. A few Mujeres and their children showed up, and as we examined the scattered "Respect Dignity Justice" boards on the park lawn, we decided to brighten them up and use the stencils to make other words as well. The men of the May 1 Alliance had given us instructions on what to do—more black stenciling of the official slogan—but left the park while the women and children actually took up the materials. Before long, we were painting pink, green, and purple flowers around the black stencils, or using the letter blocks to make other words like "Unity" or "Peace." We were attempting to intervene on the terms of struggle that would represent this very public march, the largest and most inclusive public event organized against police brutality in that period.

Some of those men came back later that afternoon to drop off three cardboard caskets, painted matte black, to be carried in the march to represent the three men who had been killed. Yesi looked at them, then looked at her grandkids and the other children nearby, making a face; the black caskets were drab and dark, seeming to suck the energy out of everything around them. Shi suggested we make *flores de papel* (tissue paper flowers) to decorate the caskets and celebrate the men's lives in a way that felt more true to Mexican and Chicanx aesthetics of grief. As Tara put it while folding and cutting sheets of red tissue paper, "Love is a color and community is love."

The morning of the *marcha*, hundreds of participants gathered at Closter Park before heading onto the route. I had loaded up a heavy canvas tote bag with apples, almonds, and water to share. Yarri carried a lit bundle of sage around to cleanse anyone who wanted her to do so. I noticed that our colorful signs had been dumped behind the rotunda and the ones with exclusively black stenciled writing offered to marchers.

It was a huge turnout. Some participants were waving white UFW *banderas* (flags), others wore all black, and some even had brown berets, a nod to the Chicano militant movement. *Danzantes* performed Aztec dances in full regalia in front of the Closter Park rotunda. Many young white people from out of town were present, some with signs or shirts that read "FTP" (Fuck the Police), distributing anarchist newsletters or abolitionist flyers. Tara asked a couple of them to please put away the FTP signs—not that she disagreed with the sentiment, but because these out-of-towners had the privilege of expressing it and still getting home safely. Most of my healing collective colleagues were running similar interference, trying to suss out the visiting *traviesos* (troublemakers) who might instigate more police violence in a community they didn't call home.

The march itself set out with the flower-covered caskets carried up near the head, and *danzantes* leading the way. I lost track of most of the Mujeres, aside from Tara, who was doing crowd control at the margin of the marchers. I found out later that most Mujeres did not actually walk. The crowd of hundreds was too hectic, or the route too long, for them or their kids, or they had other things to do. There were countless other moments that we walked together; they didn't need to do so in the march.

Figure 5.4. Preparing signs before the *marcha*. Photo by the author.

Figure 5.5. *Danzantes* (Aztec dancers) and protesters make their way during the *marcha*. Photo by the author.

Frank Alvarado Jr.

Less than two months later, in July, it happened again. I first saw the news one morning, again from Yesi's Facebook post, and immediately texted Shi—"Again? Really???"

I checked *The Californian* and there it was, headline news. With each hour that passed, from eight to nine to eleven o'clock to again around one o'clock, the newspaper updated it. Police-involved shooting. A death. An investigation by the district attorney. Frank Alvarado Jr., recently released from a correctional facility in Santa Cruz County, had been shot in the early morning hours out front of his family home in East Salinas. The police later claimed he held his cell phone like a gun, and tricked them into committing "suicide by cop."

When Shi and I talked, she sounded exhausted. I asked who she knew in the area where Alvarado was shot, a residential pocket at the southern edge of East Salinas, behind a gas station and next to a freeway off-ramp.

She knew a few folks who lived around there and said she would text them later. She added, "I'm not sure what's gonna go down, but I'm just gonna keep posted, like on standby. Let's keep each other posted."

Later she texted me back saying that she and a few other women from her old *cliqua* as well as some of the Mujeres were planning to protest on the street in front of that gas station later that day, near to where Alvarado was killed. I already had a scheduled interview with Pamela and then a meeting with the Colectiva's new interns, two young women from the local college and funded by TCE. We agreed that I would meet up with all of them and then they could join us at the protest if they felt comfortable.

Pamela's car broke down five times en route, but she made it to our interview. We chatted for an hour, and she shared parts of her "Voice of the Voiceless" journal. Shi and Rosa had devoted the last few circles to making these journals, creative and tactile work that would give us all space to decompress, talk, and process what we were feeling. Rosa brought books of poetry and prose by Tupac, bell hooks, and Gloria Anzaldúa and supplies for collaging. She had a plan for facilitating *pláticas* that would help the women articulate a narrative of their lives. Pamela had already written quite a bit in her journal, finding her words. Pamela had a way of talking in swirls that could dizzy the uninitiated. She was adamant about using her voice to address the injustices she saw and lived, from her youth in poverty through her experience working in programming and policy at Soledad State Correctional Facility over a decade, through the struggles of some of her children with mental illness, addiction, and incarceration. She told me that at a recent circle, when we had been reviewing our Colectiva Agreements, she felt it was the first time she could be herself among others, and she said it out loud emphatically so she herself could hear it. Her adult daughter Rachel was also attending consistently and didn't say much but was strengthened by being among strong women, Pamela said. She felt she belonged there, too.

When the interns started to show up, Pamela decided to stay. By way of orientation to the Colectiva, we started to talk about Frank Alvarado Jr. We watched a seven-minute clip of him speaking in front of the Santa Cruz County courthouse in which he described some of his regrets while incarcerated for the past eleven years and being released "to a family that might not respect you but still does love you." His *ganas* (desire, drive) for transformation and realness about his experience reminded me of some of the MILPA men, and it was almost unbelievable that he was the latest victim of police violence. Larissa, an intern, told us that Alvarado had been a friend of her dad's, and she cried because she didn't even realize he had been released until hearing he had been killed.

Pamela said, "We need to share Frank's message. His message is of transformation and opportunity. That's the energy we need to have in our hearts as we go out to the street."

The four of us headed for the protest. Shi and a few others were already there, along with a clutch of reporters and some of Frank's family members, gathering at a growing memorial. The sidewalk was busy, in a transitional industrial zone without a lot of foot traffic. On that hot and polluted strip of concrete, we held up signs and asked drivers of cars and trucks to honk as they rolled off the freeway. Tara was out there, one foot off the curb, waving a white *paño* (towel) around, toting a sign with so many words I could barely read it from down the sidewalk.

We decided to pick up the protest again the next morning. I met Shi in the parking lot of the 7-Eleven, where she was burning sage in a *concha* on top of her trunk, next to a stack of signs. We hung out waiting for others to arrive, and Yarri told me about how her family had been "hella pissed" at her for protesting the day before and confronted her about it when she got home. "It's all good," she stated. "I just let it roll off me."

It was a quieter start to the day, with fewer people on the sidewalk, entirely women. We had switched most of our signs into Spanish as we'd noticed the previous day that most of the people driving by were agricultural workers on their way home from the fields, and they seemed to not have enough time to understand what our signs said. While Pamela's sign was still in English—"Honk 4 Justice. Frank's Message Remember: Make a Difference," and Tara's sign had some typos that did not matter, "Quieremos Justicia," Shi's said simply, "YA BASTA" (Enough Already).

Christopher

When I got the call from Pamela on an afternoon that August, I was at the beach in nearby Marina. I could barely hear her over the crashing waves, just some keywords. I thought I heard her say that her son was hit by a train, but I couldn't believe it. I hate that I did this, but I asked her to repeat it, after she stammered through a minute or two of verbiage I couldn't understand, other than that she couldn't reach Shi and needed support from the other women. When she made it abundantly clear to me—"My son was hit by a train and is dead"—I told her I was heading back to Salinas immediately and would find Shi.

I went straight to Shi's, parking on the street and rushing up to her apartment. I was deeply relieved to see her daughter on the landing and the screen door open. Shi greeted me, surprised I was there, I could tell a bit embarrassed for being in her *chanclas* (slippers) and with a fuzzy Dallas Cowboys *cobija* (blanket) wrapped around her. I told her what had happened, that Pamela's son had died and she didn't know what to do.

Shi got on it, borrowing my phone to call Pamela first and then the local mortuary. We tidied up her apartment and Shi put on her makeup. We reached out to the rest of the Mujeres, letting them know what had happened and that we would be figuring out how to support Pamela. Some of them came to Shi's too, and when Pamela arrived, we piled onto the L-shaped couch. Shi's daughter was on my lap as I braided her hair, and Pamela told us more about what had happened. Her son, Christopher, had been released from jail in Contra Costa County, north of Oakland. He hadn't received the proper dosage of his medication while locked up. When the time came for him to be released, he basically was allowed to walk out of the facility with no support and no services, despite his mental illness and the shellshock of incarceration.[1] He was unhoused and staying by a set of train tracks.

Though Pamela's son did not experience acute state violence like the four men killed by Salinas police that year, Christopher's life was slowly taken by a state carceral system that, after having captured and neglected him, abandoned him. Abandonment is a more gradual and passive form of state killing (Povinelli 2011); the state carceral system did most of the work, and let the rest happen. Each of the four men killed that year by Salinas police, and Christopher too, had experienced forms of state abandonment prior to their deaths. Angel Ruiz and Frank Alvarado Jr. had been incarcerated and released with slim-to-no resources and faced mental health issues with tremendous barriers. Their deaths were written off by media and police as suicide by cop, attempting to render them culpable for and deserving of what was done to them. Not long before their deaths, Hernández and Mejía had made the dangerous and fraught journey to Salinas to work. They crossed borders and endured lethal challenges all along the way from El Salvador, in the absence of a safe, legal pathway to immigration to pick America's food. American immigration policy lets the desert do the work of violence (De Leon 2015), a form of deterrence that is actually homicidal abandonment. Hernández and Mejía arrived, struggled, and self-medicated, only to have their distress be interpreted as imminently dangerous by state agents.

Pamela understood this without putting it into words. Her eyes red and tired, she told us: "My son is Frank Alvarado. My son is every young man whose life has been taken too soon by the system."

We took this in. In these moments, there is nothing that can be said, only things that can be done.

"We are a sisterhood," Shi declared. Just as we had when the other four men were killed—we would be there for and with Pamela.

"Thank you," Pamela replied quietly. "This is where we walk together."

There is so much I could include here. I will note just one more moment in this account of the Mujeres' rugged world-making amid the raw wounds of this state violence. There were multiple parts to Christopher's funeral, from the showing at the mortuary, to the memorial at a Baptist church in the center of Salinas, to his interment with a local *maestro* drumming the *teponaztli* as copal smoke washed over us all. Pamela urged members of the Colectiva to attend the church memorial. She said she needed us to give her strength, so that she could look to us and we would provide her with the ability to do what she planned to do—dance for her son, at the front of the pews, to Monica's song "Still Standing," a piano- and synth-driven R & B jam featuring Ludacris.

As Pamela danced alone in front of the congregation, I cried like hell, in a mix of sadness and deep admiration for her strength and endurance. The warm breeze blew in from the open windows, and I saw Shi in the back pew, alone, sunglasses on, her cheeks wet like mine.

I'm still standing, standing, standing, standing . . .

Ya Basta; We Remember

A year later, on Día de los Muertos in November 2015, members of La Colectiva de Mujeres set out on what they called a Walk to Remember. They visited each of the four sites where Ruiz, Hernández, Mejía, and

Alvarado had lost their lives and made a stop outside of the Salinas rodeo grounds where Jose Velasco, a man with known mental illness, had been beaten and then arrested by Salinas Police Department officers in the fall of 2014. Along with the Mujeres were some of the victims' sisters, children, or parents, and at each site they and their slain loved one were honored with sage and a blessing. They walked with signs: "Knowledge Is Power," "Justicia al Pueblo de Salinas," "Respect Dignity Justice."

It was a significantly smaller gathering than the previous year's mass *marcha*. Much had happened in the wake of the homicides, like a scathing investigation and report by the Department of Justice (Santos et al. 2016), with its dozens of suggestions to the Salinas Police Department to improve their relationships with the local Latinx community. Out of that, a citywide project called Governing for Racial Equity (GRE) was born, funded in part by TCE. Through the GRE, elected leaders and community residents came together for sustained periods to develop *conocimiento* and understand how racial equity and cultural healing could be built into local infrastructure (Raschig 2018). The investigative report and subsequent formation of the GRE are often upheld as the justice wrought in that period of struggle. Pamela and Shi were part of the GRE, and before that they also spoke to investigators at the Department of Justice. But they had also made it possible for women like Angel Ruiz's sister to feel OK about talking to the investigators and then being able to go out and protest too, and not feel alone in her grief. They had prepared the space with medicine and their presence, tending the ground on which those attempts at justice could be built.

"We didn't have to understand. We just know and remember," Pamela told me, while I was finishing up this chapter years later, in 2022. I had asked her to hop on a Zoom meeting and talk more about this period again, though I struggled with whether it was justified to keep asking for this effort from her and other Mujeres. I had already written about this time extensively in journal articles. The Colectiva's actions during these police homicides was something that almost always came up whenever any configuration of us were together—there was always still more to say about it, even if it was just to acknowledge with awe how intense it had been. To paraphrase Shi as I quoted her earlier in this chapter, we know in our hearts what we did and the impact it made.

But was it, is it, OK to keep reiterating these deaths and responses again and again? Is it too much to ask of interlocutors, that they continue to go back to a place that was so painful for them and brought up so much? Is it not enough that their bodies already archive this terror and transformation?

"Let's look at it different," Pamela replied when I expressed this regret to her. "What if we didn't show up? What if we didn't come together? What if it was just like, it's OK for police to kill four people? What was next? We made our way out of nowhere . . . there was not a way that anybody showed us how to do things. So, we feel a lot."

She continued, expressing ambivalence about what she and others had fought for and what had been achieved: "But then what? Again, even with all of us, it's like, did we continue? Are the women lost now? How many of us died?"

I thought about this, and the fact of their leadership at that time, making something out of nothing, starting with a scream and moving from there. The women who were lost—Lisa, Gina, and Rachel— were among those who showed up the hardest during that period. They passed in the time since from years of stress, hard lives without access to institutional care or support. Some, like Tara once the period of homicides cooled, "fell off," returned to substance use, lived unhoused. They are also the casualties of this state violence and abandonment, and the wide reach of carceral logics in disciplining and displacing raw women. How do these women fit into the otherwise understanding of this period of police homicides?

Shi had also brought up these women when I talked to her while writing this chapter. "The women that have passed on . . . they held on to so much but they were fucking raw and they were brave for even showing up and for showing up more than once," she said, forcefully. "They were committed members, and why? Because they felt, they felt like they belonged there. We made them feel welcome. And women like that are never felt to be welcome anywhere and to have a space like that. That was very sacred. So, I don't give a fuck what anyone says."

This chapter and the understandings it opens up can be an ongoing space for these women to belong and be honored, and where these voices can stay forever. It is enough already that the Mujeres remember these events and their intensity, that we know in our hearts the impacts we made, and continue to live out that commitment to each other and others afflicted in Salinas. It is enough to know the transformations wrought at that time in our bodies and relations, as Shi, Pamela, and others have made clear over the years. And in holding up these fragments of action, and the rawness they still brought out for these women nearly a decade after they occurred, maybe there is more for us and others to see, hear, and feel in them, more to do with them.

6

The Work and Play of Healing

Making Fugitive Spaces for Joy

For Brenda

Brenda Mendoza was having a mental health crisis. She had locked herself in her beat-up Ford Explorer, parked in front of her mother-in-law's house. It was where the twenty-year-old new mom was living at the time. The Salinas Police Department tank blocked the road behind the driveway in a standoff that lasted two and a half hours. With mischievous flourishes, Brenda occasionally brandished a fake gun while bantering in a mix of Spanish and English with one of the three male officers present.

That officer, who generally struck a friendly tone, asked Brenda if he could call her on her phone so they wouldn't be yelling at each other.

"I don't think so, I want to yell," she shouted back clearly through the missing rear window, lined with tattered garbage bags.

Because she had tracked through a series of behavioral health programs and continuation schools in the city, the police on the scene should have been aware that Brenda had long-term mental health issues related to domestic abuse and poverty. Her baby had been taken away due to her continued substance use and lack of stable housing. She had postpartum depression, had run out of her bipolar disorder meds, and had expressed suicidal thoughts earlier that day. Despite these deeply worrisome and known mental health and social conditions, her social workers were not called to the standoff.

The officer and Brenda continued their repartee while the other two officers stayed posted in the tank, eyes and guns trained on where she sat, near the Explorer's rear window. She eventually closed her eyes, appearing sleepy, before gently clowning on the officers with the statement, "You guys had your chance."

The lead officer continued to banter with her, mostly in Spanish, to try to get her to get out of the car. Sometimes she responded to what he was saying, and other times she ignored it, hewing to her own narrative line. On an officer's body cam footage, she could be heard saying, "*Como—como—como—como?*" asking no one in particular, "How—how—how—how?" She flicked a fake firearm up through the back window and laughed. She was playful, fading in and out. The humorless officers yelled at her to drop the gun. Instead, she flicked it up again, taunting them to deal with her on her own terms.

Shi texted me about Brenda's death that same Friday afternoon in March 2019. I was sitting at my desk at California State University, Sacramento, where I was in the middle of my second semester as an assistant professor. Shi and I had already been texting throughout the day, partly to share ideas on the new healing circles we were planning to start up but hadn't quite solidified. She had also recently moved back to California after a year or so away in Arizona, taking distance from Salinas after she was fired from her role as facilitator of the Colectiva and the group had been defunded. In early 2016, the group lost its financial support when its funders disagreed with some key actions by the Mujeres, placing conservative limits on what constituted appropriate or respectable healing practices.

Both back in Cali, we had been talking about how to revive some version of the women's healing collective but hadn't quite found the right configuration. We didn't have a space to host it. We weren't sure who to invite. We couldn't land on the right theme, whether reunion or sisterhood or what. In the midst of this low-key ongoing planning, Shi had been venting her frustration with her housemate-turned-slumlord, a former friend she rented a room from and now referred to as "this gestapo." I had wired her some money to get away from her musty room for a couple of nights at the GoodNite Inn, a very cheap local motel that seemed mostly to function as temporary shelter for the un- or underhoused.

Shi sent me a link to the breaking news about Brenda, adding a series of expletives about the trigger-happy Salinas police. I froze, feeling a heavy, sinking sensation of déjà vu to 2014. Only this time, it was a new mother, with a documented history of mental illness, and on the tail of years of explicit efforts to build racial equity and healing in Salinas.

Another message followed from Shi before I could reply: "Mayb this wil be a perfect opportunity for wat were anticipating on doing. Let's brainstorm as more info is known."

"Omg this is crazy and horrible," I texted back. "Yes we have to work with this."

Brenda's death snapped Shi and me out of speculation and into a responsive mode, with the urgent imperative to honor Brenda by holding space for other women through which to expand possibilities for their well-being and ability to live. As we would see, these new healing circles would become a vibrant space for not only the *work of* healing but also the *play for* healing, nestled away from disciplinary oversight that renders play, ribaldry, and experimentation a threat to order or a marker of deviance. Palpable in Brenda's lighthearted back-and-forth with the officer, the activity that got Shi fired and the Colectiva defunded, or the raunchy joking that ensued in the new healing circle, play enacts, however fleetingly, a version of the world that is safe for working-class Chicanas and Latinas to air, share, and explore the deeply felt, but too quickly disqualified, knowledge of their lives. As such, play is an experiment with freedom (Cox 2015), in defiance of the gendered and racialized violence that pervades the context. Play is not separate from pain but can disentangle and remake the latter's social and affective conditions. It can be an integral part of the creative labor of healing—if supported and engaged on equitable terms. That is a massive "if." As is clear in Brenda's police-inflicted death or Shi's dismissal, among working-class women of color whose bodies and behavior are policed at nearly all turns by high-stakes respectability norms, play is too easily and treacherously misappropriated as threat. The consequences are enormous, the need for safe and nourishing space likewise critical.

Crucially, these playful new healing circles were funded not by philanthropy but by the "fugitive" redirection of an ethnographic research grant I held at the time (Harney and Moten 2013; Rosas 2019). Fugitivity, Stefano Harney and Fred Moten write, is a being that is "separate from settling"; it is a modality of movement "that has learned that organizations are obstacles to organizing ourselves" (2013, 11). As the Colectiva's defunding made all too clear, philanthropic oversight exerted stifling limitations on the range of behaviors considered appropriate to healing, doubling down on the discipline Chicanas and Latinas were subject to in this city. Philanthropy's professionalization of healing, while making possible new spaces and resources for community healing projects, had also effected new forms of dispossession in its wake. Those most impacted were women like Shi and Brenda, who were denied the institutional care and support dangled in front of them, as well as forced into dangerous and stressful housing insecurity through skyrocketing local real estate costs. This exorbitant increase in the cost of living was also due, in part, to gentrification wrought by philanthropic "improvements" to Salinas. The context of lethal structural vulnerability, and women pushed to that edge, must be understood alongside the exuberant and defiant experimentation of play in the context of healing.

In truth, it all became startlingly personal. In Brenda's life, I started to see worrying parallels with Shi's. During the months of planning and holding the new circles, Shi's housing situation fell apart. She became one of the thousands of working people in the region who could not find, let alone afford, housing that was safe and appropriate for herself and her daughter. I was terrified that my friend would end up on the street, pressed to her limits, and in danger. Supporting her in the ways I could included apportioning significant chunks of my research grant into a monthly stipend for her to run the new healing circles, as well as supplies for hosting them. The new circles, their social context and funding stream, thus cast into relief the possibilities and limitations of an Otherwise Anthropological commitment that works from the space of friendship and accompliceship to address endemic forms of structural violence. As my friend and co-thinker Laura McTighe and I have written, an Otherwise Anthropology—not only an anthropology of the otherwise—is founded through our intimate fieldwork-based kinships, inviting commitments to struggle and solidarity that exceed the expectations of research mandates in neoliberal academic settings (McTighe and Raschig 2019). These arrangements sometimes require fugitive workarounds, "stealing" from the university (Moten and Harney 2013), "trafficking" in subaltern knowledges (Rosas 2019), leveraging whatever academic privilege and capital we can muster in solidarity with a grassroots project. An Otherwise Anthropology foregrounds these commitments with the aim of developing a responsive, flexible, and complicit mode of collaborative research that strategically builds worlds alongside our interlocutors. This work happens "at the speed of trust" (a. m. brown

2017), built on a foundation of *confianza* and mutuality that emerges through play, shared joy, and material commitment, in the midst of deep struggle.

The Work of Healing

As more details of Brenda's death emerged, a familiar anguish and outrage set in among my friends in Salinas. In community responses, her murder was linked with the four of 2014, although it had its own unique and painful contours. The 2014 police homicides, in their frequency and similarities, had brought out the issue of racialized criminalization of Chicano and Latino men that harmonized with the contemporaneous rising refrain of "Black Lives Matter" and the anticarceral movement. Brenda's life and death took a differently gendered trajectory: through domestic abuse, substance abuse, and mental illness; the "behavioral" flanks of the carceral system that surveilled and failed women (J. Flores 2016); and the prevalence of homelessness or housing insecurity for single mothers in this region and state. The economic burdens facing low-income women, particularly single mothers, in Salinas and the surrounding Monterey County were intensifying as the region became increasingly and outrageously expensive. Even the way her death unfolded—her anguished play, unruly, met with police bullets—offered a stark escalation of gender-based discipline facing Chicana and Latina women in the United States. The challenges and stakes of performing the right, respectable femininity, whatever that was, had become increasingly fraught.

A series of protest, vigil, and discussion events followed Brenda's death, organized by members of MILPA and other organizations affiliated with Building Healthy Communities. Commemorations of her life and protest of its unjust end aligned with ongoing efforts and narratives countering police brutality and the carceral state. The first big event was a "Justice for Brenda" rally held the following Friday at Closter Park, chosen not only for its centrality on the East Side of Salinas but also in pointed contrast with another event planned there that same day: a celebration of the Salinas Police Department for receiving the James Q. Wilson Award for Excellence in Community Policing. The latter celebration was, rightfully, canceled. The Justice for Brenda rally featured a series of impassioned and tearful speakers, Danza Azteca, and Native American Church songs as *ofrendas* to Brenda and all present.

The following week, BHC hosted an event dedicated to the recently released book *The End of Policing* (2017), featuring a talk by the author, Alex Vitale, and the quintessential Salinas public meeting spread of tortas and pan dulce from La Plaza Bakery. The talk had been in the works for some months, but it felt fortunately timed to open focused discussion on Brenda's death and how it could catalyze structural change in the context of policing. An altar on the side of the room featured photos of Angel Ruiz, Osmar Hernández, Carlos Mejía, Frank Alvarado, and Brenda Mendoza, taped to a window above a collection of Mesoamerican figurines and medicines encircled by roses. These objects and offerings sat atop a red cloth with "Missing and Murdered Indigenous Women" written on it in white ink. In the informal time before and after the talk itself, attendees stopped by the altar to pay their respects and take a photo of the arrangement.

I was visiting with Shi that weekend, renting a room for us at the GoodNite Inn. She had decided to chill in the "momo" (motel) and avoid the nonprofit crowd that we knew would be attending the event. Still upset about the Colectiva's defunding, Shi was uninterested in seeing the people she felt had sold her out. Her daughter, then ten years old, came with me. As we snagged tortas and searched for seats she liked, we met with Rosa and a few other nonprofit leaders in the aisle, some of whom I hadn't seen for years. We hugged and caught up, and Rosa noted to me that she wished the Colectiva were still around today. She continued, "No one is organizing the women right now. If the Colectiva were here, they would make things crack off."

"Oh, definitely," I agreed, but didn't know what else to say, feeling the weight of that and other implicit "ifs." If only the Colectiva had not lost its funding. If only Shi had not felt utterly betrayed to the point of isolation, losing her job, her home, her community, and very nearly herself. If only there were more resources for women in this region to do that healing work, and if only it was safe for them to do it.

Members of the healing collectives often described healing as *work*. The labor of cultural healing is emergent and responsive to what one and others have been through, the conditions of their lives, and a sense of what healing or being healed would make possible. Such healing is a praxis that M. Jacqui Alexander notes "assumes different forms, while anchored in reconstructing a terrain that is both exterior and interior" (2005, 339). Distinctively Chicana in its blend of spirituality and *política*, healing is world-making, embodied, and collective (Facio and Lara 2014). This healing praxis exceeds the other denotation of "work," the professionalized and remunerated role of the *job*. Shi's *job* was to facilitate the healing collective, which involved a set of administrative tasks, but also to do her own healing *work* within the group and model it for others. Likewise for Yarri, a paid intern with the Colectiva through 2014 and 2015, being remunerated to attend and help organize healing circles and ceremonies, civic meetings, and movement *encuentros* made it possible for her to spend time on projects of her own healing and community justice rather than taking a less meaningful service job. But when the challenges of life as a young, single, formerly gang-involved mother took over, she could not make enough hours with the Colectiva to get her and her daughter out of a shelter and into a rental. In an insulting interaction she recalled to me years later, male counterparts involved in BHC told her that she wasn't cut out for "the work" rather than acknowledging that the job itself wasn't offering her enough support, given the cost of living and her particular gendered struggle. Women engaged in this work typically had children to care for, adding limitations to what they could give to their jobs while also driving their tooth-and-nail passion to make Salinas a more livable place.

Both Shi and Yarri had a life course that exemplified many of the challenges women face in Salinas, which was why they were hired for their positions. Shi, especially, was always transparent about her healing being an ongoing project, and the assertion that healers need healing, too. But the professionalization of the work of healing applied limits on what qualified as legitimately or appropriately healing, particularly for those being paid for it. Specifically, when Shi's *work* of healing verged into interpretation as *play*, it was deemed inappropriate in light of her professional role. Prior to the Colectiva's defunding, Shi was partying and posting about it on social media, newly separated from an abusive and controlling *machista* husband.[1] These liberatory acts, in defiance of his attempted patriarchal control, were healing, in that through them she asserted and affirmed her own will and pleasure. This play was part of "the work" for Shi, making her growth possible in ways supported by, but exceeding, what she could do in circle itself. The play was experimentation with freedom and tinkering with the world, a temporary but iterative reclamation of control (Cox 2015). Play, like humor and ribaldry, is everyday resistance to such inequities as they take shape in and on bodies of women of color, but also an iterative dismantling of those constraints. However, Shi was fired for this play, when local managers caught wind of it and aligned it with other perceived indiscretions. Since the Colectiva was considered her intellectual property, The California Endowment ceased to fund the group at the same time. Shi's play for healing was considered so transgressive that it led to the dismantling of the Colectiva as a whole, a grassroots institution making palpable impacts on the lives of local women who had limited access to dedicated spaces for healing and solidarity.

As I have argued in this book, cultural healing is potentially a radically open and inclusive category of praxis; since one's healing is situated, relational, and emergent, it will look and feel different to everyone. But as such, healing remains susceptible to capture by more conservative ideologies and institutions, and wherever it is leveraged begs examination for its disciplinary effects: What counts as healing and what becomes disqualified; how and by whom; and with what impacts? What treacherous new forms of dispossession are leveled by this reductive and conservative criteria of healing, despite its radical promise?

When Healing Inflicts Dispossession

Whether cultural healing praxis served as an ultimately disciplinary technique making possible new forms of dispossession was the persistent point of discussion in a mutual interview my friend Joaquin and I conducted, from our varying capacities, late in the summer of 2019. In recent years, he had become the communications director for BHC, while still dabbling in photography and journalism on the side. He asked to interview me for a case study he was preparing on how Salinas and its residents had fared over ten years of BHC funding. Since this question was so close to my own, we took the opportunity to treat it as a conversation, carrying on our old tradition of what we called "researchismeando," gossiping (*chismeando*) in the name of research and organizing goals. What used to happen over Tuesday beers in his backyard was now taking place in his glassy downtown Salinas office, and recorded for both of us to write up.

While acknowledging some of the major achievements of efforts funded by BHC in Salinas—like the reduced scope of the local juvenile hall; the refusal to place school resource officers, uniformed police, in schools; and the dwindling of the youth homicide rate from "Murder Capital of California" levels to almost zero (Szydlowski 2019)—Joaquin shared concerns about the benefactors of healing projects, and those who, already pushed to the margins, were definitely not benefiting, if not being actively dispossessed by them. This meant the growing numbers, hundreds or thousands, living visibly unhoused and vulnerable in Salinas's Chinatown encampment; the less-visible overcrowded slum conditions of many East Side rental units like decrepit garages populated by a dozen farmworker family members at a time; and the situations of too many single, working-class Chicana, Latina, Indigenous, and white women I knew who had lost their stable housing in the years since 2014. These were all issues that intersected in the life and death of Brenda Mendoza. How had this vast number of people been served by the philanthropic and community emphasis on healing?

"After these ten or so years of healing and whatnot, what do we have to show for it?" Joaquin asked, rhetorically. "Look, we've rehabilitated the gangsters? Everyone is fine and normal now," just in time for the new rapid rail line linking Salinas with Silicon Valley?

I looked out his office window to the gentrifying Salinas Old Town in front of us, which had come to accommodate more slick brewpubs and overpriced housing meant to appeal to the influx of residents from Silicon Valley, an hour or so up Highway 101. Since 2014, Salinans not only had faced down the devastating carceral logics of racialized criminalization and fought to have fewer police in their schools and on their streets but also had seen their rents and property values become inflated to the point of inaccessibility for many in a city where the poverty rate sat at 17 percent. While the rental vacancy rate here hung around 2.5 percent against a national average of 6 percent, the average rental cost had increased more than 50 percent over those short five years (Cimini 2019). I thought wistfully of the room I rented on a ranch just outside Salinas for $500 per month in 2013–14, how easy it was as a single white woman to live there temporarily. Meanwhile, now, Shi had left her slumlord-housemate's home and was living in a women's shelter with her daughter, after reaching the limit of three months at a different shelter in nearby Seaside. She was struggling to find an apartment that would accept her slowly improving credit score, and where she ideally would not have to prove her income was at least three times the monthly rent, averaging an outrageous $2,200 per month in the region at that time.

For some months, she could add about $800 to her income from the "consulting" work she was doing by running our new healing circles, paid for by my research grant. Under no illusions about the philanthropic funding opportunities available to our planned initiative, we took an alternative approach. Evading philanthropic surveillance and respectability norms required fugitive strategies and commitments, to seize on and live into the possibilities for radical connection and healing despite disciplinary threats all around. Without disciplinary oversight, our new circles could provide a safe space for women's play and healing, at a time when it was desperately needed.

Making Space for Play

In taking our time to launch the new circles, we mulled over whether it was worth connecting with other funded groups to use their space or gain their support. But Shi, betrayed already by this apparatus, didn't want to inure herself to the "community network" in the city, nor did she want to deal with its respectability norms. Scholars in the critical Black studies tradition have named and critiqued respectability politics for its equation of "better behavior" with "better treatment," upholding conservative mainstream values, de-emphasizing sexuality, and policing one's own community through adherence to white middle-class norms. Normative markers of respectability are often calibrated to certain notions of individual and community success: a trim and contained body and appetite (Cox 2015), the pursuit of higher education, the innocence of being "brought" to this country at a young age. The notion of being *unapologetic*—to not be sorry for "failing" to meet those conservative norms and thus to flagrantly refuse them—has risen in respectability's wake, turning refusal of such norms and the embrace of joy and pleasure into key political gestures of the late liberal era (Shange 2016; a. m. brown 2019).

In the weeks after Brenda's death, Shi told me about meeting up with another former member of the Colectiva. She described how good and healing it felt just to hang out together, smoke bud, bake cookies, and talk about Brenda Mendoza and the lack of support for mental illness among women of color. Shi's vision was generating and holding a space without the surveillance of philanthropy to determine what counted as acceptable healing behavior; she just wanted a space for women to be themselves and together, without threat of sanction. I jumped on board with this vision, eager to support her as well as hold dedicated space together as we had done before.

We decided to pilot the circles where she was employed at the time, a downtown Salinas methadone clinic. It was a nondescript, beige, and shabby space, cluttered with locked doors to rooms with internal windows for surveillance of what was going on inside. The clinic followed a harm reduction, medicine-assisted treatment (MAT) model but had empty space on its schedule on Friday afternoons, when most counselors did not have appointments, daily doses had already been distributed, and a larger room near the back was free. Our new circle was emphatically not part of the clinic's harm reduction method and therapeutic apparatus, but an opportunistic occupying of its space and engagement with its clientele on radically different terms than the biomedical. Shi's supervisor gave her the leeway to mobilize her healing-informed training without much oversight, asking us to collect demographic data on participants and submit briefs of each circle but never collecting either—which was fortunate, since we did not want to provide that data.

Through her role as a counselor at this clinic, Shi was getting to know a wide cross section of Salinas residents caught up, to varying degrees, in opioid use, increasingly common among *Mexicano*, Chicanx, and Latinx residents in the region. While they came from diverse socioeconomic and ethnic backgrounds, most of her clients were Mexican American, and a considerable proportion lacked stable housing. Twice-monthly counseling sessions were mandated alongside clients' daily methadone dosing at this clinic, and Shi, with her bold makeup and office decked out in Indigenous and Chicana paraphernalia, quickly distinguished herself there as pleasantly different from the other half dozen counselors on staff. The other counselors were generally former opioid users but had forged a solidarity among themselves defined against the active users in their care, whom they deemed manipulative, speaking to and of them in patronizing and disdainful ways. Shi, on the other hand, aligned herself with the clients themselves and grew especially close to her female clients. They seemed to appreciate her egalitarian approach and willingness to open up to them too, in particular about her experience as the daughter of a heroin user. Her father had recently passed away after a lifetime of heavy heroin use, and she found a degree of understanding and healing in exploring the different angles of this experience with her clients.

Shi had carefully assembled a list of her clients who she thought would benefit from and be receptive to the circles. From our beds in our motel room another weekend that spring, she described each to me while I took notes:

> Carmela, she's from LA, been clean for two years. She's really cool and nice. We joke that she's like my *tía* [aunt]. She has lots of trauma though. When she was young she got beat up at gunpoint, raped, they threw her out of the car, all sorts of things. She's now in her sixties. Doesn't have a mental illness but she's been having health issues, possibly breast cancer. She says, "If I die, I die"—she doesn't want to get diagnosed but knows something is wrong. If that's true, maybe getting the group of women together will give her the bravery to open up, you know? Maybe it will give her that support. Oh, and she has a little dog, like Chloe. [Chloe was Shi's beloved Chihuahua, recently deceased.] That's her emotional support. Her dog got her out of depression.
>
> Then there's Shellie. She and my dad used to use together. She went to my caseload because she didn't like her other counselor, but it's technically a conflict because we've known each other since we were young. She wants to go to residential care but she's not sure yet. I'm not sure if her kids are OK with her husband. They live in a car all together. He is hardworking, but bipolar and not on his meds, so they have their conflicts.
>
> Sophie is another one that's really cool and smart. She lives in Chinatown and everyone knows her and comes to her tent for supplies or support—she says they "come knocking at her door." She wants to write a book about the women in Chinatown. I think she's just really ready to blossom with some more support.

I nodded and scribbled down her descriptions in my notebook. Shi said that she had also told her clients about me, that I was a professor at Sac State but used to be a big part of La Colectiva de Mujeres and had been down with the group while they were out there, protesting police brutality.

"And do any of them know each other?" I asked Shi.

"Sometimes they see each other in, like, the waiting room, but not really," she said. The clinic did not prioritize group connections or social therapeutics. "But I'm selecting the ones that I think will get along with each other. Plus some of them live in the same area, so they should know who they are and build that, like, sisterhood."

Despite being held at the clinic and inviting women who were clients and actively on methadone treatment, the point of our circles was not to address their addictions or compel them to stop using, as many still were. Rather, these circles focused on honoring women in struggle and creating a safe and celebratory space for them, and Shi took a looser approach than she had in the Colectiva. Her facilitation of the circle and the configuration of women who showed up each time created a space where many women were able to be playful, ribald, hurt, and in general as excessive and effusive as they wanted. In this space, unruly affects, substance use, and sexuality could be expressed without penalty of social sanction or death, beyond the conservative limits of the biomedical clinic, the carceral state, and philanthropically funded healing. Here, abundance, togetherness, and the play for healing took up our time and became the primary purpose of each circle.

Reunited . . . and Raunchy

Our third circle at the methadone clinic opened much like the others before it. Shi saw clients on Friday mornings, and I ran around town beforehand to gather supplies: sandwich trays, snacks, and roses from Safeway, small goodies from the Dollar Tree to entertain any kids who were brought along, extra bundles of sage and sticks of *palo santo* from the *botánica* (a store that sells religious or spiritual goods) for the women to take with them afterward. Creating an atmosphere of abundance with good food and small gifts for everyone to feel comfortable and honored became fundamental to the circle itself, especially as we realized that the women we invited were often unable to make it reliably each session or on time. Trouble arranging a lift, childcare issues, "the devil throwing things in the way," as one of them put it, distraction, substances, or any number of reasons kept many from attending consistently.

Paring down and adjusting our plans with each circle, the imperative was holding space to honor the women present, and enjoying a couple of hours of affirmation and connection with each other, as well as lunch, rather than advancing particular teachings or cumulative art and activist projects as we had done with the Colectiva. We saw it as a space where whoever showed up, showed up, and whatever emerged was what had to be discussed that day. We learned on the fly to minimize our own ordering and disciplinary urges to keep the healing praxis in order and on schedule. As the following account should demonstrate, this approach could be unwieldy, but it also allowed for a variety of themes to come out and be addressed. It gave space for us all to understand each other and ourselves a bit better, without expectation of any particular trajectory of healing.

After running all of the pre-circle errands, I arrived at the clinic, and Shi's daughter helped me carry the bags from my car. Shi had already begun setting up the room, moving furniture toward the walls and assembling a few chairs in a circle. The room was decorated with posters in outdated colors and styles, illustrating how various substances affected human bodies, whiteboards, and windows lining the hallway side. The clinic's other counselors occasionally strolled by and peeked in. They were curious about the party-like atmosphere of food, decorations, and laughter that we somehow created in this drab clinical space, and sometimes grabbed a sandwich. We humored them but were not eager for their attention.

One of our circle regulars, a woman in her sixties named Ana, was early as usual; she picked up her weekly take-home methadone dose on Fridays at noon and stuck around the clinic until our circle began at 1:30. Ana was talkative and open. She eagerly began sampling the sandwiches, dips, and cookies as soon as I set it all down. With long-term health troubles and an ongoing family dispute over an inheritance she felt had been stolen from her, she was quick to offer me her updates, as well as share stories about her sassy toddler granddaughter. Ana lived with her sister but hated it, and each week obsessed over the murky legality of her stolen inheritance as she longed for the financial security to live alone.

While Ana sat with a plate of food on her lap, I started to set up a scarf as an altar on the floor, carefully arranging the conch shell, bundles of sage, and crystals that Shi and I brought to each circle. Meanwhile, Shi came in with Annie, a new client in Shi's caseload who was attending the circle for her first time. Her deeply tanned skin was complemented by a brown T-shirt that stated, in capital letters, "LET ME DRINK ABOUT IT," and it was her birthday. I had come prepared with a small chocolate cake from Safeway. Shi was excited because she knew that Annie and Ana were former sisters-in-law who hadn't seen each other in years. As they greeted each other, both seemed thrilled to be reunited, having lost each other's phone numbers years ago. They chatted animatedly and snacked while we finished setting up the space. Shi put some early 1990s hip-hop on her phone, then switched it to rattle-driven peyote music. We waited around a bit in case anyone else stopped in but soon realized that it would just be the four of us today, and that would be fine.

Shi began by lighting the bundle of sage on the altar and explaining why she sent it around for everyone to hold, encouraging Ana and Annie to wave the smoke toward themselves and take calming, quiet breaths. "Just go with the flow . . . we're just sending our energy out and just having positive thoughts. And if you guys want to take some sage, to bless yourselves . . . ," she trailed off as she passed the bundle to Annie on her left.

Ana didn't skip a beat when she got a good look at the smoldering bundle. "Does that remind you of anything?" she asked her former sister-in-law, with mirth in her nasal voice.

"She's bad!!" Annie exclaimed, while we all chuckled. The sage did look like a giant joint.

Ana defended herself, "I can't help it! Since I turned sixty-two, I'm going crazy!"

Annie waved the smoke toward Ana and said quietly to herself, "You gotta bless her."

Normally, passing around the sage is the point at which healing circles become hushed and sacralized, when everyone has a moment with the medicine and takes the cues to be quiet and introspective. This time, it heralded the beginning of the jokes. Ana found it the ideal moment to share that she "had a dream and I woke up like . . ." and here she panted, as if out of breath. "And I did it! I got off! It's been a long time!"

Shi laughed out loud and exclaimed, "What?!"

Under her breath, Annie said with a sly smile, "Oh my God, she had a wet dream."

Ana confirmed this, and then began talking about her collection of sex toys, to which Annie and Shi added points about how ugly they are. I asked if Ana's granddaughter ever stumbled upon her stash. After some moments of hilarity and the vision of a mousy older woman like Ana taking the batteries out of her red sex toy so it wouldn't turn on if found by a small child, Shi tried to rein us in and back to the saging.

"So we're just gonna bless ourselves, we want to honor our time, we wanna honor Annie, all of us, for being here. We're just gonna use the space for whatever we need today and then just go from there. And just say prayers, this is the medicine, sage and *palo santo*, to cast out the negative energy and bring in the good ones, where sometimes we block 'em out for a reason, but this is a good energy and we try to bring it in."

Ana, quietly and seriously this time, said, "I don't wanna be hateful no more."

We moved toward the check-in part of the circle, where each person is asked to share a *carga* and a *regalo*, baggage that is bothering them and a gift, whatever they are grateful for on this day. As we have seen, this ritual of *descargando* was an incredibly potentiated phase of each Colectiva *círculo* and an integral part of the group's embodied praxis of mutuality and world-building. Shi prompted Annie for her gift first.

"I dunno, I'm really going through it right now. But I got good people in my life. That's a gift. Good people."

"And, do you have any baggage?"

"Oh, I got too much baggage! You don't want my baggage." We left it there.

Ana went next. "Mine's just that, I'm happy that I'm alive, I'm sixty-two." Annie joked that "everyone says that" but let her continue. "My baggage is that I'm still waiting for SSI and I have to find out where that money went to." She was referring to her inheritance, which "my daughter has, because SSI won't give me any money until we figure out where that is. . . . So, I'm just waiting for money."

This disturbed Annie greatly. While Shi and I knew all too well about Ana's inheritance issues, it was new to Annie, and she began questioning Ana about who she had talked to about it. Annie vowed to help her former sister-in-law by connecting her with her lawyer, and planned to call him after the circle. They exchanged numbers, calling over Shi's daughter to tap Ana's number into the other's phone. Ana lamented that her lack of money was preventing her from moving out from her sister's place, informing Annie that "the good sister" died two years ago and she was left with this one, wondering, "Where will I live after my sister dies if I don't have that money?! I don't even have a car. I don't want to live in a recycling box . . ."

Annie told us that she often slept in her car, and then it was Ana's turn to be appalled. "I'm gonna call our landlord for you! He owns a bunch of places and he's gotta have something for you."

It was my turn for gifts and baggage, and I shared the good news that I had eloped with my partner, but given the housing insecurities that had just surfaced, I left out that we partly did so in order to buy a house together. I didn't feel like dropping that stark inequity into this space so blatantly—it would create distance between us when the joking was bringing us closer. Shi already knew about our homeownership plans and smiled peacefully, while Ana asked enthusiastically if he was cute. I replied yes. No baggage for me, I said, and turned the floor over to Shi.

Shi's *carga* was that she missed cooking for her kids, and that she hardly saw her adult sons anymore, now that they had lost their place and she was living in a shelter with just her daughter. But "once we all come back together we can appreciate each other more, and I'm happy about that." She also shared that an important anniversary approached, June 20, the day some years back she had seen a young man pass away in front of her, as a first responder dispatched to a gang-related shooting. It was his death, and the connection she made with the young man's girlfriend, that pushed Shi toward Chicanx-Indigenous cultural healing as integral to her life and work. Through the story, she transitioned from her *carga* to a broader framing of what we were doing in the circle, telling us, "I'm happy you're all here. . . . I know it's a little bit difficult, life happens, crisis, pain, lots of things kick in, and it's really hard to tell sometimes. But thank you for trusting us, for being here. We wanted to talk today about honoring yourself, your inner child, your person, but things shift and we want to keep it open, just kind of checking in and having that conversation, but also having it guided to build on the strengths that we have already. Because sometimes we don't see our strengths or we don't acknowledge who we are as women. Personal experience should be honored, it should be recognized."

Reading the room and deciding not to get too deep into any particular topic, she signaled to me to start closing the circle by asking the group what other kinds of topics they might find useful to talk about in future circles. I mentioned some themes that had already emerged, like financial insecurity. Annie piped in immediately, "Yeah, housing! Like seeing what kind of grants we could get to find help."

Shi interjected, "Yes! When we had our old Colectiva, we did a lot of advocacy work. You just mentioned most of the time you sleep in your car. Who else would know how to advocate for homelessness support?" She was emphasizing the value of experiences that are often denigrated, trying to reframe them and imagine other possibilities for them to be acted upon, so they could be seen as resources of wisdom. "You could maybe get a position to advocate from your experiences, you've already been through that . . . for everyone in Chinatown."

Annie lit up at this idea, sharing that she had long wanted to be a motivational speaker of sorts, "like to go into the juvenile hall and talk to the kids that haven't really got too deep into gangs yet, tell 'em how it really is. They don't give a shit about you, the gangs."

"So we could have a workshop about telling your story a certain way," I suggested, bringing up an idea that had been popular in the original Colectiva. Annie somewhat ignored the suggestion, which made me think she didn't see herself needing any help telling her story or offering it to youngsters to warn them away from the life she'd had. She launched instead into a story about how she had deterred her own daughter from becoming a Norteña by taking her to a grimy flophouse filled with heroin users, people who "smoked KJ" and had just got out of prison.

"The next day, she turned mod!!" Annie roared. "She was scared straight!" The four of us laughed, and we asked for more details about her daughter, which Annie provided, while telling us about her niece as well.

But as she told stories about her niece, her voice got thick, and we could see she was starting to cry. "It just hurts so much," she said, explaining her tears. Her niece, we found out then, had been hit by a train in Chinatown three or so weeks before this, while high and hanging out in the encampment. Chinatown, a shorthand for the hub of tents and shelters at the center of Salinas, was built around the Amtrak line and formed the center of the local drug trade. It was active and tumultuous there after dark, and news of people being shot, overdosing, or dying on the tracks was common if often thin on description. The city had recently begun locking the public toilets there overnight due to lack of funding for security, making the nighttime an increasingly dangerous period for the women who lived or hung out in Chinatown and needed to venture into the darkness to relieve themselves.

Shi had not known about Annie's niece beforehand. We caught each other's eyes, clearly surprised at the affective pivots in what Annie had shared. She said a bit more about her niece and told some stories about their relationship over the years before Shi asked each of us to say something positive and supportive to Annie as clearly she was feeling a lot of pain. When it was my turn to speak, I said to Annie that she seemed to really enjoy telling those stories and encouraged her to focus on the good memories. Shi reminded us that each day is a celebration of life and especially so that day, as it was Annie's birthday. It was time for cake.

We finished up the circle eating chocolate cake, chatting, laughing, and listening to doo-wop oldies on Shi's phone, eventually stepping out to the alley behind the clinic so we could all sage off and Annie could have a cigarette. The scent of the tobacco and sage, two medicines, intermingled as we stood around in the interstice, enjoying the afternoon sun and the connections we'd made or rekindled. The two sisters-in-law were making plans to help each other out with their various situations, and telling a few more dirty jokes for us while they had the chance. As we cleaned up, everyone took home extra food, sage, and roses, to be enjoyed themselves or, as Shi suggested at the end of each circle, shared with another woman who couldn't be in the circle that day.

The flow of this circle, and the themes that emerged in what the four of us shared, laughed, and cried about, sketch out the important work of making space for various aspects of these lives we could categorize in the zeitgeist vernacular of "a little extra" even as they emerge from profound insecurity, isolation, and fear. Ana and Annie's playfulness let them connect and carry on as, presumably, they had when they were younger, while approaching deep-seated struggles in their lives. They let Shi and me in on their jokes and shared their pain, having established connections through an abundance of laughter, pleasure, and tasty food. This play was not done solely in the service of healing but contributed to it in essential ways: surfacing pain, connecting individuals into resurgent coalition, and smoothing the path forward.

Honoring Play and Pleasure

Norma Mendoza-Denton, in her ethnography *Homegirls* (2008), writes lovingly of clowning and raunchy linguistic play among her interlocutors as an intimate part of working-class Chicana social life and the stoic chola ethos of "laugh now cry later." However, she concludes her analysis sharply with the observation that such "speech routines lead to instances of misrecognition and stereotyping," suggesting that these perceived transgressions ultimately harm the young women themselves. She does not make a claim for these forms of play as a legitimate part of a gendered praxis of self-determination, or a vital experimentation with liberation in the face of violence. What would it mean, as part of an anthropological praxis, to imagine and enact a world made safe for these expressions? Or, even better, how could we imagine and enact a world where these expressions are encouraged, acknowledged, and honored?

That imagination, or rather its expansion and enactment, is the implicit goal of this chapter. In examining three ludic, pleasurable moments with radically divergent outcomes—Brenda Mendoza's killing, Shi getting fired but returning to healing on her own terms, and Ana and Annie reconnecting and building new forms of presence for each other in an emphatically ribald circle—it becomes clear that there is immense but variable potentiality in play. It should also be clear that playfulness involves dramatically high stakes for women of color who are subject to the stringent criteria of respectability or deservingness of care, whether as adjudicated by the carceral state or by conservative private sector philanthropy. The gendered and racialized context of the instances of play featured here—housing insecurity, trauma and mental illness, recreational drug use, and the default carcerality of social services—is a widely shared set of conditions for life in late liberal California and the United States more broadly. It can all seem intractable, impossible to chip away at. Yet through ethnographic attention and a fugitive research agenda that attempts to support and help to sow these practices and spaces, we hold together the pain of these women's experiences alongside their refusal to let it overwhelm them. We amplify the ways they build play and indulgence into their lives when they can, and direct material and epistemological capital to this abundance.

Movement scholar adrienne maree brown writes about how she has come to realize that "facts, guilt and shame are limited motivations for creating change, even though those are the primary forces we use in our organizing work. I suspect that to really transform our society, we will need to make justice one of the most pleasurable experiences we can have" (2017, 33). Her subsequent text, *Pleasure Activism* (2019), is a dialogic treatise on the critical role of bodily pleasure in social justice work, with pleasure broadly defined to encompass practices that spark happiness and satisfaction. Drawing on Audre Lorde's (2007) theorizing of the erotic as power, brown reminds us that the sharing of joy connects those who have been individualized and isolated, founded in deeply embodied knowledge of what we each need to live with integrity. She argues that though all deserve pleasure, the pleasure of those most impacted by oppression should be prioritized. "Where we have been socialized to believe only scarcity exists," or been disqualified for care or life when centering bodily pleasures like these forms of play, brown argues for building spaces and relations that allow us to tap into those deep wells of abundance, energy, and power (a. m. brown 2019, 13).

The play tracked in this chapter should be understood through this framework of pleasure and erotics and, accordingly, as powerful and critically important in emergent enactments of an otherwise. Whether successfully or not, these instances of play were experiments with new relationships and forms of presence—novel attempts to affirm embodied experience and defiance of norms, in recognition of the deep wounds inflicted by gendered and racialized experiences of structural and interpersonal violence. Though there were times when I left these new circles wondering how "effective" they had been, realizing that the presence and playfulness made possible in each was enough helped me to shake off those latent liberal expectations of progress and its proof. As experiments, the impacts of each circle were unknown from the outset, unlimited by predefined criteria. These are the intimate abolitionist practices that can accrue and grow into more durative aspects of an anticarceral world or at least, per local parlance, a "healthy community."

There are distinct limitations to this effort: Ana and Annie, and women like them, need more support than a fun Friday afternoon and a good lunch. Shi remains largely unacknowledged and unremunerated in Salinas for her brilliant ability to hold cultural healing space for women. Most acutely, Brenda Mendoza should still be alive and present with her daughter. But as Shi put it, "We're just planting the *semillas* [seeds] in these circles. We don't know what's going to take root, or for who, but something is going to grow from it. Even if we don't see it." We have had to be satisfied with this, even if we would like the world to be otherwise more quickly and more discernibly. These circles, at least, were a taste of freedom for some women, an experimentation with a beautiful and nourishing otherwise in Brenda's name, making space to be playful and connected and to celebrate life in the process.

Conclusion

Closing the Circle

With a heavy paper bag of snacks from Target in one arm, and my three-month-old, Alice, in the other, I entered Eli's warm house. Pamela squealed, approaching me from the living room, and we hugged, hands and hearts full.

It was good to see her. It was sad to see her. I had last seen Pamela four years earlier, in 2018, when I had just moved to Sacramento, and her daughter Rachel was entering a residential addiction program a short bike ride from my house. I met them both there for a visit and had coffee with Pamela afterward, as she shared her plans to move in with her daughter and keep her on a good track.

It didn't work out as hoped. Pamela ended up moving to Florida to live with her other daughter. Now she was back in Salinas in tragedy. Rachel had passed away, and Pamela was here to inter her daughter next to her son, Christopher, at a cemetery in South Salinas.

When I learned this sad news, posted on Facebook, I wrote to Pamela but quickly texted Shi as well. Rachel and Shi had been close when the Colectiva was still active. Pamela and Rachel were almost always there in circle, and they reliably showed up for the group's advocacy work. Where Pamela was fiery and outspoken, Rachel was often silent, but present, and took in her surroundings. She didn't share much, but when she did it carried weight. As we learned, she had felt—had been—excluded from or diminished within so many spaces that were supposed to be supportive. Like others, she felt punished rather than cared for by counseling, rehousing, and addiction services, spaces that evidenced the "wraparound" reaches of the state carceral apparatus (J. Flores 2016). When she landed with the Colectiva, it was a relief to be accepted for who she was, not diminished by what she had been through. She quietly thrived being surrounded by other strong women who were open about their struggles. That gave her strength, too. Shi and I set in motion plans to hold a memorial circle to honor Rachel and support Pamela.

I want to stop dwelling in loss, but there has been so much of it in this decade of work with the healing collectives. These deaths permeate this project and cannot be ignored, deflected, or absorbed into jargon or analysis. As I hope to have shown, however, there is always more than pain at stake in the losses grieved and endured by the Mujeres, underscoring how much they continue to honor and fight for each other's lives and distill possibility from their relationships. And beyond this integrity to what has happened, thinking through Rachel's memorial circle sketches out some answers to the questions that have emerged in this book: What justice, relief, or transformation has cultural healing made possible? What ground has the Ollin remade, and what now is the terrain of struggle? What can be learned through this attempt to develop and convey an Otherwise Anthropology—a commitment to liberatory projects that exceeds conventional academic mandates or slim versions of solidarity—and what are its limits?

In this book, I have shown how the members of the Salinas healing collectives, and especially the Mujeres of the Colectiva, have walked together. Borrowing Patrisia Gonzales's terms (2012), I have attempted to amplify how re-membering cultural healing praxis generated affirmative reframing of ancestral knowledges and collective futures. This integration of *cultura* into everyday life generated a framework for feeling, knowing, and doing otherwise, growing all that was already beautiful in Salinas but had perhaps been obscured. In times of acute struggle and diffuse, ongoing violence, the Mujeres have re-membered Chicanx-Indigenous cultural healing praxis to reframe their understandings and relations, creating new possibilities in the process. They have done this in the quotidian and ceremonial spaces of their days, while addressing, refusing, and dismantling the carceral institutions and logics that permeate their lives and kinship. Sometimes these logics surfaced as criminalization or dispossession, or misogyny laced with classism, disrespect, or disdain for raw femininity; the misrecognition of incredible strength and fugitive knowledge as disqualifying excess or liability. Showing how they address this violence, I have sought to convey the distinct sense of possibility, love, and otherwise that often suffused our gatherings and connections.

Eli had made *pozole verde* and filled sturdy Styrofoam bowls to the brim for each of us. We decorated our bowls with avocado and slathered tostadas with crema while we waited for everyone to arrive and got caught up. Pamela was asking Yarri about her new job, working with *cultura* at a youth wellness organization in nearby Watsonville, in still-more-progressive and better-resourced Santa Cruz County. We all chimed in periodically with sounds of pride and encouragement at this new gig and how well she and her young family were doing, as she brought cultural healing into the lives of the next generation. The conversation turned to Pamela's career at Soledad State Correctional Facility with "the lifers," as she called them, successfully advocating to have their sentences reduced so they could go free. As always happened when we gathered in any configuration of Mujeres, we talked about the police homicides in 2014, reminiscing about all the actions and bitter disputes of the time. Pamela noted how the homicides "made so much possible," bringing new funding and energy to the community, clearing space for new projects to be grown.

Rosa arrived with bundles of medicine for all of us, which she had harvested from her East Salinas backyard. We each received long sheaves of lavender with a sprig of *romero* in each, and she had brought an extra bunch of *ruda* for Pamela with the instruction to bathe with it. Rosa sat next to me and took Alice on her lap so I could scoop up the last bit of broth in my bowl. She was wearing a cloth mask due to the ongoing COVID-19 pandemic, but her eyes danced with delight at this new life. I remembered how much I could learn about the world just from the affect conveyed in Rosa's reactions.

Next to the dining table, chairs and a couch surrounded a coffee table on which Pamela had begun placing items in Rachel's memory, like the ceramic heart Shi had given Rachel years ago. She asked me to take a picture of it to send to Shi, who couldn't attend. I brought out the photos I had developed for this altar, images of Rachel among other members of the Colectiva. Pamela smiled as she flipped through them, recalling the moments outside of the sweat lodge or just after a Board of Supervisors meeting where one or another photo was taken. We arranged each carefully on the table. The sadness was starting to slice into the joy of our reunion.

"Rachel should be here," Pamela grimaced. "She isn't in a better place."

Rosa opened the circle, honoring the four directions, thanking the plants for offering themselves and for rooting us. She directed smoke from the sage toward our eyes, so we could see; our ears, so we could hear; hearts, so we could feel; our bellies, so we could digest; and our legs, so that we could walk forward. Sage burned in a small bowl as we stayed quiet for a time, letting Pamela express herself.

Her head bowed, she nodded sadly for a long moment. When she was ready, she whispered, "I can't scream anymore. Remember when I screamed and yelled that sorry wasn't enough, this pain never goes away, that this was how we speak out?" That *grito* opened this book and echoes throughout.

Pamela gestured upstairs where her daughter Serenity was trying to sleep. Still whispering, she said, "I can't scream. I need to support her and help her feel strong so she can rest." She thanked Rosa and all of us for bringing medicine, and for letting her and her daughters be part of these "cultural" ways. She emphasized that there would be no pastor at Rachel's funeral the next day, just medicine.

We went around the circle sharing our memories of Rachel. Holding the *palabra* piece, I struggled, trying to say something that conveyed what I felt and remembered of Rachel, while also not speaking too loudly to wake Alice sleeping on my chest. I felt that nothing I could say sufficed to express the ways I would remember Rachel or how much she had been loved in the Colectiva—a familiar feeling of inadequacy for anyone who has tried to write about love. Just as she had expressed when the Colectiva was still active, Pamela reassured me: it's not what you say, it's how we walk together. It's not about being here for you, but about being here with you.

* * *

Projects like La Colectiva de Mujeres are precious, and precarious. Many working on the nonprofit scene in Salinas have recognized that the Mujeres were doing the "real work" of cultural healing as a form of social change: working intimately within families, making space for multigenerational *cargas* to come down, evolving and nourishing their relationships of affiliation, and celebrating each other as a practice of nurturance in a weathering world. But that theory in the flesh clashed with The California Endowment's philanthropic theory of change. This disciplinary edge to healing, revealing health philanthropy's entrenched respectability ethos, suggests the incompatibility of decolonizing and anticarceral embodiments of power with liberal institutional tools in criminalized and stressed communities working on abolition.[1]

This incompatibility, however, is not inherently a limitation. Beyond the Colectiva's existence as a funded group, the relationships fostered through it ran deep and became embedded in our lives. "We really are a family," as Yarri put it in that circle for Rachel. "We may not see each other all the time, but we come together and nothing has changed." The Colectiva's trajectory reminds us that otherwise transformations are humble and ever partial, and that a project's potentiality can take many directions and iterations as it is "lived into" (Crawley 2016). At Rachel's circle, I was reminded in new ways that the point of the Colectiva was not to get back together in the same exact formation but to keep moving through our own lives and spaces, embodying its core understandings in our various endeavors and relationships. Or, as Shi had said, "*ponemos las semillas*" (we're planting the seeds), and we don't even know what kinds of wild and unexpected otherwises might take form. Erstwhile members of the Colectiva embodied and lived into its possibilities in myriad ways as they turned to medicine, recalled teachings, stayed connected and sowed strong relationships with other women, and affirmed their own and one another's worth. They continued to hold space for each other. They could see and know themselves differently, through a framework of power and relation; living into that understanding, they could remake the world around them to reflect and reproduce it. The Mujeres' everyday and often unremarkable "spiritual activism" was an emphatic and deeply embodied refusal of oppression that surged with joy, pain, and sisterhood (Anzaldúa 2015). In these ways, symbolic and epistemic shifts are enacted, becoming worldly and tangible.

Nevertheless, as this book has shown, there are distinct limits to epistemic frameworks when material resources are thin. Rachel has passed, as have Lisa and Gina, other raw women who found a home among the Mujeres. Their deaths were premature, induced by chronic stress, substance use or abuse, inaccessible health care, and poverty. If the Colectiva had endured, would these women have made it longer as well? To what lengths can we trace out or imagine the impacts of this life-affirming group and its cultural healing praxis? How can we make the world less exhausting, less weathering for each other? These are questions that get at the indefinite time lapse between symbolic and epistemic shifts, and material transformation.

In contrast with the Colectiva, MILPA, the other Salinas healing collective featured in this book, has become an embedded community institution in the decade since it was founded in 2013. It has a multifaceted and ever-growing set of offerings, as well as connections with other Indigenous organizations around the United States and world. It has earned widespread recognition for its impacts and outlived the Building Healthy Communities era. The work of MILPA is firmly grounded in cultural healing and is explicitly anticarceral: from the juvenile hall reduction, to the support MILPA offers local residents in expunging their criminal records through Proposition 47, to successfully advocating for local school districts to refuse funding for school resource officers (in other words, defunding uniformed police in schools).

Though some of these initiatives could be interpreted as "reformist reforms" on their own, attempts that ultimately rearrange and reproduce rather than dismantle carcerality (Gilmore 2007), their alignment with MILPA's other projects to create new formations of presence and affirmation indicate a deeper "nonreformist" core. Telpochcalli, for example, is an in-house curriculum for systems-impacted youth to learn more about their cultural heritage as well as cultivate critical consciousness, imparting a liberatory and transformative, healing education. Juan and I, along with our colleague Desiree, began conducting collaborative research into the impacts of Telpochcalli, which means "House of Youth" in Nahuatl, in 2020. Our findings demonstrate how the program directly counters the sense of negation and criminalization that many Chicanx and Latinx youth experience in mainstream schools, where white supremacist norms of behavior, bodies, knowledge, and success are imposed on them at the expense of their own self-worth.[2] This is just one example of how MILPA's work and praxis generate otherwise realizations and engagements for youth in the region daily. And, perhaps because of the threats to existing norms posed by MILPA's transformative work, its members also continue to weather the threats to their organization and themselves, as local media and police resort to slanderous criminalizing tropes and falsely associate MILPA, its members and staff, or its anticarceral campaigns with gang activity. Carceral logics, honed to efficacy over the modern era, continue to be mobilized by state agents to ensnare those who have worked hardest and most creatively to dismantle them.

While the two healing collectives have taken radically different trajectories, their respective approaches to and embodiments of cultural healing offer a few conclusions. One is that the philanthropic context of their initial emergence and relative (dis)continued support did not overdetermine their impacts or potential, though it did shape the interventions each collective could envision and enact. Like the post–Chicano Movement era relationship between health conversion foundations and Chicanx-Indigenous groups discussed in chapter 2, The California Endowment and Building Healthy Communities offered resources to the Salinas collectives that mattered at the time, making it possible for some residents to run with and build out their own visions. The ever-savvy MILPA was largely able to sustain its philanthropic investment while sowing transformative spaces, relations, and practices, expanding upon and doing more than expected with TCE's epistemic and material resources. As Shi summed it up to me, "BHC put a lot of money into our community. They had a lot of money for everything you wanted, like, whatever, there was so much money." However, ever recursive to philanthropy's liberal foundation, this money was bound up in stark disciplinary norms. The raw women of the Colectiva were punished for being the least beholden to bureaucracy and most willing to fight, scream, and dream for radical change. "We were driven by our own agenda," as Shi continued. "We were pretty raw and uncut. And we held space." I hope the vitality of the Mujeres' approach, untethered to and in defiance of philanthropic constraint, suffuses this book like the smell of rosemary and lavender in the air.

The distinct, enduring, and diverse approaches of MILPA and the Colectiva, among other groups that took up the work of cultural healing, make clear that healing was never simply a product of top-down philanthropy-approved campaigns, but a movement forwarded by the former and continuing residents of Salinas in a variety of ways and sites. This book has depicted a snippet of that long movement, the sometimes-slow rumble of the Ollin, ever shifting the terrain of struggle in Salinas and the Chicanx-Indigenous struggle to decolonize and decarcerate. The work is obviously not complete. Aiming to reject, reduce, or eliminate police presence in the region, and demand alternatives to incarceration and carceral logics as they permeate all social life, must be unfolded alongside the work of building otherwise, being present with and honoring one another, and living into another world as the deep violences of the old one are eroded. This sounds like the Indigenous resurgence described and desired by Leanne Betasamosake Simpson, where Indigenous ways of knowing and relating are placed at the center of world-building in everyday forms, aside from any claims on the state. "I'm interested in alternatives," she writes, in refusal of a concept of justice thoroughly steeped in settler colonialism and state recognition. "I'm interested in building new worlds" (2016, 31). That everyday resurgence is in motion in Salinas and elsewhere in Chicanx-Indigenous spaces.

* * *

It is important to close a circle, so that all present can disperse feeling renewed and cohered, not burdened or in turmoil.

At Eli's house, as we closed the circle for Rachel's memorial, Pamela took the lead. She reminded us that whenever someone gets in her car, she asks them, "What is it that you want? What is it that you *really* want?" Yarri brought up how she was in Pamela's car when she first heard, years ago, that her college tuition funding was coming through and that she got approved for an apartment, so she and her daughter could move out of the shelter and she could pursue an associate's degree. Something about the story was almost mystical: the Mujeres really did make the world otherwise for each other in those moments, eliciting and amplifying each other's potential. So, what was it that we all really wanted to take with us from the circle?

Eli said, "Courage."

I offered, "Groundedness."

Yarri, "A moment of peace or stillness."

And Rosa, "Collective awakening."

To close this book, I suggest a few final takeaways. In a project oriented by Otherwise Anthropology, my goal has not been to know more: to know what members of MILPA or the Mujeres were doing for the sake of data itself, exercising a kind of ethnographic surveillance that only builds social capital for the author. Rather, my goal has been to know differently: to evoke and share how the healing collectives' wide repertoire of cultural healing practices did the iterative and everyday work of undoing carcerality, a deeply entrenched system of power, prone as it is to expansion.

I may be the sole listed author of this text, but the vast majority of it was fomented collaboratively, in conversation and consultation with key members of both La Colectiva de Mujeres and MILPA. By providing an account of cultural healing practices and scenes with interlocutors, writing up our interpretations, and circulating them to new audiences, I hope this text has forwarded some of the goals held by these collectives and the broader movement. The interventions on carcerality made through cultural healing have limits, but that does not discount its impact, nor does it foreclose its potentiality, especially in localized contexts and particular lives and relations. In the understandings offered in these pages, I have intended for the potentiality of cultural healing as decolonial, anticarceral, and abolitionist world-making to be held open and expanded. As Alexis Shotwell (2011) argued, knowing otherwise enlarges collective consciousness about what transformation looks like and how it happens. Knowing otherwise comes through shared bodily practice and the divergences it can produce, but also through relational modes like *conocimiento* and *descargando*, getting to know the lives, experiences, and visions of people like Shi, Pamela, Juan, and so many others. This endeavor of knowing differently, I hope, provokes conscription and complicity in a set of ideas and a political vision, as we slowly undo the carceral frameworks of our world and get into different relation with each other.

This effort can't bring back Rachel, or Brenda Mendoza, or the four men killed by the Salinas Police Department in 2014, but it can plant seeds in their honor. The knowledge and ways of knowing generated and conveyed through an Otherwise Anthropology are an invitation: to let these teachings land in readers' own lives; to consider the ways we are all impacted by the malignancy of our abiding carceral systems; to realize the habits or unexamined ways of thinking that reproduce carceral logics; and to build otherwise in alignment, accordingly, like "constellations of co-resistance" across time and space (Betasamosake Simpson 2016).

To push further, I want to amplify the call for active coalition and fugitivity, made possible through community-led anthropological collaboration, grounded in shared bodily praxis. An Otherwise Anthropology nurtures engagement that runs deeper and is more durative and less disciplined than performances of solidarity. These engagements, which will look different in each field site and per the ethnographer's relative positionality, should be tended and nourished throughout the manifold aspects of academic labor and inequality, and made transparent. This is not to turn it into a spectacle of doing good—especially when the ethnographer is in a position of relative privilege or benefits from whiteness—but to make clear and normalize practices like codesigning research projects; writing employment or funding for our interlocutors/collaborators within grant applications; strategizing with these same key co-thinkers about how, where, and why we share our findings; and other equitable distributions of social and material capital.[3]

We may now call these strategies "fugitive" because they tend to contradict the supposed autonomy or authority of the scholar, or may be interpreted as tampering with sociocultural phenomena we should primarily be documenting. These are among the ways that ethnographers can be a conduit to academia and elsewhere for the transformations provoked by the otherwise projects we "study." The revolution will not be funded (see INCITE! Women of Color against Violence 2009), and the academy will definitely not "win" the revolution. However, we can attempt to rework the relations of anthropological research and the communities we endeavor to understand and affirm, as we find and foreground ways to be in right relation with, and accountable to, the otherwise projects remaking the world around us.

ACKNOWLEDGMENTS

Every bit of researching, imagining, writing, and rewriting this book has been a labor of love. Thank you to all who have brought your care and good spirits to this process.

I was taught in Salinas to name my parents first. Thank you, Petra and Moses, for the support and space to embark on a series of peregrinations that led me to Vancouver, Amsterdam, Salinas, Charlottesville, and Sacramento. Thank you to my grandparents, Pilwi and Max, and Sarah (Carmen) and Solomon, for giving us rich lives filled with nourishment, possibility, and curiosity.

I am immensely grateful to folks in Salinas for sharing so much with me over the years. Shi, it is a true honor to be your friend, *comadre*, confidante, and collaborator. Pamela, your strength and kindness inspire me every single day. Juan, I am grateful to call you a brother and a teacher. Jesús, I could not have begun this research without your friendship and support navigating life in Salinas. To the folks at MILPA past and present, especially George, Rene, Elias, Airam, Edgar, Desiree, and Keylin, thank you for showing me what it means to have *palabra*. Yarri, Vicky, Juanita, Maria G., Maria B., Diana, Araceli, Willow, Tatyana, and all of the Mujeres both featured in and inspiring this book, thank you for trusting me with your stories over the years. I appreciate you all beyond words.

To my teachers: thank you to Patrick Moore at the University of British Columbia, for early guidance and inspiration, and to Yolanda van Ede at the Universiteit van Amsterdam, for modeling incredible passion and creativity for this impressionable anthropologist-in-training. Thank you to Jarrett Zigon, whose support for my PhD came to me first in a dream somewhere along the Camino de Santiago and who has never ceased to be a great mentor and friend.

A big shout-out to the co-thinkers, close friends, and communities who have supported this work as it unfolded over many years: Lex

Kuiper and Stine Grinna, my colleague-soulmates; Sylvia Tidey and Annemarie Samuels, true icons; brilliant and wonderful fellow PhDs Hasan Ashraf, Annelieke Driessen, Mark Hann, Hanna Henao, Efecan Inceoglu, Willemijn Krebbekx, Justine Laurent, Carola Tize, and maybe too many others to name at the AISSR; and Boudewijn Snoeck, whose friendship and memory I treasure. I am especially grateful for the brilliance and levity of collaborators and dear friends Laura McTighe and David Flood. Megan Farren, thank you for running a daycare that is a second home for my children; without your labor of care this book could not have been completed during these very full years.

Huge appreciation goes to the student assistants at Sac State who have offered research (and moral!) support along the way—Katelyn Graff, Jovan Virag, Victoria Heyn, Rebecca Machain, Amie Yebra, and Rebecca Estrada. I deeply value your insights and care with this work. Thank you to my fantastic colleagues at Sacramento State, especially Terri Castañeda, Ana Gutierrez, Clara Scarry, and Michael Walker, for your support and enthusiasm for this work.

Parts of this book were greatly enhanced by the feedback gained through presentations at the University of California, Los Angeles; Dartmouth University; the London School of Hygiene and Tropical Medicine; and the London School of Economics, as well as too many AAA panels to name. Funding from the Wenner-Gren Foundation, the Spencer Foundation, the Universiteit van Amsterdam, and California State University, Sacramento has been very much appreciated. Thank you to the many anonymous reviewers who have so generously engaged with my work, and the editors who have shepherded it along, especially Jennifer Hammer at NYU Press.

Finally, Matt, Jonathan, Carmen, and Alice, my big-little family: your love and chaos keep me grounded and teach me about the world in wild new ways. I am grateful to have had so many beloved distractions while writing this book.

NOTES

INTRODUCTION

1. MILPA is the acronym for Motivating Individual Leadership for Public Advancement. The word *milpa* also refers to a traditional Mesoamerican system of agriculture.
2. A chola, in this context, is a girl or woman who is gang-identified, typically with a strong relationship to where she is from (her barrio or neighborhood or block). Cholas are associated with an iconic aesthetic of wing-tipped eyeliner, drawn-on eyebrows, and particular lipstick and hairstyle choices associated with their gang.
3. Most names have been changed, in keeping with interlocutors' preferences.
4. In California, there are two broad associations of Mexican and Mexican American gangs, Norteños and Sureños, or Northerners and Southerners/Southsiders. Norteños skew Mexican American and are associated with the Nuestra Familia prison gang. Sureños typically present themselves as more *Mexicano/a* and are connected to the Mexican Mafia prison gang.
5. Caló is an argot rooted in post–World War II Chicano cultural and linguistic practice, with origins in the Pachuco subculture of Los Angeles and Southern California.
6. In official US racial categories, Latinx/Hispanic is typically offered as a secondary ethnic modifier rather than a primary racial category. This is often though not always replicated in carceral demographic data collection instruments. The quality of ethnic data collected across state carceral systems is wildly variable, with some states, including California, leaving ethnicity out of their data collection entirely (Urban Institute 2016). Latinx people are thus excluded or erased from much data collection and analysis, with the implication that Latinx populations held in carceral facilities are often counted as white (Raschig 2019; Loudenback 2020a; Hernandez 2019). This minimizes or obscures the racial disparities that exist in US carceral systems. At various points in modern American history, Latinx groups have sought to be recognized as white to access or accrue the privileges of whiteness (Salinas 2015; Haney-López 2004; Escobar 1999). However, the legal and social constructions of race and whiteness often do not align, and even if they are "counted as white" in flawed demographic data, many Latinx people will continue to face discrimination based on their appearance and identity (Salinas 2015, 19).
7. Before deciding where exactly I could conduct my research, in January 2013 I visited a few potential field sites around California: the Imperial Valley, Bakers-

field, and Salinas. Each site is home to significant populations of farmworker families and a variable number of community organizations. I met with some of these organizations in each stop during this preliminary visit to introduce myself, learn about what they did, and see if they would support me conducting research in their programming. I was initially interested in the work of *promotoras de salud* (health promoters), or residents who volunteered to educate others in their community about various health and wellness strategies. I was interested in how these *promotoras* shared political ideas and grew critical consciousness through these intimate engagements, at a time when the Affordable Care Act was being implemented and expanded for low-income and undocumented people in the United States. Though I received the go-ahead from one of the directors of a health promotion program in Salinas, when I moved there later that year, I found myself unable to meaningfully access or connect with many of its staff and began to engage in other sites around Salinas to broaden my focus.

8   With some key members of the healing collectives, I conducted two to four interviews. While I did not formally interview all members, I have engaged in ongoing conversations over months or years with many of them.

9   DACA is the acronym for Deferred Action for Childhood Arrivals, the policy that granted temporary protected immigration ("deferred action") status to young people who were "brought" to the United States and who meet a variety of criteria. U visas grant a nonimmigrant status to victims of certain kinds of crimes who work with law enforcement in investigating criminal activity.

10 "The only possible relationship to the university today is a criminal one," announces a heading in chapter 2 of *The Undercommons: Fugitive Planning and Black Study* (Harney and Moten 2013, 26). This means to realize one's place "in" the university but not "of" it, making use of its resources while subverting its neoliberal imperatives.

11 A *comadre* is a person, gendered female, with whom one has a relationship of shared responsibility and care. It is a term of endearment and literally means a co-mother.

12 Obsidian is a volcanic rock associated with the Nahuatl figure of Tezcatlipoca, often translated as "Smoking Mirror." Obsidian's black surface, cut at the right angle, is highly reflective and has been used in prophetic and ritual work to reveal that which is as yet unseen.

CHAPTER 1. OCCUPYING THE NARRATIVE

1   Gilmore's analysis is thoroughly Marxist, relying on Karl Marx's articulation in *Kapital* of how the "relative surplus labor population" is in fundamental service to capitalism and its goals of securing cheap labor through suppressed wages. Robert D. Weide (2022) discusses at length the transgressive potential and thus constant risk of this laboring population contesting those individuals and systems that keep them oppressed; invented notions of crime and enforcement of capture and incarceration aim to neutralize this threat. Even more insidiously, Weide shows,

this invention of crime among the working class serves to "divide and conquer" these populations along racialized axes. These invented racialized divisions are reproduced, unwittingly, through identitarian movements that affirm racial differences, resting on symbolic gains in the absence of material redistribution that would actually challenge capitalist order.

2   These names reflect broad territories, which today may be organized into a variety of tribes and nations. This information was sourced from interlocutors at MILPA, www.native-land.ca, and the websites of local tribes.

3   Journalist Roberto M. Robledo (2014), opening a feature in the local newspaper showcasing East Salinas, described the area as

a mural, banda music, slam poetry, jingle of an ice cream vendor's bell, Spanish tile roofs, a gunshot, police siren, smell of deep frying carnitas, waft of field-fresh strawberries, blue-suited cops, black-hooded criminals, quinceañeras, funerals, church-going immigrants, soccer as religion, women with babies in strollers. [East Salinas] is a sea of stucco houses, it is garages and sheds crammed with families; idled, dirt-poor Mexican laborers, coiffed Latina entrepreneurs in spiked heels, it is pot holes and computerized schools, wayward teenagers, Chicano college coeds, graffiti-scarred fences, green parks.

Robledo concludes his description with a nod to the uncharted possibility of the area as "low expectations and high hopes—and so much more."

4   "The State of the Nation's Housing, 2016," a report by the Joint Center for Housing Studies of Harvard University, listed Salinas as the fifth-most expensive place to live in the United States.

5   Police departments around the United States cultivate this vigilance and compel communication with police as an act of "good citizenship," as noted by Thijs Jeursen in *The Vigilant Citizen* (2023). These forms of "lateral surveillance" corrode community cohesion and enact everyday policing practices that extend beyond police officers themselves (Jeursen 2023, 67–68), demonstrating the pervasive reaches of the carceral state.

6   I made the conscious decision to not engage with members of the Salinas Police Department in conducting and writing up this research. Excellent ethnographies of police and policing exist and contribute to our critical understandings of this central and contested social institution (Cattelino 2004; Jeursen 2023; Mutsaers, Simpson, and Karpiak 2015). I am less interested in their perspectives on police brutality, state violence, and the disproportionate incarceration of *Mexicano*, Chicanx, and Latinx people in Salinas and elsewhere in California and feel that this police department has a strong platform of its own to communicate its message.

7   Perhaps the best-known program combining criminal justice and public health perspectives is Ceasefire, which was developed in Chicago and then adopted around the United States, including in Salinas (Ritter 2009; Roseman n.d.). Ceasefire and other programs like it that combine criminal justice and public health strategies are data-driven and enlist community partners alongside law enforce-

ment to "interrupt" violence as well as promote preventative behaviors. Though some consider Ceasefire to have been moderately successful in Salinas, many members of the healing collectives strongly criticized the approach for disseminating carceral logics in the community and building troves of data on residents that could later be used against them, while posturing as a trust-building and health-oriented effort. In focusing entirely on changing resident behaviors, while centering law enforcement and ignoring structural and societal racism, disinvestment, and legacies of colonial oppression, Ceasefire neglects the root causes of violence in communities like Salinas.

8   The Native American Church is a syncretic and pan-Indigenous religion, founded by Indigenous peoples in the nineteenth century as a response to the impositions and impacts of the reservation system and displacement from ancestral land (Calabrese 2013). Integrating peyote as a sacrament, Native American Church practice combines elements of Indigenous beliefs and Christianity though centers the former, and has been an important space for Indigenous self-determination, power, and alterity (Dawson 2018).

9   Literally "flower and song," *flor y canto* refers to poetic communication and performance, part of the Chicano Movement's artistic legacy.

CHAPTER 2. MAKING THE MOVEMENT OF HEALING

1   A *limpia* is a spiritual or energetic cleansing, often performed by a family member or *curandero/a/x* to determine the cause of an illness, or aim to correct a felt imbalance. The term comes from the Spanish verb *limpiar*, which means "to clean."

2   This recuperation can also be recognized as acts of "mestizo mourning," which Cotera and Saldaña-Portillo characterize as "a psychic restoration of an indigenous past denied [to Chicanx peoples] by exigencies of US colonial history and law" that does not inherently reproduce imperial logics (2014, 563).

3   As Lourdes Alberto notes, "Even radical and counter-hegemonic narratives rooted in *mestizaje*, while liberating for many Chicanos/as and Latinas/os, can feel oppressive for Indigenous Latinas/os" (2017, 252).

4   Many scholar-activists have convincingly revealed a symbiotic relationship between nonprofit and carceral systems, which they articulate as the nonprofit-industrial complex and the prison-industrial complex. The nonprofit-industrial complex has grown out of the tremendous wealth inequities in California made possible in part through carceral capitalism (Rodriguez 2009). Nonprofit organizations, in their dependency on wealthy donors and imposition of bureaucracy, often function to corral, contain, and neutralize any radical threat to the current order of power posed by community organizing. Less notorious but still deeply influential, the cluttered scene of philanthropic foundations and community endeavors known as the nonprofit-industrial complex claims to address the inequalities and injustices wrought by the prison-industrial complex (and other endemic forms of structural violence).

5 California's Three Strikes Law created automatic sentence "enhancements" (lengthening) for those convicted of one, two, or three felonies. A person convicted of a second felony would receive a sentence of double the length specified for the crime, whether or not the second crime was a violent offense. If convicted a third time, a person would receive an "indeterminant prison term of 25 years to life" (Bird et al. 2022). Some juvenile crimes were considered a strike under this adult penal code law, which could result in the young person's transfer to the adult system, where the penalties are more harsh and the young person has even fewer supports. Three Strikes resulted in many individuals being incarcerated for prolonged periods. It is not believed to have contributed to declining crime rates in California.

CHAPTER 3. *CARGAS* COMING DOWN

1 For as much as many residents resented the disproportionate and constant presence of police in East Salinas, they also resented that the police did not seem to value their lives enough to investigate violent crime when it affected them.
2 In 2014, the healing collectives and other BHC groups successfully advocated for the bed count to be reduced from 150 to 120, as documented in chapter 2 of this text. In 2020, that number was further reduced to 80, with housed populations significantly dwindling (Loudenback 2020b).

CHAPTER 4. HOMEGIRL *NOBLE*

1 "Homegirl" is a term of affinity prominent in this context to describe girls or women who embody and practice love and solidarity for their community and people, and typically have been or remain gang-affiliated.
2 Joan W. Moore's (1991) work with Chicanx street organizations in Los Angeles has been celebrated for its longitudinal approach, built on her strong relationships with interlocutors. However, in focusing on substance use and work (or lack thereof), exemplified in her chapter "Growing Up," her examination of women's and men's gang affiliation beyond adolescence reproduces the criminogenic biases of its generation of sociology.
3 In edited volumes on gang studies, research on girls and women in gangs is often relegated to the sole chapter examining themes of gender and sexuality (Decker and Pyrooz 2015; Decker, Pyrooz, and Densley 2022). This research seems preoccupied with enumerating the prevalence of girls' and women's participation, and understanding macro-level gender dynamics across contexts.
4 Following up with women to keep them accountable to these agreements was part of my role as a co-facilitator.
5 Translated as "deer's eye" beads, *ojos de venado* are sourced from liana vines and offer protection to the wearer, much like an evil eye. One *ojo de venado* would be included on each necklace, with multicolored seed beads along the rest of the strand.

CHAPTER 5. THIS IS WHERE WE WALK TOGETHER

1 Being released from incarceration and set up to fail has been noted as a feature of the prison-industrial complex, rather than a bug or an issue of individual behavior. Jennifer M. Ortiz and Hayley Jackey (2019) describe the "prisoner reentry industry" as a set of purportedly rehabilitative state agencies and nonprofits that continue the work of the carceral system in new sites and guises. They argue that this industry is an intentional and ongoing form of structural violence that ensures the "continued oppression" of the (formerly) incarcerated.

CHAPTER 6. THE WORK AND PLAY OF HEALING

1 *Machista* describes someone who performs a toxic masculinity known as *machismo*.

CONCLUSION

1 At the same time, health equity frameworks have been mobilized in powerful ways to do meaningful anticarceral work: at the grassroots level as cover for projects of spiritual healing like the Colectiva, but also in key state institutions. For example, California's Division of Juvenile Justice was slated to dissolve by 2023, with its mandate to be taken over by the Health and Human Services Agency. For those involved in healing projects in Salinas, the announcement of this plan was bittersweet: a "win" in the fight for affirmative carceral alternatives that focus on healing in underresourced Latinx communities, but also a risk for carceral disciplines to shape-shift under the guise of health into pathologies of disorder or deviance. The rich polysemy of health is something that Chicanx-Indigenous activists can adapt and deploy for their own abolitionist strategies aligned with ancestral etiologies, though not without the very real possibility that health will be used to frame disposability in new and dangerous ways.

2 Some of our preliminary findings from this project can be heard on episode 20 of season 2 of the *Building Justice* podcast (Gomez, Raschig, and Rosas 2023).

3 For anthropologists racialized as white, who inevitably inherit aspects of the colonial legacy and debts of this discipline when they study "the other," humility and a commitment to coalition and repair can mean leveraging privileges in material and epistemic ways to generate benefit to interlocutors and their projects across a long horizon of time. This approach may be interpreted as a "move to innocence" common among white people eager to perform their solidarity (Tuck and Yang 2012). This is a very fair critique and should spur those racialized as white to make themselves accountable to interlocutors in a long-term relationship, and continuously check in with their own desires to be virtuous while critically reflecting on the work of hope as it figures in whiteness (Jeske 2022).

BIBLIOGRAPHY

Acosta, Frank De Jesus. 2010. *The History of Barrios Unidos: Healing Community Violence*. Houston: Arte Publico Press.

Akins, Damon B., and William J. Bauer Jr. 2021. *We Are the Land: A History of Native California*. Oakland: University of California Press.

Alarcón, Daniel Cooper. 1997. *The Aztec Palimpsest: Mexico in the Modern Imagination*. Tucson: University of Arizona Press.

Alberto, Lourdes. 2016. "Nations, Nationalisms, and Indígenas: The 'Indian' in the Chicano Revolutionary Imaginary." *Critical Ethnic Studies* 2 (1): 107–27.

———. 2017. "Coming Out as Indian: On Being an Indigenous Latina in the US." *Latino Studies* 15 (2): 247–53.

Alexander, M. Jacqui. 2005. *Pedagogies of Crossing: Meditations on Feminism, Sexual Politics, Memory, and the Sacred*. Durham, NC: Duke University Press.

Alexander, Michelle. 2012. *The New Jim Crow: Mass Incarceration in the Age of Colorblindness*. New York: New Press.

Anzaldúa, Gloria. 2009. *The Gloria Anzaldúa Reader*. Edited by AnaLouise Keating. Durham, NC: Duke University Press.

———. 2015. *Light in the Dark/Luz En Lo Oscuro: Rewriting Identity, Spirituality, Reality*. Edited by AnaLouise Keating. Durham, NC: Duke University Press.

Baker, Lee D. 2021. "The Racist Anti-racism of American Anthropology." *Transforming Anthropology* 29 (2): 127–42. doi/full/10.1111/traa.12222.

Battaglia, Giulia, Jennifer Clarke, and Fiona Siegenthaler. 2020. "Bodies of Archives / Archival Bodies: An Introduction." *Visual Anthropology Review* 36 (1): 8–16. doi/full/10.1111/var.12203.

Berry, Maya J., Claudia Chávez Argüelles, Shanya Cordis, Sarah Ihmoud, and Elizabeth Velásquez Estrada. 2017. "Towards a Fugitive Anthropology: Gender, Race and Violence in the Field." *Cultural Anthropology* 32 (4): 537–65. doi/abs/10.14506/ca32.4.05.

Betasamosake Simpson, Leanne. 2016. "Indigenous Resurgence and Co-resistance." *Critical Ethnic Studies* 2 (2): 19–34. doi.org/10.5749/jcritethnstud.2.2.0019.

Bettie, Julie. 2014. *Women without Class: Girls, Race and Identity*. Berkeley: University of California Press.

Bird, Mia, Omair Gill, Johanna Lacoe, Molly Pickard, Steven Raphael, and Alissa Skog. 2022. "Three Strikes in California." California Policy Lab. August.

Blackwell, Maylei. 2011. *¡Chicana Power! Contested Histories of Gender and Feminism in the Chicano Movement*. Austin: University of Texas Press.

Blackwell, Maylei, Floridalma Boj Lopez, and Luis Urrieta Jr. 2017. "Introduction." In "Critical Latinx Indigeneities," special issue, *Latino Studies* 15 (2): 126–37.
Bradley, Rizvana. 2015. "Other Sensualities: An Introduction to *The Haptic: Textures of Performance*." *Women and Performance* 23 (2–3): 129–33. doi.org/10.1080/074077 0X.2014.976494.
Brotherton, David. 2015. *Youth Street Gangs: A Critical Appraisal*. Abingdon: Routledge.
Brotherton, David C., and Luis Barrios. 2004. *The Almighty Latin King and Queen Nation*. New York: Columbia University Press.
brown, adrienne maree. 2017. *Emergent Strategy: Shaping Change, Changing Worlds*. Chico, CA: AK Press.
———. 2019. *Pleasure Activism: The Politics of Feeling Good*. Chico, CA: AK Press.
Brown, Carolyn E., dir. 2014. *The Salinas Project*.
———. 2023. "The Salinas Project." https://carolynebrown.com.
Brown, Wendy. 2015. *Undoing the Demos: Neoliberalism's Stealth Revolution*. New York: Zone Books.
Burton, Orisanmi. 2015. "To Protect and Serve Whiteness." *North American Dialogue* 18 (2): 38–50.
Cacho, Lisa Marie. 2012. *Social Death: Racialized Rightlessness and the Criminalization of the Unprotected*. New York: New York University Press.
Calabrese, Joseph D. 2013. *A Different Medicine: Postcolonial Healing in the Native American Church*. New York: Oxford University Press.
Calderón, Dolores, and Luis Urrieta. 2019. "Studying in Relation: Critical Latinx Indigeneities and Education." *Equity and Excellence in Education* 52 (2–3): 219–38. doi/abs/10.1080/10665684.2019.1672591.
Carlson, Liane. 2019. *Contingency and the Limits of History: How Touch Shapes Experience and Meaning*. New York: Columbia University Press.
Carson, Dena C., and J. Michael Vecchio. 2015. "Leaving the Gang: A Review and Thoughts on Further Research." In *The Handbook of Gangs*, edited by Scott H. Decker and David C. Pyrooz, 257–75. Chichester, UK: John Wiley and Sons.
Castillo, Ana. 2014. *Massacre of the Dreamers: Essays on Xicanisma*. Albuquerque: University of New Mexico Press.
Cattelino, Jessica. 2004. "The Difference That Citizenship Makes: Civilian Crime Prevention on the Lower East Side." *PoLAR: Political and Legal Anthropology Review* 27 (1): 114–37.
Cimini, Kate. 2019. "Rent in Salinas Is Practically Double the National Average." *The Californian*, March 23. www.thecalifornian.com.
———. 2020. "California Housing Crisis: Salinas Farmworkers Struggle to Make Homes." *The Californian*, January 21. www.thecalifornian.com.
Colen, Cynthia G., Qi Li, Corinne Reczek, and David R. Williams. 2019. "The Intergenerational Transmission of Discrimination: Children's Experiences of Unfair Treatment and Their Mothers' Health at Midlife." *Journal of Health and Social Behavior* 60 (4): 474–92.

Cotera, María Eugenia, and María Josefina Saldaña-Portillo. 2014. "Indigenous but Not Indian? Chicana/os and the Politics of Indigeneity." In *The World of Indigenous North America*, edited by Robert Allen Warrior, 549–68. New York: Routledge.

Coulthard, Glen Sean. 2014. *Red Skin, White Masks: Rejecting the Colonial Politics of Recognition*. Minneapolis: University of Minnesota Press.

Cox, Aimee Meredith. 2015. *Shapeshifters: Black Girls and the Choreography of Citizenship*. Durham, NC: Duke University Press.

Crawley, Ashon T. 2016. *Blackpentecostal Breath: The Aesthetics of Possibility*. New York: Fordham University Press.

Critchley, Simon. 2013. *Infinitely Demanding: Ethics of Commitment, Politics of Resistance*. New York: Verso Books.

Dawson, Alexander S. 2018. *The Peyote Effect: From the Inquisition to the War on Drugs*. Oakland: University of California Press.

Day, Elizabeth. 2015. "#BlackLivesMatter: The Birth of a New Civil Rights Movement." *The Guardian*. July 19. www.theguardian.com.

Decker, Scott H., and David C. Pyrooz, eds. 2015. *The Handbook of Gangs*. Chichester, UK: John Wiley and Sons.

Decker, Scott H., David C. Pyrooz, and James A. Densley. 2022. *On Gangs*. Philadelphia: Temple University Press.

De Leon, Jason. 2015. *The Land of Open Graves: Living and Dying on the Migrant Trail*. Berkeley: University of California Press.

Dill, Katherine. 2014. "The Most and Least Educated Cities in America." *Forbes*, September 16. www.forbes.com.

Duan, Mary. 2016. "Community Program Aimed at Community Cooperation with Police Misfires." *Monterey County Weekly*, November 3. www.montereycountyweekly.com.

Escobar, Edward J. 1999. *Race, Police, and the Making of a Political Identity: Mexican Americans and the Los Angeles Police Department, 1900–1945*. Berkeley: University of California Press.

Espinoza, Dionne, Maria Eugenia Cotera, and Maylei Blackwell. 2018. *Chicana Movidas: New Narratives of Activism and Feminism in the Movement Era*. Austin: University of Texas Press.

Facio, Elisa, and Irene Lara. 2014. *Fleshing the Spirit: Spirituality and Activism in Chicana, Latina, and Indigenous Women's Lives*. Tucson: University of Arizona Press.

Ferris, James M., and Elizabeth A. Graddy. 2001. "Health Philanthropy in California: The Changing Landscape. Vol. 1, No. 3." Center on Philanthropy and Public Policy, University of Southern California. cppp.usc.edu.

Flores, Edward Orozco. 2013. *God's Gangs: Barrio Ministry, Masculinity, and Gang Recovery*. New York: New York University Press.

———. 2016. "'Grow Your Hair Out': Chicano Gang Masculinity and Embodiment in Recovery." *Social Problems* 63 (4): 590–604.

Flores, Jerry. 2016. *Caught Up: Girls, Surveillance, and Wraparound Incarceration*. Berkeley: University of California Press.

Gálvez, Alyshia. 2020. "Taking *Susto* Seriously: A Critique of Behavioral Approaches to Diabetes." *American Anthropologist* 122 (3): 651–52. doi/abs/10.1111/aman.13443.

Gilmore, Ruth Wilson. 2007. *Golden Gulag: Prisons, Surplus, Crisis, and Opposition in Globalizing California*. Berkeley: University of California Press.

Gilmore, Ruth Wilson, and Craig Gilmore. 2004. "The Other California." In *Globalize Liberation: How to Uproot the System and Build a Better World*, edited by David Solnit 381–96. San Francisco: City Lights Books.

Giroux, Henry A., and Brad Evans. 2015. *Disposable Futures: The Seduction of Violence in the Age of Spectacle*. San Francisco: City Lights Books.

Gomberg-Muñoz, Ruth. 2018. "The Complicit Anthropologist." *Journal for the Anthropology of North America* 21 (1): 36–37. doi/abs/10.1002/nad.12070.

Gomez, Juan, Megan Raschig, and Desiree Rosas. 2023. "Telpochcalli: Racial Justice in Education with MILPA." March 6. *Building Justice*. Podcast. open.spotify.com.

Gonzales, Patrisia. 2012. *Red Medicine: Traditional Indigenous Rites of Birthing and Healing*. Tucson: University of Arizona Press.

Haney-López, Ian F. 2004. *Racism on Trial: The Chicano Fight for Justice*. Cambridge, MA: Belknap Press.

Harney, Stefano, and Fred Moten. 2013. *The Undercommons: Fugitive Planning and Black Study*. Wivenhoe, UK: Minor Compositions.

Hernandez, Colin. 2019. "We Need More Data to Understand the Impact of Mass Incarceration on Latinx Communities." Vera Institute. October 14. www.vera.org.

Hernández, Kelly Lytle. 2017. *City of Inmates: Conquest, Rebellion, and the Rise of Human Caging in Los Angeles, 1771–1965*. Raleigh: University of North Carolina Press.

Horton, Sarah Bronwen. 2016. *They Leave Their Kidneys in the Fields: Illness, Injury, and Illegality among U.S. Farmworkers*. Oakland: University of California Press.

INCITE! Women of Color against Violence. 2009. *The Revolution Will Not Be Funded: Beyond the Non-profit Industrial Complex*. Cambridge, MA: South End Press.

Jeske, Christine. 2022. "Introduction: Hopes of and for Whiteness." *Journal for the Anthropology of North America* 25 (2): 54–73. doi/full/10.1002/nad.12172.

Jeursen, Thijs. 2023. *The Vigilant Citizen: Everyday Policing and Insecurity in Miami*. New York: New York University Press.

Jobson, Ryan Cecil. 2020. "The Case for Letting Anthropology Burn: Sociocultural Anthropology in 2019." *American Anthropologist* 122 (2): 259–71. doi/full/10.1111/aman.13398.

Joint Center for Housing Studies of Harvard University. 2016. "The State of the Nation's Housing, 2016." www.jchs.harvard.edu.

Kaba, Mariame. 2021. *We Do This 'til We Free Us: Abolitionist Organizing and Transforming Justice*. Chicago: Haymarket Books.

Kendall, Mikki. 2020. *Hood Feminism: Notes from the Women That a Movement Forgot*. London: Penguin Books.

Kohl-Arenas, Erica. 2015. *The Self-Help Myth: How Philanthropy Fails to Alleviate Poverty*. Oakland: University of California Press.

Lethabo-King, Tiffany, Jenell Navarro, and Andrea Smith. 2020. *Otherwise Worlds: Against Settler Colonialism and Anti-Blackness*. Durham, NC: Duke University Press.

Lorde, Audre. 2007. *Sister Outsider: Essays and Speeches*. Berkeley, CA Crossing Press.

Loudenback, Jeremy. 2020a. "Latinx Youth in the Juvenile Justice System Face Census Undercounting." *The Imprint*, August 26. imprintnews.org.

———. 2020b. "Monterey County Downsizes Its New Juvenile Hall." *The Imprint*, June 10. imprintnews.org.

Maffie, James. 2015. *Aztec Philosophy: Understanding a World in Motion*. Boulder: University Press of Colorado.

Magdaleno, Johnny. 2016. "Welcome to the Youth Murder Capital of California." *VICE News*, July 27. news.vice.com.

Massey, Douglas S., and Zai Liang. 1989. "The Long-Term Consequences of a Temporary Worker Program: The US Bracero Experience." *Population Research and Policy Review* 8 (3): 199–226.

Mattingly, Cheryl. 2018. "Ordinary Possibility, Transcendent Immanence, and Responsive Ethics: A Philosophical Anthropology of the Small Event." *HAU Journal of Ethnographic Theory* 8 (1–2): 172–84.

Maynard, Robyn, and Leanne Betasamosake Simpson. 2022. *Rehearsals for Living*. Chicago: Haymarket Books.

McKibben, Carol Lynn. 2022. *Salinas: A History of Race and Resilience in an Agricultural City*. Palo Alto: Stanford University Press.

McTighe, Laura, and Megan Raschig. 2019. "An Otherwise Anthropology: Introduction." *Cultural Anthropology*, Fieldsights, July 31. culanth.org.

Mendenhall, Emily. 2012. *Syndemic Suffering: Social Distress, Depression, and Diabetes among Mexican Immigrant Women*. Abingdon: Routledge.

Mendoza-Denton, Norma. 2008. *Homegirls: Language and Cultural Practice among Latina Youth Gangs*. Malden, MA: Blackwell.

Million, Dian. 2009. "Felt Theory: An Indigenous Feminist Approach to Affect and History." *Wicazo Sa Review* 24 (2): 53–76.

———. 2013. *Therapeutic Nations: Healing in an Age of Indigenous Human Rights*. Tucson: University of Arizona Press.

Miranda, Deborah A. 2013. *Bad Indians: A Tribal Memoir*. Berkeley, CA: Heyday Publishing.

Miranda, Marie. 2003. *Homegirls in the Public Sphere*. Austin: University of Texas Press.

Moore, Joan W. 1991. *Going Down to the Barrio: Homeboys and Homegirls in Change*. Philadelphia: Temple University Press.

Moraga, Cherrie, and Gloria Anzaldúa, eds. 1983. *This Bridge Called My Back: Writings by Radical Women of Color*. New York: Kitchen Table/Women of Color Press.

Mutsaers, Paul, Jennie Simpson, and Kevin Karpiak. 2015. "The Anthropology of Police as Public Anthropology." *American Anthropologist* 117 (4): 786–89.

National Compadres Network. 2012. "Lifting Latinos Up by Their 'Rootstraps': Moving beyond Trauma through a Healing-Informed Model to Engage Latino Boys and Men." nationalcompadresnetwork.org/.

Ortiz, Jennifer M., and Hayley Jackey. 2019. "The System Is Not Broken, It Is Intentional: The Prisoner Reentry Industry as Deliberate Structural Violence." *Prison Journal* 99 (4): 484–503. doi.org/10.1177/0032885519852090.

Panfil, Vanessa R., and Dana Peterson. 2015. "Gender, Sexuality, and Gangs: Re-envisioning Diversity." In *The Handbook of Gangs*, edited by Scott H. Decker and David C. Pyrooz, 208–34. Chichester, UK: John Wiley and Sons.

Pina-Cabral, João. 2015. "Names and Naming." In *International Encyclopedia of the Social and Behavioral Sciences*, edited by James D. Wright, 183–87. Oxford: Elsevier.

Povinelli, Elizabeth A. 2011. *Economies of Abandonment: Social Belonging and Endurance in Late Liberalism*. Durham, NC: Duke University Press.

———. 2012. "The Will to Be Otherwise/The Effort of Endurance." *South Atlantic Quarterly* 111 (3): 453–75.

Ralph, Laurence. 2014. *Renegade Dreams: Living through Injury in Gangland Chicago*. Chicago: University of Chicago Press.

Rankine, Claudia. 2014. *Citizen: An American Lyric*. Minneapolis, MN: Graywolf Press.

Raschig, Megan. 2017. "Triggering Change: Police Homicides, Community Healing, and the Emergent Eventfulness of the New Civil Rights." *Cultural Anthropology* 32 (3): 399–423.

———. 2018. "'You Don't Know That': Refusals of Community Policing and Criminalization in California." *Journal for the Anthropology of North America* 21 (1): 5–20. doi.wiley.com/10.1002/nad.12065.

———. 2019. "Of Other Times." *Cultural Anthropology*, Fieldsights, July 31. culanth.org.

Reynolds, Julia. 2014. *Blood in the Fields: Ten Years Inside California's Nuestra Familia Gang*. Chicago: Chicago Review Press.

Rios, Victor M. 2006. "The Hyper-criminalization of Black and Latino Male Youth in the Era of Mass Incarceration." *Souls* 8 (2): 40–54.

Risling Baldy, Cutcha, 2018. *We Are Dancing for You: Native Feminisms and the Revitalization of Women's Coming-of-Age Ceremonies*. Seattle: University of Washington Press.

Ritter, Nancy. 2009. "CeaseFire: A Public Health Approach to Reduce Shootings and Killings." National Institute of Justice. nij.ojp.gov.

Robledo, Roberto M. 2014. "Agents of Change Fan Out in Alisal." *Salinas Californian*, May 16. thecalifornian.com.

Rodriguez, Dylan. 2009. "The Political Logic of the Non-profit Industrial Complex." In INCITE! Women of Color against Violence, *The Revolution Will Not Be Funded: Beyond the Non-profit Industrial Complex*. Cambridge, MA: South End Press.

Rosas, Gilberto. 2019. "Fugitive Work: On the Criminal Possibilities of Anthropology." *Cultural Anthropology*, Fieldsights, September 26. culanth.org.

Roseman, Julie. N.d. "Cultivating Peace in Salinas: A Framework for Violence Prevention." The Prevention Institute. preventioninstitute.org.

Saldaña-Portillo, María Josefina. 2001. "Who's the Indian in Aztlán? Re-writing Mestizaje, Indianism, and Chicanismo from the Lacandón." In *The Latin American Subaltern Studies Reader*, edited by Ileana Rodriguez, 402–23. Durham, NC: Duke University Press.

———. 2016. *Indian Given: Racial Geographies across Mexico and the United States*. Durham, NC: Duke University Press.

Salinas, Lupe S. 2015. *U.S. Latinos and Criminal Injustice*. East Lansing: Michigan State University Press.

Sánchez Walsh, Arlene M. 2001. "'Normal Church Can't Take Us': Re-creating a Pentecostal Identity among the Men and Women of Victory Outreach." *Journal of Hispanic/Latino Theology* 9 (2): 48–78.

Santiago-Irizarry, Vilma. 2001. *Medicalizing Ethnicity: The Construction of Latino Identity in a Psychiatric Setting*. Ithaca, NY: Cornell University Press.

Santos, Roberto, Rick Gregory, Leocadio Cordero, and Gerald Richard. 2016. *An Assessment of the Salinas Police Department*. Collaborative Reform Initiative. Washington, DC: Office of Community Oriented Policing Services.

Sedgwick, Eve Kosofsky. 2003. *Touching Feeling: Affect, Pedagogy, Performativity*. Durham, NC: Duke University Press.

Seif, Hinda. 2008. "Wearing Union T-Shirts: Undocumented Women Farm Workers and Gendered Circuits of Political Power." *Latin American Perspectives* 35 (1): 78–98.

Shanahan, Jarrod, and Zhandarka Kurti. 2022. *States of Incarceration Rebellion, Reform, and America's Punishment System*. Chicago: Reaktion Books.

Shange, Savannah. 2016. "Unapologetically Black?" *Anthropology News* 57 (7): e64–e66.

Shange, Savannah, and Rosann Liu. 2019. "Solidarity-as-Debt: Fugitive Publics and the Ethics of Multiracial Coalition" *Cultural Anthropology*, Fieldsights, July 31. culanth.org.

Sharpe, Christina. 2017. "The Weather." *New Inquiry*, January 19. thenewinquiry.com.

Shotwell, Alexis. 2011. *Knowing Otherwise: Race, Gender, and Implicit Understanding*. Philadelphia: Penn State University Press.

Simpson, Audra. 2014. *Mohawk Interruptus: Political Life across the Borders of Settler States*. Durham, NC: Duke University Press.

Smith-Oka, Vania. 2014. "Fallen Uterus: Social Suffering, Bodily Vigor, and Social Support among Women in Rural Mexico." *Medical Anthropology Quarterly* 28 (1): 105–21.

Smith, Christen A. 2016. "Facing the Dragon: Black Mothering, Sequelae, and Gendered Necropolitics in the Americas." *Transforming Anthropology* 24 (1): 31–48. doi/10.1111/traa.12055.

Sojoyner, Damien M. 2021. "You Are Going to Get Us Killed: Fugitive Archival Practice and the Carceral State." *American Anthropologist* 123 (3): 658–70. doi/full/10.1111/aman.13615.

Stevenson, Lisa. 2014. *Life beside Itself: Imagining Care in the Canadian Arctic*. Berkeley: University of California Press.

Strong, Tracy B. 2013. *Politics without Vision: Thinking without a Banister in the Twentieth Century*. Chicago: University of Chicago Press.

Szydlowski, Joe. 2019. "Salinas, Former 'Murder Capital,' Sees 89% Drop in Homicide Rate." *The Californian*, July 12. www.thecalifornian.com.

Tapias, Maria. 2006. "Emotions and the Intergenerational Embodiment of Social Suffering in Rural Bolivia." *Medical Anthropology Quarterly* 20 (3): 399–415. doi.wiley.com/10.1525/maq.2006.20.3.399.

Taylor, Diana. 2003. *The Archive and the Repertoire: Performing Cultural Memory in the Americas*. Durham, NC: Duke University Press.

Thomas, Deborah A. 2011. *Exceptional Violence: Embodied Citizenship in Transnational Jamaica*. Durham, NC: Duke University Press.

———. 2019. *Political Life in the Wake of the Plantation: Sovereignty, Witnessing, Repair*. Durham, NC: Duke University Press.

Tronto, Joan C. 1995. "Care as a Basis for Radical Political Judgments." *Hypatia* 10 (2): 141–49.

Tuck, Eve, and K. Wayne Yang. 2012. "Decolonization Is Not a Metaphor." *Decolonization: Indigeneity, Education and Society* 1 (1): 1–40.

United States Census Bureau. 2022. "U.S. Census Bureau QuickFacts: Salinas City, California." www.census.gov.

Urban Institute. 2016. "The Alarming Lack of Data on Latinos in the Criminal Justice System." Urban Institute. apps.urban.org.

Valdez, Avelardo. 2007. *Mexican American Girls and Gang Violence: Beyond Risk*. New York: Palgrave Macmillan.

Valenzuela, Jesus, Jamila Bradshaw, and Tenoch Ortiz. 2016. "Building the We: Healing-Informed Governing for Racial Equity in Salinas." Race Forward. www.raceforward.org.

Van Gelder, Sarah. 2016. "The Radical Work of Healing: Fania and Angela Davis on a New Kind of Civil Rights Activism." *YES! Magazine*, February 18.

Vargas, Edward D., Melina Juárez, Gabriel R. Sanchez, and Maria Livaudais. 2018. "Latinos' Connections to Immigrants: How Knowing a Deportee Impacts Latino Health." *Journal of Ethnic and Migration Studies* 45 (15): 2971–88. doi.org/10.1080/1369183X.2018.1447365.

Vargas, Roberto. 1984. *Razalogía: Community Learning for a New Society*. Oakland, CA: Razagente Associates.

Villarejo, Don, and Gail Wadsworth. 2018. "Farmworker Housing Study and Action Plan for Salinas Valley and Pajaro Valley." California Institute for Rural Studies. June. cirsinc.org.

Vitale, Alex. 2017. *The End of Policing*. London: Verso Books.

Weide, Robert D. 2022. *Divide and Conquer: Race, Gangs, Identity, and Conflict*. Philadelphia: Temple University Press.

Yancy, George, and Judith Butler. 2015. "What's Wrong with 'All Lives Matter'?" *New York Times*. January 12. archive.nytimes.com.

Yee, Min S. 1973. *The Melancholy History of Soledad Prison: In Which a Utopian Scheme Turns Bedlam*. New York: Harper's Magazine Press.

Zigon, Jarrett. 2008. *Morality: An Anthropological Perspective*. New York: Routledge.

———. 2018. *Disappointment: Toward a Critical Hermeneutics of Worldbuilding*. New York: Fordham University Press.

———. 2019. *War on People: Drug User Politics and a New Ethics of Community*. Oakland: University of California Press.

———. 2021. "How Is It between Us? Relational Ethics and Transcendence." *Journal of the Royal Anthropological Institute* 27 (2): 384–401. doi/full/10.1111/1467-9655.13496.

INDEX

Page numbers in italic indicate photos.

abolition, 4, 10, 11, 13, 49, 61, 66, 72, 77, 116, *134*, 169, 173, 182n1; Chicanx-Indigenous grassroots abolitionist approach 5, 8, 22, 91; in Black radical tradition, 10; contemporary social movements, 11, 124
Academia Ollin, 29
accompliceship, 16
Acosta Plaza (AP), 66
activism history in Salinas area, 7
addictions. *See* substance use
Affordable Care Act, 177–78n7
African American civil rights, 50
agriculture, 8, 30, 34
Alberto, Lourdes, 180n3
Alexander, M. Jacqui, 149
allostatic load, 74
allyship, 16
Alvarado, Frank, Jr., 2, 135–37, 138, 139–40
American Indian Movement, 50
anthropology, 16, 18–19, 77–78, 125, 146, 173–74, 182n1 (Conclusion)
antiterrorism laws, 103
Anzaldúa, Gloria, 50–51
appreciation, 84
appropriation, 49, 50–51
Armenta, Fernando, 69, 70
Aztlán, 50–51

Bad Indians (Miranda), 29–30
Barrios, Luis, 33
Barrios Unidos, 52–54
behavioral "problems," 55
Berry, Maya J., 77
Black Lives Matter (BLM), 13–14
Black Panthers, 7, 32
Blackwell, Maylei, 123
book overview, 4–5, 11–12, 15–17, 21–26, 166, 172–74
Borderlands/La Frontera, (Anzaldúa), 50–51
boycotts, 32
Bracero Program, 31–32
Bradley, Rizvana, 86
Brotherton, David, 33
brown, adrienne maree, 163
Brown, Michael, 13
Building Healthy Communities (BHC), 39, 55, 122, 147–48, 149, 150–51

Calcagno, Lou, 69–70
The California Endowment (TCE): overview, 39–41; defunding of La Colectiva, 144, 145, 148, 150, 168–69, 171; Governing for Racial Equity (GRE), 140; history of, 53; and La Colectiva history, 122; and MILPA, 49, 60
California Wellness Foundation, 53
California's Division of Juvenile Justice, 182n1 (Conclusion)
Caló, 6–7, 177n5
capitalism, 178–79n1
carceral data, 177n6
carceral logics. *See* carcerality

193

carceral systems. *See* incarceration
carcerality, defined, 5; American carcerality, 8–9; California carcerality, 32; as part of otherwise and abolitionist work, 12–13, 124; carceral logics, 10, 21, 42, 61, 71, 74, 141, 151, 172; cultural healing as intervention, 48–49, 55, 60, 71, 170, 173
cargas: overview, 73, 74–75; ancestral, 80; of Esme, 80–85, 86–87; and haptic force, 85–86; inherited, 104–6; at methadone clinic *círculos*, 158–60; as picked up, 80. See also *descargando*
Carlson, Liane, 85
Carmel Mission, 29–30
Ceasefire, 179–80n7
ceremonies: Academia Ollin, 29; bridge, 111–13; Danza Azteca, 58; and gourd rattles, 43; at protests, 1; tepee ceremony, 58; Xinachtli closing ritual, 108. *See also* sage
César Chávez (film), 118
chanunpa, 59
Chávez, César, 32, 63
Chicana Movidas (Espinoza, Cotera, and Blackwell), 123
¡Chicana Power! (Blackwell), 123
Chicanas, defined, vii
Chicano Brown Berets, 7
Chicano Civil Rights Movement: overview, 123; Chicano psychology, 52; and health, 52; and Indigeneity, 49; as inspiration, 14; and institutions, 51–52; machismo of, 117; *marcha*, 133–34, *134*, *135*
Chicano psychology, 52
Chicanx, defined, vii
Chicanx-Indigenous, defined, vii
chimal, 58, 109
Chinatown encampment, 151, 161
cholas, defined, 100, 177n2
Christianity, 10, 180n8

chronic stress, 23, 73–77, 81, 85, 101–2. See also *cargas*; *descargando*
círculos, 29, 60–62, 79, 84. See also various *círculos*
City of Inmates (Hernández), 9
coalition, 74, 86, 162, 173, 182n3; feminist coalition, 90
Colen, Cynthia, 75
collective power, 60, 72
colonialism, 9–10, 30, 41, 56–57; colonial and carceral logics, 10, 74, 76
comadre, defined, 178n11
community health, 37–38, 39–40, 53, 179–80n7
"The Complicit Anthropologist" (Gomberg-Muñoz), 16
conocimiento, 38, 140
contingency, 77, 85; and possibility, 80
convivias, 78
copal, 1, 11, 29, 112, 139
Cotera, María Eugenia, 123, 180n2
Coulthard, Glen, 13–14
counterinsurgency, 32
Crawley, Ashon, 11
criminalization: overview, 10, 35; and colonialism, 30; defined, 34–35; and dehumanization, 35; of gangs, 33; internalizing, 35–36, 71–72; Pachucos in LA, 31; of working classes, 178–79n1
critical hermeneutics, 18–19
cultura: defined, 48; and everyday life, 166; in institutions, 54–55; and Ollin, 4; reclaiming, 65; re-membering/re-framing, 42; and TCE, 40–41. *See also* ceremonies; Indigenous Knowledge
cultura (es) cura, 2, 53
cultural healing, defined, 11–12. *See also* healing; healing collectives
the cultural piece, 8–11, 40. *See also* ceremonies; *cultura*; Indigenous knowledge

Danza Azteca, 58
danzantes, 134, 135

Deferred Action for Childhood Arrivals (DACA), 16, 178n9
dehumanization, 35
Department of Behavioral Health, 54–55
descargando: overview, 73, 74; Esme's, 84–85; in gangs, 79; heritable experiences, 104–5; individual/collective, 80; at methadone clinic *círculos*, 158–60; and Otherwise Anthropology, 77, 78. See also *cargas*
disposability, 34–35, 40, 74, 76, 89, 96, 182n1 (Conclusion)
dispossession, 5, 8, 10, 22, 41, 74, 76, 87, 146, 151
Divide and Conquer (Weide), 51
Division of Juvenile Justice, 182n1 (Conclusion)

El Movimiento. *See* Chicano Civil Rights Movement
The End of Policing (Vitale), 148
Espinoza, Dionne, 123
ethics of care, 95
ethnography, 19

family care, 10
farmworkers, 63–64, 151
Fathers and Families (cultural healing organization), 118
feminism: ethics of care, 95; and selective Indigenous tropes, 50–51; of La Colectiva, 79, 87; and racialized/gendered stress, 75–76; solidarity, 77
Flores, Edward Orozco, 95–96, 107
Floyd, George, 13
food, 64
fugitivity, 145, 146, 173–74

"gang recovery," 42, 95, 104, 107, 114
gangs, 92; as belonging, 102; criminalization of, 33; deterring family, 160; dismissal of shootings, 35; as empowerment, 33; enhancements, 94; exiting, 95–96, 101, 103, 107, 114; gender performances, 95–96; history in Salinas, 33; incarceration and prevention, 103; and intergenerational trauma, 105; and Julian's death, 94, 97–98; look of, 93; parental cause stereotypes, 63–64; prevention programs, 104; privileges, 102; as public health problem, 39; "raw" women, 79; refusal of oppression, 33; rehabilitation, 116; respect, 102; scholarship on, 95–96, 99, 101, 116, 181n3; as solidarity, 6; as "street terrorism," 32; tattoos, 94, 100. *See also* homegirl *noble*; Norteños; Sureños
gender: and care, 95; and gang scholarship, 95–96, 99, 181n3; and healing circles, 22; MILPA leadership, 63; performances, 95–96, 99; and stress, 75–76
gender equity, 117
gentrification, 144, 151
Gilmore, Ruth Wilson, 178n1
girls like T-Rex, 99
God's Gangs (Flores), 95–6
Gomberg-Muñoz, Ruth, 16
Gonzales, Patrisia, 9, 11
gourd rattles, 43, 44
Governing for Racial Equity (GRE), 140
grant money, 146
Great Depression, 31
greenlighting, 101
guest worker programs, 31

hapticality, 85–86
harm reduction, 153
Harney, Stefano, 86, 145
Haskie, Sara, 109
healing: as feeling good, 10; funders deciding, 144, 145–46; healing healers, 149; as individualizing, 41; and play, 145, 149–50, 161–63; safety as, 57; vs. self-determination, 41; vs. therapy, 89–90; as work, 148–49

healing collectives: overview, 6–7; as abandoned, 17; Barrios Unidos, 52–54; *conocimiento*, 38; dispossession of, 151; goals of, 12; healing as work, 148–49; La Cultura Cura, 52–55; as liberatory, 9; and play, 145, 161–62; regaining practices, 41–42. *See also* La Colectiva de Mujeres; MILPA

health, 39, 52, 64–65, 74–75. *See also* chronic stress

health equity: overview, 40–41, 49; and anticarceral work, 182n1 (Conclusion); in *círculos*, 61, 64–67; MILPA and TCE, 60. *See also* community health

"Health Happens Here" slogan, 37–38

hermana/sister status, 17

Hernández, Kelly Lytle, 9

Hernández, Osmar, 2, 3, 125–28, *127*, 138–40

Hispanic, as term, viii; in carceral demographic data, 10, 177n6

homegirl, as term, 181n1

homegirl *noble*: overview, 92; and gang connections, 102–3; and incarcerated men, 98; intergenerational trauma, 105–6; letting go of, 106–7; as older women, 93, 94–95, 96, 98–99, 100, 102–3; refusing norms, 115; respect, 102. *See also* gangs; *mujeres nobles*

Homegirls (Mendoza-Denton), 99, 162

homegirls, scholarship on, 181n3

Horton, Sarah, 75

housing: Acosta Plaza (AP), 66; affordability, 34, 146, 152; Chinatown encampment, 151, 161; *círculos* at methadone clinic, 159, 160; and single mothers, 147; support for, 160

Huerta, Dolores, 118

identitarian movements, 51, 179n1

immigration, 16, 178n9

incarceration: AP as, 66; and Ceasefire, 179–80n7; and Christopher's death, 138; and colonial expansion, 9–10; data, 177n6; and DJJ closing, 182n1 (Conclusion); gang enhancements, 94; as gang prevention, 103; and lack of support, 182nn1 (Chap. 5, Conclusion); needing bodies, 8; and nonprofits, 53, 180n4 (Chap 2), 182nn1 (Chap. 5, Conclusion); and race, 177n6; rates of, 10; reentry, 182nn1 (Chap. 5, Conclusion); and romantic relationships, 98; Telpochcalli, 170; Three Strikes Law, 53, 181n5. *See also* chronic stress

Indigeneity, 11–12, 49–51, 53, 108, 180n2

Indigenous, as term, 8–9

Indigenous knowledge: disrupted, 9; as inherited, 9; Medicine Wheel, 63; Native American Church, 180n8; and resurgence, 13; and world-building, 172. *See also cultura*

Indigenous Peoples: and Chicano Movement, 49, 50–51; history in Salinas, 30–31; and *mestizaje*, 180n3; in Mexico, 57. *See also* Native American Church

infrastructure, 39

intergenerational trauma, 104–6

Jackey, Hayley, 182n1 (Chap. 5)

Jackson, George, 32

James Q. Wilson Award for Excellence in Community Policing, 147

Jeursen, Thijs, 179n5

Joven Noble, 108

Justice for Brenda rally, 147–48

juvenile hall expansion, 36, 68–71, 87, 181n2

Kaba, Mariame, 72

Kapital (Marx), 178n1

La Colectiva de Mujeres: overview, 5, 22, 90, 124–25, 166, 168–70, 171; beginnings, 7; *cargas* inherited, 104–5; *cargas* into action, 86–91; and chronic stress,

73–77; closing the circle, 165, 167–68, 169, 172; defunded, 144, 145, 148, 150, 168–69, 171; as erased, 122–23, 133; Esme's *cargas*, 80–85, 86–87; gang sociality, 104; *gritando*, 120; healing circles, 2–4; healing vs. therapy, 89–90; history of, 78–79; as homegirl *noble*, 100–101; judgment of, 59; and La Cultura Cura, 87–88; meeting of, 1–2; MIPLA on, 90; poem, *113*; police violence protests, 126–28, 131–34, *131*, 136, 137; and Rachel, 165–66; Raschig as co-facilitator, 17; Stockton *encuentro*, 121; support from, 59, 137–38, 139, 141; suspicions of, 111; as too "raw," 35, 122; Walk to Remember, 139–40; women's leadership, 117–18, 120–24, *131*, 132–33; Xinachtli, 108–13, 114. *See also* homegirl *noble*
La Cultura Cura, 52–55, 78, 87–88, 108
la vida loca, 94
labor movement, 7
languages, 57, 137
Las Hijas de Cuauhtémoc, 123
lateral surveillance, 35, 36, 179n5
Latinx, defined, viii, 177n6
lettuce boycott, 32
liberalism, 13–14, 36, 39
limpias, 46, 180n1
"Living in Fear" press conference, 35–36
Lorde, Audre, 162

machismo, 117, 121, 182n1 (Chap. 6)
May 1 Alliance, 133
McTighe, Laura, 12, 146
Medicine Wheel, 63, 109
Mejía, Carlos, 2, 128–29, 138–40
Mendenhall, Emily, 75
Mendoza, Brenda, 25, 143–45, 147–48, 153, 164
Mendoza-Denton, Norma, 99, 162
mental health issues, 138, 140, 143
mestizaje, 50, 180n3
mestizo mourning, 180n2

methadone clinic circles, 153–60
Mexica, defined, viii
Mexican Americans, defined, vii
Mexican-American War, 30–31
Mexicano/as, defined, vii
migration, 31–32, 138–39
Million, Dian, 41
MILPA (Motivating Individual Leadership for Public Advancement): overview, 170–71; Academia Ollin, 29; beginnings, 7, 38; *círculos*, 61–67; on La Colectiva, 90; meaning, 177n1; police violence protest, *127*–28; presentation in redwoods, 42–44; "rootstrap" thinking, 60; San Diego road trip, 45–47; and TCE, 49, 60
Miranda, Deborah A., 29–30
Miranda, Marie "Keta," 99, 115
missions, 30
Moore, Joan W., 181n1
Moten, Fred, 86, 145
mothers' stress, 74–6, 101–2
mujeres nobles, 114–15

Nahuatl: cosmology, 4, 14, 46, 51, 109; language, 6, 29, 46, 55, 58
Native American Church, 43, 62–63, 109, 180n8
Native Americans. *See* Indigeneity; Indigenous Knowledge; Indigenous Peoples
Naval Postgraduate Academy, 32
nicknames/*placasos*, 93, 105–8
noble, 92
nonprofit industrial complex, 53, 180n4 (Chapter 2)
norms, 152
Norteños, 33, 66, 94, 177n4
North American Free Trade Agreement (NAFTA), 65

obsidian, 25, 178n12
occupying the narrative, defined, 39–40
Ohlone peoples, 30

ojos de venado, 111, 181n3
Okies, 31
Ollin: overview, 14–16; Academia Ollin, 29; in *círculos*, 62; defined, 4–5, 8, 27; as ever shifting, 171–72; and La Colectiva, 90
Ometeotl, 3
Operation Garlic Press, 103
Ortiz, Jennifer M., 182nn1 (Chap. 5)
otherwise, as term, 11, 12, 14
Otherwise Anthropology, 15–16, 17–20, 24–25, 26, 125, 146–47, 173–74

palabra, 43, 44
Palabra Comunitaria, 132–33
peyote, 180n8
philanthropy organizations, 40, 53, 145–46, 152, 171. See also *specific organizations*
pirul, 45, 46
placasos, 105–8
play, 143–44, 145, 156–58, 161–63; clowning as linguistic play, 162; and "the work" of healing, 149–50
pleasure as political gesture, 152, 162
Pleasure Activism (brown), 162
police: and lack of investigation, 82, 181n1; award for policing, 147; and good citizenship, 35, 36, 179n5; and Raschig's research, 179n6; in schools, 151
police violence: overview, 2; and Alvarado's death, 135–36, 137; and Angel's death, 119; and Brenda's death, 143–45, 147–48; Department of Justice investigation, 140; and "Living in Fear" press conference, 35–36; and Mejía's death, 128–31, *130*, *131*; and Osmar's death, 125–28, *127*; and Salinas gang narrative, 33; UFW strikes, 32. See also protests: police violence
positivity, 83
possibility: abolitionist, 4–5; sense of possibility, 10, 11, 19, 166; cultural healing as praxis of possibility, 12, 39, 52, 71, 76, 80; otherwise possibility, 12, 15
poverty, 31, 34, 151. See also housing
prisons. See incarceration; juvenile hall expansion
privilege, 77–78, 146, 182n1 (Conclusion)
probation officers, 54, 58
professionalization, 40, 146, 149
Proposition 47, 87, 170
protests: elders disapproving of, 59; *marcha* protest signs, 133, *134*; police violence, 1, 2–3, 59, 120–22, 125–28, *127*, 130–31, *131*, 132–34, *134*–35, 136, *137*, 147–48
public toilets, 161
Purépecha language, 57

Quintero, Otilio, 53

race, 51, 70, 177n6, 179n1
racism, 63–64, 74–75
radicalism, 180nn3, 4
rain sticks, 109
Ralph, Laurence, 102, 106
Rarámuri people, 57
raw or rawness, 22, 79, 116, 120, 122
Razalogia (Vargas), 52
reciprocity ethics, 102
Red Medicine (Gonzales), 9
reframing, 11, 42, 58
rehabilitation, 116
relational ethics, 95–96, 102–4
re-membering, 11, 42, 48, 55–56. See also Indigeneity
renegotiation, 106
research sites, 177–78n7
resilience, 36, 60, 75
respect, 116
respectability, 42, 116, 145, 152
resurgence, 13
revising narratives, 36
revolution, 70, 174
Robledo, Roberto M., 179n3

"rootstrap" thinking, 60
Ruiz, Angel, 2, 119, 138, 139–40

safety, 66–7
sage, 2–3, 62, 69, 73, 74, 78, 83, 121–22, 128, 133, 137, 157–58, 168
Saldaña-Portillo, María Josefina, 51, 180n2
Salinas overview, 8, 30–34, 151, 179nn3–4
The Salinas Project (film), 36
screaming, 4, 123, 168
Sedgwick, Eve Kosofsky, 125
self-hate, 56–7
settlers' history, 30–31
sexual assault, 83, 105
sexual harassment, 81
sexuality, 155, 158, 162, 181n3
Shotwell, Alexis, 173
Simpson, Leanne Betasamosake, 172
Smith, Christen A., 75
Soledad State Prison/Correctional Facility, 7, 32, 167
solidarity, 19, 51, 77, 99
stereotypes, 162
Stevenson, Lisa, 106
stigmatization, 35
Stockton *encuentro*, 118–19, 121
stress, 23, 73–7, 81, 85, 101–2. See also *cargas*; *descargando*
strikes, 7
substance use, 153–54, 161
Sureños, 6, 33, 93, 101, 177n4
surveillance: philanthropic, 152–3; ethnographic, 172; lateral (in policing), 179n5
sweat lodge, 46, 57–58

tattoos, 94, 100
Tello, Jerry, 54, 55, 56, 58, 87–88
Telpochcalli, 170
temezcal, 46, 57–58
tepee ceremony, 58
Therapeutic Nations (Million), 41
thick solidarity, 19
Thomas, Deborah, 125

Three Strikes Law, 53, 181n5
Treaty of Guadalupe, 31

U visas, 16, 178n9
The Undercommons (Harney and Moten), 86, 178n10
undocumented people, 34
United Farm Workers (UFW), 32, 118
universities, 178n10

Vargas, Roberto, 52
Velasco, Jose, 140
Victory Outreach, 107
The Vigilant Citizen (Jeursen), 179n5
violence, 66, 82, 101, 145, 179–80n7. See also police violence
Vitale, Alex, 148
Vizcaíno, Sebastian, 30
"Voice of the Voiceless" journal, 136

Walk to Remember, 139–40
water, 29, 34
Weide, Robert D., 51, 178–79n1
white anthropologists, 182n1 (Conclusion)
white supremacy, 55, 56
whiteness, 177n6
Witnessing 2.0, 125
Women's Healing Collective. See La Colectiva de Mujeres
women's leadership, 117–18, 120–24, *131*, 132–33
World War II, 31
world-building or world-making, 23, 51, 52, 91, 116, 123, 157, 172; healing as world-making, 40, 149, 173

Xicanas, defined, vii
Xinachtli, 108–13

Yaqui people, 11, 108
youth as threat, 66

Zigon, Jarrett, 18–19, 95

ABOUT THE AUTHOR

MEGAN S. RASCHIG is Assistant Professor in the Department of Anthropology at California State University, Sacramento.

www.ingramcontent.com/pod-product-compliance
Lightning Source LLC
Chambersburg PA
CBHW020029040426
42333CB00039B/591